The Twilight
of the
Primitive

By the same author

IN SEARCH OF THE PRIMITIVE

PASSPORT TO ADVENTURE

AMAZON HEAD-HUNTERS

ZANZABUKU

Lewis Cotlow

The Twilight
of the
Primitive

THE MACMILLAN COMPANY
NEW YORK, NEW YORK

Portions of this work originally appeared
in *Playboy* magazine

The Macmillan Company
866 Third Avenue, New York, N.Y. 10022
Collier-Macmillan Canada Ltd., Toronto, Ontario

Library of Congress Catalog Card Number:
74-156992

First Printing

Printed in the United States of America

for CHARLOTTE

Acknowledgments

In addition to those not mentioned elsewhere in this book, the author also wishes to express his appreciation for generous help and advice he received from the following:

Dr. Robert Caneiro, American Museum of National History;

Ambassador Galo Plaza Lasso;

Dr. Frederick J. Dockstader, director, Museum of the American Indian, Heye Foundation;

The Honorable A. Burks Summers;

The Honorable Spruille Braden;

Bishop I. F. Pintado of Ecuador,

Father Carollo of Ecuador,

Father Anthony Togoochi, and

Father Edward Capeletti, all of the Salesian Mission of St. John Bosco;

General Matthew B. Ridgway, former Chief of Staff, U.S. Army;

Colonel William Cameron, commander, U.S. Military Group, Ecuador;

Captain John E. Lowell, U.S. Naval Mission, Ecuador;

Major Allyn C. Houltry, intelligence adviser, U.S. Military Group, Ecuador;

Bodo Wuth, Quito, Ecuador, who accompanied me as cameraman on my last three expeditions to the Upper Amazon;

Dr. Charles Wagley, Institute of Latin American Studies;

Maria Yolanda Umburanas;

John N. Lindskoog, director, Instituto Linguistico de Verono, Quito, Ecuador;

Major General Robert R. Linvill, commander, U.S. Military Group, Rio;

Colonel William P. Renny, U.S. Embassy, Rio;

Henry B. Ryan, U.S.I.S., Rio;

Dr. William R. Wood, president, University of Alaska;

Dr. Max E. Brewer, director, Naval Arctic Research Laboratory, Barrow, and members of his staff;

Acknowledgments

Dr. Maynard M. Miller, professor of geology, Michigan State University;

Vice Admiral Bernard H. Bieri, Jr., U.S.N. ret.;

Max Britton;

Harold Gray, former chairman, Pan American Airways;

Australian News and Information Service for the use of photographs of natives of Australia and New Guinea;

The Honorable David Hay, C.B.E., D.S.O., administrator, Territory of Papua-New Guinea;

Sir James Plimsoll, C.B.E., former secretary, Department of External Affairs, now Australian ambassador to the U.S.;

Bryan Perkins, director, Mt. Hagen Radio Station;

R. I. Skinner, former district commissioner, Mt. Hagen, Papua, N.G.

Randal Heymanson, C.B.E., chairman, American-Australian Association;

Dr. Matthew W. Stirling, Smithsonian Institution;

R.K.O. Radio Pictures for permission to reproduce some still pictures from my South American film *Jungle Headhunters*;

Republic Pictures for permission to reproduce some still pictures from my African film *Zanzabuku*;

Dr. A. H. L. Lovink;

Sydney Cohen for editorial help in preparing this book.

Contents

Maps

Preface

INSTANCES OF VANISHING PRIMITIVE cultures far exceed those I have described in this book. Their disappearance is really a news-story, one that is taking place swiftly, right now. It is perhaps too complex a story to be covered by one man. Nevertheless, the telling of even a part of the story cannot wait. In a decade or so there may not be much left to tell about.

I came along at a time when it was still possible to see people living as they had for ten, twenty, perhaps a hundred centuries. I cannot say often enough how lucky I regard myself to have lived at a time when modern technology made possible for me trips that would once have taken years of preparation and sapped the energies of much stronger men. Paradoxically, this same technology has contributed to the demise of the cultures I have described here.

The sad truth is that we are witnessing the end of primitive man, man as he has lived for much of his time on earth—at least since he first learned to use tools and to communicate his ideas from one generation to another. While individual primitive men may die off during the next few years in bitterness and confusion, it is not for them that we need compassion. In my view it is already much too late to do anything but help new generations find their own way in a rather maddening world—we may have already helped the older generation too much.

The principle of living that we define as civilization may call not for a hymn of triumph but for a dirge. Man as a primitive has done quite well if we use time as a yardstick: the cultures I have described have endured for a far longer time than has Western civilization. And civilization, after all, may yet have to be tested.

To take this thought a step further, the very civilization most responsible for the end of primitive life is now itself facing disaster. Stanford University biologist Paul Ehrlich puts it this way: "There is *no*, I repeat, *no* conceivable technological solution to the problems we face." Other civilizations have risen, had their day and left the stage. But what other civilization in history has been "advanced" enough to drag down with it the primitive sources that could one day perhaps replenish its sapped vitality?

We have absorbed primitive man into a system of life which is considerably more fragile than his own tradition-oriented cultures. Hence, it is not wholly clear to me why we should congratulate those peoples who have succeeded in making an adjustment to modern life, who have given up the ways of their ancestors and joined us in our precarious dependence on the complex instrumentalities that now rule our lives. Yes, we can congratulate them for having withstood our superior weapons, our whips and diseases; we can admire their flexibility and intelligence in learning to play our games. Are we so sure, however, that we want them to follow our lead?

Not only have we been engaged in destroying indigenous cultures the world over, we have done it while saying that if these children of nature had any sense they would follow our example. And this may turn out to be, at the very least, one of the boldest pieces of ignorance—or simple falsehood—in man's history. It has become appallingly clear that in order to sustain our idealized "standard of living" we must draw from the earth's total resources at a rate that is fifty, perhaps one hundred times greater than the primitive's modest demands on his environment. Moreover, it is increasingly the primitive man's environment that we have been tapping. And if a high standard of living means almost limitless consumption, then those who can afford it will become fewer and fewer. It is probably too late, but would it not be better to begin asking what primitive men can teach us?

Western nations have long deluded themselves with the prideful and foolish notion that they were best suited to regulate the lives of primitive peoples. But since the frightful world wars which culminated in the holocaust of Hiroshima, Western man has begun to question in earnest his own moral superiority as well as his faith in the benevolent qualities of his machines, his cities, his institutions and even his philosophies. And it has become terrifyingly clear that we stand in danger of using up our air, fresh water and living space. The inevitability of disaster does not seem to be in question—only the timetable.

This is the final irony: we are losing faith now in the very values which we have been attempting to impose upon primitive man. Our governmental, religious and educational values have been questioned on every side. Our youth are rebelling not only against routinized and uninspired occupations but against the materialism which creates them and makes them necessary. Perhaps the bitterest irony of all is that the very machines with which we have awed primitive man have now begun to frighten us as though they were visitations from some alien world rather than the products of our own ingenuity.

So one must ask the inevitable question: Whose twilight is it?

1 They Will Not Pass This Way Again

LET US SUPPOSE that a favorite fantasy of science fiction writers actually came to pass: beings with a most advanced technology invade the earth and impose upon man an alien and entirely incomprehensible way of life, relegating the erstwhile "Lords of Creation" to the ignominious roles of servants, slaves or, at best, museum curiosities. How might human beings be expected to react? Some, of course, would try to learn about the invaders' superior techniques (assuming we were given the opportunity). Some, no doubt, would be horrified at the prospect of becoming second-class beings in a world in which they had once been supreme. They would seek places to hide or would even fight a certainly tragic, losing struggle to affirm their sense of "human dignity." We would all yearn to survive, but only as men and only as we have learned to define our humanness.

We like to think that perishing in behalf of a way of life is nobly tragic: defeat at the hands of a superior force brings out human capacities of which most peoples on this earth have been traditionally proud. Yet, in our Western regard for the winner, and in our belief that God is on our side, we often forget that in this hemisphere people whom the earliest explorers mistakenly dubbed Indians have endured a five-century-long encounter with an alien civilization not unlike the fanciful invasion described above.

The continents of North and South America were uninhabited by man when the first Asians migrated across the skimpy land bridge connecting Alaska and Siberia thousands of years prior to the arrival of Christopher Columbus—or Leif Ericson—in the New World. For these first Americans there were no waiting tribes, friendly or hostile, on hand to trade furs, skins, corn, planting techniques or valuable real estate for bits of colored glass. The mantle of ice had barely retreated from the continent when the first waves of these nomadic hunters opened the trails, discovered sources of food, the habitable valleys and plains and the hunting grounds in an unknown and often inhospitable new world. With simple Stone Age weapons they pursued huge mammoths, mastodons and other great land mammals, inadvertently helping them to extinction.

These groups of early Americans undoubtedly arrived with different abilities, religious and social customs, and sought living space that would suit their cultures. Moving on without covered wagons or supporting armies, they invaded the Arctic lands of the north, the plains and mountains to the south, and eventually the east coast of North America; then the lands of Central and South America until they attained the tip of Tierra del Fuego—a distance of over ten thousand miles, encompassing an area of millions of square miles.

Eventually the wandering stopped when they came upon territories hospitable to their way of life, lands in which they could survive within the limits of their knowledge, their tools, their beliefs and superstitions. Perhaps they had no clear idea where they were heading; at first they followed animal trails and wandering herds of bison, drawn by the promise of warmer climates and ice-free valleys, the beckoning foothills and the lure of the seemingly endless grasslands.

By the time white Europeans began arriving in the New World during the fifteenth and sixteenth centuries, the first Americans had produced such a variety of cultural styles, levels of technical achievement and political sophistication that it is difficult to generalize about them in comparison to the "more advanced" Europeans. The Indian tribes of the Americas did share some obvious deficiencies: they lacked gunpowder, horses and artillery. And they were unarmed in quite another sense: they could not understand—nor could they have ever anticipated—the unquenchable thirst for land and resources that would possess the invaders. They were totally unprepared for the righteous cruelties that the Spanish, French, Dutch, English and Portuguese would inflict upon them in the name of civilization.

The pattern of barbarities that stains the history of the Americas right up to the present was begun by men who came to take what was not theirs to take. Columbus found the Arawak Indians of the Caribbean islands to be "a loving people." Peter Farb, author of *Man's Rise to Civilization as Shown by the Indians of North America*, has commented: "But in their haste to exploit the new abundance of the Americas, the Spaniards set the loving and gentle Arawak to labor in mines and on plantations." He adds that "whole Arawak villages disappeared through slavery, disease, and warfare, as well as by flight into the mountains. As a result, the native population of Haiti, for example, declined from an estimated 200,000 in 1492 to a mere 29,000 only twenty-two years later." This has been the unhappy pattern on both continents. The only difference is that in South America much of the decimation of the Indian peoples has taken place in recent decades. And it is still going on.

The headhunting Jivaro of Ecuador cuts off the head of his enemy after a raid and shrinks it to the size of a fist, and many civilized people are appalled at this. Yet the Puritans of New England in 1703 paid about $60 for Indian scalps, while later in that century Pennsylvanians offered $134 for a male Indian's scalp, $50 for a female's. Although they have been thought to typify the bloodthirsty savage of the New World, the Jivaros could never conceive of killing in this commercially systematic way. The Jivaros believe that they must avenge the spirits of their kin slain in raids by rival clans; they mark individual enemies for death and decapitation. When they prepare for a raid, they have to work themselves into a frenzy by means of dancing and drugs. But bounties for dead enemies, killing by other indirect methods—the slaughter of game, gifts of poisoned food or of clothing and blankets infected with smallpox—are more the ways of the European than of the American savage.

By the time the Spaniards had completed their ravishment of the West Indies some six million Indians were reported to have been wiped out. It is said that there are no longer any "true" Indians there. Those who survived the slave labor, torture, rape and disease became mixed with their conquerors and with the Negro slaves imported to take their places. Jesuit missionaries record instances of Indians who, believing that the real god of the Spaniards was gold, addressed prayers to chests of that metal in a vain attempt to placate their tormentors.

In Brazil enslavement was already in progress as early as 1511. Portuguese slave raids along the coast, numerous and bloody after 1547, comprised what the historian Artúr Ramos called "one of the greatest massacres in the history of the contacts of peoples in the world." So great was the Portuguese colonists' dependence upon slave labor that even the severest censures of the Church had no deterrent effect. In 1639 when Pope Urban VIII threatened anyone who enslaved an Indian with excommunication, the citizens of Rio de Janeiro rioted at the Jesuit college, nearly murdering some Paraguayan fathers; in Santos there was violence and in São Paulo the Jesuits were run out of the city.

Thousands of square miles in the São Paulo area were stripped within the first century and a half of colonization—two million Indian inhabitants were captured or slain. Sometimes the Indians were herded in chains on brutal death marches. Certain converted Guarani Indians were tricked into slavery by raiders costumed as Jesuits, complete with rosaries, crosses and black robes. There are numerous reports of Indians who were made to turn over their own war captives. In 1696 Portuguese raiding the upper Amazon offered iron tools to the Yurimagua in exchange for slaves. When the chiefs refused to turn over captive Indians, the tribe itself was threatened with captivity. Some of the chiefs found it necessary to drug themselves in order to be able to cooperate. The Yurimagua, like other tribes, could not continue this collaboration, and eventually deserted their lands. On this same expedition the Portuguese raided Indian settlements far up the Amazon, leaving a trail of death and destruction everywhere behind them.

Early in the 1700s the Portuguese built forts at the confluence of the Amazon and its tributary, the Negro, where Manáos now stands. From here they were able to command the upper Amazon and depopulate the region systematically. Not even mission settlements were spared. Indians who were in the process of learning the ways of civilization were either captured, killed or—if they were fortunate—escaped into the more remote parts of the forest. There they might survive—if they could quickly reeducate themselves in the ways of the jungle.

Slavery was officially ended in 1888—for the record. Reports of forced labor have persisted right up until the present. At the turn of the century during Brazil's great rubber boom one of the cruellest forms of slavery, peonage, took root at Manáos and strangled Indian life as far upriver as the Putumayo in Peru.

Rubber boots, invented by Amazon basin Indians who molded the latex right on their feet, had been introduced in the United States early in the nineteenth century. But it was not until the advent of the horseless carriage that the demand for tires, inner tubes and other rubber products was responsible indirectly for the orgy of lawless greed and inhumanity that makes other terrible episodes in history seem pale by comparison. Upon reviewing the report of Roger Casement, the British consul at Rio de

Janeiro, on the atrocities, James Bryce, British ambassador to the United States and a social commentator of some note, declared that "the methods employed in the collection of rubber surpasses in horror anything hitherto reported in the civilized world during the last century." According to Casement's report, the Putumayo rubber output of 4,000 tons between 1900 and 1911 was directly responsible for the deaths of 30,000 Indians. The total population of the area shrank during this same period from 50,000 to 7,000. It was estimated that every ton of rubber from the Amazon valley—gathered primarily by and for British and American firms—had been produced at the cost of two human lives.

This was a time when a canoe-load of wild rubber was worth $2,500, when astronomic fortunes were made almost overnight, when the citizens of Manáos were sending their laundry as well as their schoolchildren to Europe, when a grand opera house was prefabricated in England, shipped and reconstructed in the capital, opening with a memorable consecration by the great Caruso.

For his share in delivering that canoe-load of rubber, the Indian was permitted to buy from traders food, clothing and trinkets marked up 1,000 percent over their original cost. Yet he was somehow never able to bring in quite enough rubber to pay for everything he wanted; he was perpetually in debt. His master, the patron, would set up a store filled with enticing trade goods all available on credit—take a lifetime to pay!

If he balked at the arrangement, the Indian was often given a fatal flogging. Or he might be decapitated or drowned, burned alive, starved, hanged or used as a target by a sadist with a pistol. Nor were his wife and children spared. Women were violated, sometimes publicly if their husbands had defaulted on a debt; mothers were beaten if their children were too young to withstand a flogging. To punish parents their children's brains might be dashed out. Even when the Indian managed to work hard enough to escape punishment he might very well be tortured anyway for the sport of it. And those who escaped the white man's violence had a very good chance of succumbing to one of the contagious diseases of civilization.

The Europeans justified their treatment of the native Americans by the casuistic argument that because the Indians were nontechnological, non-Christian and nonwhite, they could be dealt with as nonpeople. (This despite the widely held romantic picture of the Indian as a Noble Savage that had been painted by poets and philosophers.) Actually, the New World's first inhabitants possessed a broad range of skills and accomplishments, and when some were given a chance to demonstrate these (before their cultural pride had been destroyed), they proved to be able adaptors to the ways of the white man. A good example of this can be found in the Cherokees of Georgia. Before they were prodded into unwanted wastelands by the Removal Act of 1830, they had developed a memorable record of industry, agriculture and learning. A Cherokee named Sequoya had perfected a syllabary notation for writing their language. They had prepared their own tribal constitution and by 1828 were printing a newspaper.

The Cherokee achievement was not the rule, however. Most American Indian tribal groups found it impossible to adapt to white European culture. Even if they had been able to demonstrate that they were prepared to abandon their own traditions, there was little chance of their ever being integrated into American society of the nineteenth century. Neither in North or South America could they hope to be treated as anything but hated and feared "savages"—as inferior beings by most, as benighted heathens, candidates for conversion to Christianity, at best.

Proof of the Indian's inferiority could be found in his "backwardness," his primitiveness and the religious, social and political customs that—when their existence was even acknowledged —seemed "barbaric." That the Indian had achieved so little in the Western sense of achievement was attributed to his innate laziness. (Of course, the corollary was that a lazy individual did not deserve to control his own destiny and therefore needed a strong-handed taskmaster.) Yet anyone who has spent much time among primitive peoples, as I have, knows that what often seems to be laziness in Western eyes is really a highly practical and time-tested way of meeting human needs in a particular environment. Hunting peoples, for example, may spend many hungry days in tracking game; then, because they lack the means or the ability to preserve meat, will spend days gorging themselves on their quarry.

The Indians of the Americas do not need apologists for their so-called backwardness. Their contributions to the accumulated body of human knowledge are indeed impressive. The great Amazon basin alone, where many of the most primitive people of the earth are still gathered, has given to medicine curare as a treatment for paralysis and as an anaesthetic; the Indian pharmacopoeia also includes cocaine from the coca shrub, salicylate (aspirin) derived from the bark of the willow, digitalis from the foxglove plant, quinine from cinchona bark. Brazilian Indians discovered important drugs used to treat ulcers, wounds and skin diseases including scurvy, eczema and leprosy; and drugs to induce sterility long before "the pill" became a part of our vocabulary. The list is virtually endless because "civilized" medicine has still not completed the task of searching out and testing primitive drugs.

Foods that have become staple items around the world since their discovery in the New World are equally important. Men who came to South and Central America for riches brought back knowledge of fruits and vegetables such as corn, pepper, guava, pineapple, pumpkin, tomato, squash, most types of beans and such important tubers as potato, sweet potato, oca and manioc. Indians had been eating "Irish potatoes," "Spanish sauce" and "Hungarian paprika" long before Europeans were aware that American Indians existed. In the New World they found not only cotton and rubber and chicle but tobacco, the use of which spread so rapidly from the time it was brought to Europe in 1558 that by the early 1700s the Eskimos were getting their supply through trade with Siberia.

Unhappily there are some Indian practices which were not taken over so completely by the white invaders: hospitality, generosity and kindness. Even among those tribes who have the best reasons for distrusting the white man, I have found a genuine willingness to accept each newcomer on his own merits once it has been demonstrated that he means no harm. Stories of lost or injured white men who have been cared for by Indians are legion. All things considered, a lone white man would stand a much better chance of remaining alive if he stumbled into a group of Indians than if it were the other way around.

The Bororo Indians, on the verge of extinction, have good reason to be suspicious of white intruders. Yet they were happy to feed me, to take me with them on hunting trips and to perform their sacred funeral rites before my camera. I owe my life to a Jivaro family who nursed me through a serious case of dysentery with as much care as if I had been one of their own. The leader of this family, a chieftain with many heads to his credit, died in an attempt to help me. He was bitten by a bushmaster while traveling to a distant medicine man or *wishinu* who had once made a white man well.

This is not to suggest that primitive Indians have a monopoly on courtesy and kindness. And sometimes their social and moral codes are difficult for an outsider to understand—much less live by. We may find some primitive communal attitudes—the Indian's insistence that he share your goods, that you share his—not consonant with Western man's concept of property rights. Or we may find it difficult to fathom the primitive's sudden anger, his strange practical jokes and his seemingly unnecessary fears. But he is more than likely to apply the standards he lives by to the visitor. The primitive expects the outsider to play by his rules; if he does the reward is usually genuine friendship.

The white invader has not, on the whole, been as consistent. For example, Indians have often learned about the white man's lofty moral and religious ideals from missionaries; then they are confronted by a group of bullies with rifles and pistols who deprive them of their land, their women, their dignity and—if they object—their lives. It has been recorded that a certain Caribbean chief was being told by a priest of the glorious life that awaited him in Heaven; he was at that moment tied to a stake and about to be burned alive by the Spaniards. "Let me go to Hell," he countered, "that I may not come where they are."

Franz Boas, the trail-blazing anthropologist and ethnologist, explained earlier in this century that achievement and aptitude do not go hand in hand, that a four- or five-thousand-year delay in cultural advancement could be explained by variations in the life history of peoples. Such a time lag appears insignificant when set against the entire span of man's occupation of this planet. "What does it mean, then," wrote Boas, "if one group of mankind reached a certain stage of cultural development at the age of one hundred thousand years and another at the age of one hundred and four thousand years?"

The date of man's first appearance has been pushed back even further since Boas's time—by Louis S. B. Leakey and others into perhaps millions of years—and the gap between civilized man and primitive man seems even less significant. Moreover, as Boas also remarked (and as Arnold Toynbee has since made common knowledge) peoples of a given culture, color or physique have shown particular capacities for growth during certain periods but not during others. For example, the Arabs excelled in medicine, science and mathematics during the early Middle Ages and were in many ways more advanced than the northern Europeans, who were not to reach their peak until hundreds of years later.

When Columbus arrived in this hemisphere, the Indians living in southern Mexico and Peru were the most culturally advanced. The Aztecs, Mayans and Incas had not only developed well beyond other Indian peoples, but in many ways their wealth, artistic achievement, communication systems, agriculture, city planning, mathematics, science and political systems were the equal of—if not better than—the accomplishments of their contemporaries elsewhere in the world. What levels of civilization might have been attained if the Spanish conquistadores had not plundered the cultures of the Andes and Central America is an intriguing question. It is quite likely that the influence of these high cultures would have been communicated to other parts of the Americas. In other words, a few hundred years more might have changed the story of European-Indian contact considerably. As it happened, the Inca empire was destroyed in 1532 by a small army under Francisco Pizarro who kidnapped the emperor,

Atahualpa; and when the huge ransom in gold had been paid the Spaniards treacherously murdered him.

Other peoples of the Americas were able to hold out against the incursions of Europeans, to delay for perhaps a few centuries their eventual destruction. Ironically, the conditions which saved them from subjugation also inhibited their cultural advancement: their isolation deep within jungles or beyond inaccessible mountain ranges, their warlike proclivities, their xenophobia or their inability to extract valuable resources. The Jivaros, secluded on the Ecuadorian-Peruvian border, had their first and, until recent decades, their last confrontation with gold-hungry white men late in the sixteenth century when a handful of conquistadores, led by Juan de Salinas, penetrated Jivaro country, set up towns and established themselves briefly as absolute rulers.

Salinas died in 1599, and the new governor was not only cruel and greedy for gold but also made the fatal mistake of not assessing the Jivaro temperament correctly. These ever-feuding head-hunters made peace among themselves—"buried the lance" —and burned the Spanish towns in a nearly complete massacre of between twenty and thirty thousand inhabitants. When the Jivaros took the governor prisoner, they assured him that he would be well supplied with the gold that he was seeking. After stripping and binding him, his captors forced his mouth open with a bone and poured molten gold down his throat. The Spanish made no attempt to settle among the Jivaros again, leaving the headhunters undisturbed and free to war upon one another in their traditional way.

The Camayuras are another primitive people who were able to escape, until recently, the incursions of white men. They live deep in the Mato Grosso of Brazil, in what is still one of the least penetrated areas of the world. Here the South American Indian, with the help of sympathetic and knowledgeable Brazilians, is making a last stand before the inevitable meeting with civilization. The Camayuras were protected by 500 miles of jungle to the north and by the once-warlike Chavantes to the south. These are the same Chavantes who, only twenty-five years ago, were pictured from the air aiming bows and arrows at low-flying airplanes. There is now an airstrip in the midst of Chavante territory, and the Camayuras, when I visited them recently, numbered·only 110. Since my earlier visit there in 1949, the white man's illnesses—pneumonia, smallpox, influenza, and tuberculosis—had taken a terrible toll. The isolation that so long protected these and other primitive peoples of South America has unhappily contributed to their susceptibility to civilization's diseases.

So it is in Brazil, Ecuador and Peru that we find peoples in the twilight period of primitive life, peoples who have not quite lost their ancient cultural identities, but who will undoubtedly vanish within a few short years, to be found only in anthropological texts and museums. Let us examine briefly what has been happening to some of them lately.

The modern conquistador—the *civilizado*—is likely to be a hard-headed businessman or government official with a twentieth-century look but with methods and rationalizations for exterminating Indians that are not much more subtle than those of his sixteenth-century predecessors. His aim is "economic development," but it often has little to do with the economic health or the physical well-being of the Indian. The *civilizado* wants the rich lands that happen to lie within his national boundaries for the rich resources they contain, for cattle to graze upon, for settlement by agricultural pioneers. He is, above all, many different people, and this has made it nearly impossible for the Indian to understand his adversary.

It has been said that there is no inherent evil in moving the frontiers of civilization into the huge Amazon basin. At any rate it seems to be almost inevitable. This immense area, stretching from the Atlantic coast to the Peruvian Andes, has the land and resources to feed the men and fuel the machinery of the world. It has been estimated that Brazil could accommodate some 900 million people. And what government would, for the benefit of a declining population of primitives, abandon such richly endowed lands when the economic watchword seems to be to expand or perish? The United States has not been the only nation to cast covetous looks at South American iron, copper, manganese, petroleum, rubber, industrial diamonds, tungsten, zinc, hardwoods, vegetable oils—to name but a few of the resources there. Nor is it a question of ideology; no nation, whether capitalist or socialist, has ever allowed primitive peoples to retain their own lands simply because of a "moral" claim to them.

So those primitive peoples who held out the longest must now prepare to meet the thrust of the *civilizado*. The Indian has a kind of Hobson's choice. If he is in the path of the resource-extractor, he can expect to deal with a man of checkered origins, who arrives without family or a sense of law. Not all the Indians of South America are as fortunate as the Auca. In 1968 when I visited the Napo River area in Ecuador, the Texaco exploration parties had come to an impasse. The oilmen had been warned by a missionary that any intrusion into Auca territory was certain to be met by fierce resistance, so they were willing to wait until the Aucas could be cleared out before proceeding with their geological survey. Usually the extractors attempt to "hire" the Indians (whether they want to be employed or not), and destroy community life in the process. The Indians are either required to help locate forest products or to serve as rowers or bearers, while the women do the cooking or are made concubines.

The Indian may encounter another group—the herders who will clear him off the land to make room for cattle. If the Indian happens to be a member of a hunting community, he must abandon his traditions (and learn that the white man's cattle are not to be hunted). Or the Indian's lands might be appropriated by agricultural pioneers, in which case he is quickly made to understand that he is an obstacle to progress. His best course is to move his village before the farmers arrive in great numbers with heavy mechanical equipment. The Indian who chooses to remain soon must cope with a changed environment and he discovers, perhaps for the first time in his people's history, what it is like to be a member of an unwanted minority.

In the face of such wrenching confrontations, it is a rare Indian who will not have his spirit broken. It does not seem to matter whether the intentions of the *civilizado* are benign or malignant. In the case of primitive cultural life, the result is usually a lingering death. Those who are concerned with the problems of primitive peoples cannot agree whether it is better to prepare the primitive at once for his inevitable encounter with economic change or to fence him off in splendid isolation.

There are some, notably missionaries, who feel that the Indian's best interests are served by his abandoning his traditional way of dress—or lack of it. I have returned to some villages after an absence of ten or fifteen years to find once-proud bodies looking more like slum products draped with sorry-looking hand-me-downs. The most brutalized contacts, however, occur between the Indian and those who intend to enslave or exterminate him. This is still common in areas where the intruder is his own policeman and makes his own law.

In fact, the *Journal do Brasil's* disquieting report that the Indian Protective Service was no longer shielding the Indian but was assisting his enemies brought me back to South America in 1968 and indirectly inspired this book. This respected newspaper fearlessly charged that recent administrations of the IPS had aided the systematic genocide of primitive peoples in order that their lands, guaranteed to them under the Brazilian constitution, might be taken over by private interests.

Indians, according to *Journal do Brasil*, had been clubbed to death, inoculated with smallpox, shot down and even massacred by explosives dropped from airplanes. In Rio Grande do Sul the Guarani and Kaingang Indians had been systematically robbed of forests once rich in pine trees. There is not enough timber there now to build a single house for an Indian family. Instances were common of the enslavement of Indians—600 Ticunas, for example—by farmers who proceeded to whip or starve them if they did not work. The rationalization in such cases was always the same: the Indians were lazy and had to be treated harshly. It did not matter that the Indians had been given neither tools nor the skills to use them. Even when the Indians evidenced a willingness to work hard, the farmers still maintained that a good beating had a salutary effect.

Foreign land speculators aided by bribed officials were able to clear Patacho Indians off lands on the coast of Brazil. When members of one village objected to being dispossessed, they were inoculated with smallpox, for they had learned to trust the men who came with little black medical bags. With insidious efficiency their infected clothing was later distributed to a neighboring village. When the Patachos complained to the IPS, their complaints were ignored. Angered, they retaliated with spears, bows and arrows. Their persecutors quickly had what seemed to be a change of heart; the following day *civilizados* appeared with sacks of sugar which were happily received. Within forty-eight hours more than fifty additional Patachos were dead; the sugar had been laced with arsenic.

One reporter learned of Indians in a farming community who had been enslaved and tormented. Near one farm a group of terrified children were herded to the bank of a river and forced to take part in an orgy. When one child escaped she was quickly captured and killed; her dismembered body was thrown piecemeal to the piranhas. One rubber plantation owner was accused of kidnapping girls from the Ticuna tribe and exporting them as prostitutes.

A group of Cintas-Largas Indians who had been enlisted as slave laborers in a mining camp were on the brink of rebelling after having been fired upon for disobedience. They made the mistake of holding a meeting on a jungle plateau. The miners learned of the meeting and sent up an airplane loaded with dynamite. Before the Indians could escape, they were blasted to bits from the air.

Hadn't Luis Neves, former head of the IPS, been charged with forty-two counts of corruption, among them the taking of $300,-000 in bribes? I knew that some of the most dedicated men I had ever known, men like the Villas Boas brothers who would give their lives to help the Indians, were themselves connected with the IPS. Yet a picture of sorts was emerging; apparently the *civilizado* was coming in for the kill—too impatient to wait for Indian life to come to an end through disease, loss of will or social disorganization. The stakes were high indeed, so why wait for someone else to grab the Indian's lands.

More recently the Brazilian government has emphatically denied any complicity in the mass slaughter of Indians. Certain IPS men, the government conceded, may have been bribed by unscrupulous commercial interests to look the other way while the Indians were disposed of, but it insisted that the government itself bore none of the blame. Officials pointed out that Indian territory is too big, hence too expensive, to police properly. Men in the upper echelons of government did acknowledge a limited responsibility inasmuch as they did not know what was going on. Clearly, no one wants to accept much of the guilt, but there seem to be very little grounds for anyone to feel pious.

What I found on my return to the primitive peoples of Peru, Ecuador and Brazil in 1968 convinced me more than the headlines that the Indian's days were numbered: the son of a fierce Jivaro chieftain who wanted to teach school, a now-mendacious Bororo chief who had lost his former majestic air, the once-secluded Yagua Indians on a tourist itinerary, Chavantes working under the stern gaze of men who they had once sworn would never set foot on their territory. And behind all the changes lay the grim message of statistics. A numbers game, perhaps, since the data on primitive depopulation are so often disputed; yet the discrepancies are never as significant as the compelling fact that the graphs all point the same way—down, and out.

There were perhaps 10 million Indians living in the Amazon basin five centuries ago. Today there are scarcely 200,000. (During this same period the world's total population has gone from less than 500 million to more than three billion.) In Brazil, the Indians numbered three million in 1500; less than a tenth of that number were living there by the turn of this century. There are about 78,000 living in Brazil today. The Bororos were still a people 5,000 strong in 1900; victims of contagious diseases, they are now down to less than 150. The Nhambiquara tribe once numbered 10,000; only 1,000 remain, tragic victims of genocide. In two centuries the Carajas of Brazil have declined from 500,-000 to 1,200 for the same reason. The Guarani of Parana were reduced by slavery and torture. In ten years they have declined from 5,000 to about 300 (and by the time you read this that figure is likely to have dropped still more).

In Belém I spoke to the Brazilian anthropologist Edward Galvao, who told me that since 1960 big business organizations, having accumulated new fortunes in Rio de Janeiro and São Paulo, have begun to penetrate the *terra incognita* of the Mato Grosso. In this once-inaccessible sanctuary of the Indian these companies are purchasing huge tracts of land for speculation, mining and cattle raising. Unlike the old-style pioneer who needed cheap labor to help locate and extract minerals, semi-precious stones and forest products, these huge operations have little need for the services of the Indian since modern equipment is now available. Such companies have both the motivation and the money to corrupt IPS officials to secure the removal of the Indians from vast stretches of the Amazon basin. The IPS, unlike the Villas Boas brothers, failed to survey and record title to the lands of various Indian groups. Big companies knowing this paid the legal registration fee and claimed these huge tracts of land. Thus they drove out both the Indians and the casual white settlers.

Since the Indian is patently unable to catch up with the rapidly paced mechanization taking place in Brazil, he finds himself on a treadmill to oblivion. He cannot assimilate because he is too unskilled for a genuinely productive role in an industrial society. Neither does his world view accord with a routinized, machine-tending life, and he is discouraged from undertaking farming, which might suit him. Wherever he is or wherever he has moved turns out to be directly in the path of progress. And his instruction in the ways of civilization is usually just enough to disrupt his traditional life but not enough to prepare him for its dizzying pace. Almost every contact with the outside world endangers his health, diminishes his pride and disorganizes his community. He finds himself a misfit.

Is there anything that can be done to postpone his fate? Perhaps little. But the interested reader might do well to look more closely at a few of the peoples I have known in the course of my travels, peoples who will soon be disappearing from this earth. They will not pass this way again.

2 Jivaros: Still Undefeated

THE PRIMITIVE IS DOOMED to come off second best in any encounter with civilization. He has neither the machines, the weapons nor the large organized populations to hold out for very long against an invader—unless he has somehow acquired a reputation, deserved or not, for outdoing his would-be conquerors in brutality. To this reputation for savagery add a natural fortress denied his North American Indian cousins; add, as well, a passionate pride in his own cultural identity, and you have a few of the reasons why the Jivaros of eastern Ecuador and neighboring Peru have survived when more trusting, more docile, more accessible peoples have vanished. They withstood armies of gold-seeking Incas; they defied the bravado of the early conquistadores; they stood up against the enslaving rubber barons at the turn of the century. And they have yet to surrender to the blandishments of oil seekers who are impatient to drill wells in their resource-rich lands.

Notwithstanding their proud history of independence and resistance to conquest—a history of which the Jivaro himself is
only vaguely aware—the visitor to a Jivaro clan will not find
large numbers of men, regimented and ready to swarm upon the
intruder. There are no villages, no concentrations of population
and fighting power. There is just a single oval-shaped hut, called
a *jivaria*, perhaps forty to sixty feet in length, with a thatched
roof supported by walls of chonta logs, designed for defense—
not against white men, but against other Jivaros who live in
similar huts some miles away. The men, women and children of
four or five nuclear families live in such huts. There will be
lances and blowguns in evidence, perhaps an antiquated shotgun
or two—equally dangerous at either end.

Something else about these warriors detracts, at first sight,
from the fierce Jivaro image. While the women are working in
the fields of manioc the men will be casually engaged in the
domestic art of basketweaving. Furthermore, they appear to be
excessively vain; each man carries his own cosmetic pouch, and
his face is ornamented with the red dye of the achiote seed. His
head is girdled by a fur band, out of which sprout the brilliantly
colored feathers of the toucan. Yet this vanity—or pride, if you
will—explains what the real weapon of the Jivaro is.

Each Jivaro is a self-contained military unit and more. He is a
vitally important actor in a drama that has been taught to him,
along with his superb fighting skills, since early childhood. His
essential role in life is to maintain always the dignity of his
family, particularly that of his ancestors and close kin who have
fallen in combat with other Jivaros. He is something of a Hamlet,
but without Hamlet's confusion. For him, life is a never-ending
vendetta, a continuous state of siege. His home is quite literally
his castle, his fortress. And so long as he maintains his identity as
a Jivaro he must be prepared for a raid—in retaliation for a raid
of his own on some other clan.

The natural environment seems to have fostered his isolation
and siege-mindedness. To the west the land rolls and hunches,
then vaults up above the clouds. To the east 3,200 miles of dense

Amazonian jungle separate him from coastal populations. Even today the Jivaro is a difficult man to reach.

You sense this, well before you meet him, as you approach his *jivaria*. You move along narrow trails as though they had been mined. On my first visit to a Jivaro community I stumbled into a mantrap, the *mosertinyu whua* ("hole of death"), intended to deter surprise attacks. One moment I was walking along, dodging branches and elephant ear leaves; the next I was scrambling through the air. The pit was about four feet deep and three feet square. At the bottom were three hardwood lances tipped with poison. Fortunately the lances were old and broke under my weight; what poison was left was ineffective. Other deterrents include *tambunchi* traps—eight short chonta spikes aimed at the face or chest—that are sprung when the intruder steps on the liana trigger on the ground.

Still other precautions must be taken: you must forewarn the Jivaro of your arrival and that you come in friendship. Before I ever met a Jivaro I found myself shouting *Whee-dee*—"It's me—I come as a friend"—at the top of my voice as I approached. And when you meet, he presents himself to you with a formalized shout using a formalized dialogue. You say: "I have come. I am here!" He answers: "Is that so?" You respond: "I have traveled many miles." And as he answers, he spits with amazing accuracy through his fingers—always emphatic, disliking what seems doubtful. This man tells you at once that he is a person who fully understands the role he must play in his world.

For him there are only two kinds of people—friends and foes. It is as simple as that. Or perhaps not so simple: sometimes foes work through witchcraft. Then the special skills of the shaman, or *wishinu*, are called into play. He must decide who has cast the spell that caused the Jivaro to fall ill, or to have been bitten by a snake or to have simply disappeared in the surrounding forest. It is highly desirable for an outsider to make friends with the *wishinu*, if possible. He is most likely to be suspicious of strangers, their influence and—if you have come from the world of the white man—competing forms of magic.

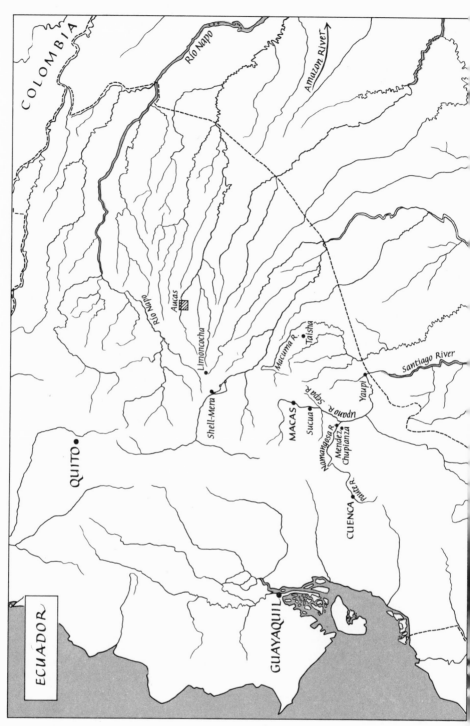

COLOMBIA

Río Napo

Amazon River

Río Napo

Aucas

Limoncocha

Macuma R.

Taisha

Santiago River

Shell-Mera

Yaupi

QUITO

MACAS

Sucua

Upano R.

Sapua R.

Numangosa R.

Méndez

Chupianza

Paute R.

CUENCA

GUAYAQUIL

ECUADOR

One can get a glimpse of the Jivaro life style in the ritualized hospitality ceremony that for me preceded a deeper friendship. He will offer to share with you his famous *nijimanche* drink, a manioc beer fermented after the admixture of the spittle of his women. You drink, you are a friend. If you can demonstrate your good intentions, you may come to the conclusion, as I did about thirty years ago, that the Jivaros are among the most misunderstood people on earth.

Making friends with these remarkable people is not done with gifts alone. All primitive peoples appreciate things like mirrors, fishhooks, fabrics, scissors and knives, and the Jivaros are no exception. Giving and sharing are generally fundamental parts of primitive life. But with gifts one buys cordiality and cooperation, not friendship. Most Jivaros are willing to give generously of themselves once they have decided that you really find them as fascinating as they find themselves—or rather that you respect them for what they are and will not deprive them of what they have, their traditional way of life. If you live as they live, show a genuine interest in their families and talk with them (they love to talk) about their lives and yours, you will be treated like a brother.

A case in point is my own friendship with Peruche, the *curaka* or elder (typically, the independent Jivaros have no word that quite stands for the concept of chieftain) of a *jivaria* in the Paute River area. It was 1945; the war had ended and I was anxious to get back to Jivaro country, the scene of my previous expedition in 1940. That time I had slid down the eastern slopes of the Andes on a mule, the only beast, aside from man, hardy (and foolhardy) enough to attempt that route.

When I reached the first *jivaria*, armed only with cameras and gifts, my boots caked with mud and shrunken tight, my body a mass of fatigue, I was given a friendly reception, then spent the night on a Jivaro wooden platform bed (made for a man five and a half feet tall). In the morning, however, I was forbidden by the old *curaka* to take any pictures, a rather common prohibition among primitive groups. One of my guides suggested that nearby there was a great *curaka* who might understand that my cameras would not deprive any of his people of their souls if I explained their operating principles to him. We moved on and at the second *jivaria* we were greeted by Peruche himself. He waved at us—a particularly good sign, for I had never seen a Jivaro wave. Peruche was pleased with the gifts I had brought, most of all by an odd-looking hat which I had bought on impulse in a shop at Cuenca. It was something of a cross between an overseas cap and a fez, very fancy and colorful. Peruche put it on his head and seldom took it off. I'm sure he even wore it to bed. He was wearing it when he died in the jungle while on his way to a *wishinu* who he was certain would know how to cure my dysentery.

Peruche was willing to dispense with the long and tediously formal introductions (which serve partly as a very effective way of sizing up the visitors) once he had decided that my guides, whom he trusted, would not enter his territory with anyone who was not trustworthy. He agreed to let me film a simulated *tsantsa* ritual—the traditional celebration after a headhunting raid—in part because he was willing to be convinced that my cameras would not harm the soul of his people, in part because it was an excuse for him to throw a party (which he loved as much as talking or performing his role as *curaka*), but also because we had taken to each other right from the start.

For three weeks I was his guest and we would talk for hours about the differences in our two cultures. Even now I remember him with affection and admiration as one who lived a full and useful life according to his code. He was one of the most open-hearted and quick-minded people I have ever known. At seventy, or thereabouts, his lined face showed fine laugh wrinkles that played about his eyes. He was a Jivaro of great reputation, a warrior with many heads to his credit, a hunter of exceptional skill and cunning. I thought then, and still do, that he was the most self-confident of all the Jivaros I have known. His pride in his own nature was such that he could afford to be exceedingly gentle and loving without surrendering his essential Jivaro dignity.

He had four wives, ranging in age from about twenty to fifty-five. After I had been his guest for a day or so Peruche offered me the youngest of them for the duration of my visit. He simply led her to me—Abanasa was her name—and with a smile of friendship that needed no translation he joined our hands. The best way to decline the offer politely, I decided, was to explain through my guide that this was impossible for me, that it was a taboo of my world to take a woman of another tribe. Peruche understood, and demonstrated that he had a fine sense of where lines of propriety had to be drawn. Although I could not take Abanasa as my wife, he argued, she might be useful in other ways.

And she was. Jivaro women are accustomed to doing heavy tasks, partly because the Jivaro animistic philosophy assigns male and female souls to all animals, plants and objects. Since many of the plants which the Jivaros cultivate have female souls, they are tended by women. Two kinds of baskets are made from plants having male souls, and therefore the men are the basketweavers. The fruit of these plants, on the other hand, have female souls, and the women carry the baskets and their contents. Men undertake the cultivation of corn and plantain, but women tend the female-souled peanuts, sweet potatoes and many other crops, including the staple, manioc, which they masticate in the process of making *nijimanche*.

Women do the cooking because fire is female; they make the pots, too, because the clay is taken from the female earth. Jivaro men, however, are not idlers. Aside from their basketweaving, spinning and planting chores they remove the hardwood trees of the forest when a new clearing is to be made. They hunt, too, and sometimes spend ten or fifteen days away from the *jivaria*, sleeping in the jungle at night, covering scores of miles. When a family is traveling the women carry the heavy loads in large baskets supported by tumplines over their heads. But then the men are at all times ready to repel an attack or to kill game along the way. Jivaro men work hard at tasks that are not regarded as "work," for example the wars of extermination and the bloody feuds, with all their complex preparations and accompanying rituals, not to mention the total psychological readiness always required.

Peruche believed that it was not fitting for a man to do the chores assigned to Abanasa: preparing the meals, hauling water and firewood, carrying supplies on hunting trips. She was robust and muscular, attractive by Jivaro standards, and, by comparison with the men, rather unconcerned about enhancing her appearance. Despite Peruche's gracious offer, Jivaro wives are severely punished for infidelity. Many interclan feuds have been brought on, like the Trojan War, by an indiscretion or an abduction. Women are taken as prizes in raids—they are too valuable to kill. And for the same reason infidelity is usually not punished by death. Women are personal property and may be bartered, loaned or given in friendship, but only at the behest of the husband. Polygamy among the Jivaros seems to operate as a means of maintaining a favorable balance between births and the high mortality rate that accompanies a vendetta culture.

It is not true, however, that Jivaros are callous husbands, that they regard their wives merely as workhorses and chattel. I have never seen a more devoted husband, father and grandparent than Peruche, and although the concept of romantic love and monogamy is foreign to Jivaro thinking, there is as much tenderness in a headhunter family as you are likely to find in any group. The wives get along without much apparent jealousy. In fact, young Abanasa was selected for Peruche, as is the custom, by his three older wives.

If the Jivaro is capable of deep affection, loyalty and generosity to those of proven friendship, his enemies, real or imagined, are the objects of implacable hatred and vengeance bordering on obsession. Rarely have the Jivaros made peace among themselves; when they have, it has only been in the face of a common, external threat—as in 1599, when they revolted against the Spanish, killing the governor and massacring the settlers who had invaded their lands.

So far as I am aware, the only time in recent years when the feuding clans have joined in a common purpose took place before my eyes and camera in 1949. On this trip, during the filming of *Jungle Headhunters* for RKO, I was to meet Utitiaja, described to me by none other than Peruche as the greatest living headhunter. Perhaps only the opportunity to appear in a motion picture could have induced him to cooperate.

I had been reading about Utitiaja in Quito, where I had found in a copy of *El Commercio* the news that the section of the Upano River to which I was heading had seen an increase in assassinations and wars of revenge. Responsible for much of this slaughter was Utitiaja, who alone had taken fifty-eight heads.

At Sucua, an outpost near the edge of Jivaro territory, my crew and I were put up at a Salesian mission. There we found about seventy-five Jivaro boys and fifty Jivaro girls attending school; in almost every case they were there because their families had been wiped out. The Roman Catholic Salesians had done what they could to erase the memories of Jivaro traditions from the minds of the children, but bitter hatreds still remained. I heard that one boy, having graduated from the mission school and wearing a cross and a Catholic medal, returned to the jungle and killed four men to avenge the deaths of his father and brothers.

As recently as 1968 the Salesians told me about a Jivaro boy who had been given the name Juan Maestro, because he had become a master mechanic under their tutelage. The Salesians, proud of this young Jivaro as an example of what patient teaching could accomplish, sent him to Rome where he told the Pope in faultless Spanish what the mission had done for him. Back in Ecuador, Juan decided to return to the Jivaro way of life. As a concession to his Christian training he took only one wife, and perhaps because of the veneer of civilization that had been applied, he brought along his mechanic's tools. His *jivaria* was the traditional oval hut, surrounded by a seven-foot-high balsa-log fence. Before long it was the scene of the inevitable siege by the enemies of his family. Juan, though outnumbered, fought it out with the raiders and was able to survive and keep his head intact by a bit of strategy he was not likely to have learned at the mission. Juan climbed the palm pole which supported the thatched roof of the hut, and from there was able to lift up the palm leaves overhead and aim his gun directly at the opposing chief. With the leader of the attack out of the way, the siege quickly ended and the raiders retreated.

One of the young men at the Salesian mission in 1949 was named Shuara. It was he who eventually brought me together with Utitiaja. *Shuara* is the name the Jivaros apply to themselves and means "the people," not at all an uncommon self-designation among preliterate groups. Shuara was given this name because when he appeared from the jungle as a child it was the only word the missionaries could make out. Although Shuara became Christianized, he kept up his jungle contacts. As a Christian he had renounced all desire for revenge, and because his entire family had been killed, he had no enemies—fine credentials for a diplomat. Moreover, he knew both Spanish and the Jivaro tongue and was intelligent and resourceful. I chose him as my guide. Shuara assured me that the reports in the Quito newspaper were quite correct. There had been many raids and much feuding lately in Jivaro territory. But he was sure that I would be welcomed, even surer when he got a look at the copy of *Life* magazine I had brought along.

In this issue was a series of color pictures I had taken on my 1945 trip which showed Peruche and others from the Paute region. Shuara told me that these pictures might very well serve as my passport among the feuding Jivaro clans. Thanks to Shuara's help, they served even better than I dared hope. My party had been to several *jivarias*, but we found only five or six men in each. The *curaka* of one of the larger *jivarias* of the Sepa group (Jivaros who live along the Sepa River, a tributary of the Upano) assembled about twenty-eight men from other *jivarias* in his clan. But something was still missing; we needed a commanding personality, someone like Peruche.

Shuara suggested that he take the copy of *Life* to some of the other *curakas* in the vicinity, including Utitiaja. These pictures, he told me, might tempt the great headhunter and the leaders who were his rivals to bury the lance for a few days and come together at the Sepa *jivaria*, an ideal setting for a film. Shuara understood the Jivaro temperament well. He would tell Utitiaja and the others that the pictures I took in 1945 of the Santiago and Paute Jivaros had been seen by people all over the world, that I had come back to the Upano group because I had heard that they were the greatest of all Jivaro warriors—and their pictures would soon be seen far beyond the seas.

Shuara returned with news of success after six days—six restless days, I might add, for the members of the Sepa clan. Utitiaja would soon be arriving with his group from the Chupientsa territory. Unbelievable as it seemed, the host Sepa group was also to be joined by members of the Cambanaca and Tutanangosa groups—four feuding Jivaro tribes in all. I asked Shuara how he had managed to get Utitiaja to come. "I told him," Shuara explained, "that you could not have a successful film without the greatest warrior of the Jivaros."

I had no difficulty picking out Utitiaja, although there was very little about him to suggest the savage headhunter of fifty-eight *tsantsas*. He was in fact a slender man with fine features and not the slightest trace of ferocity or cruelty in his expression. He was rather gentle and soft-spoken, but his self-assurance and air of genuine leadership immediately set him apart from the others. When he saw me standing alongside my tent, he came to me holding out his hand in a gesture of friendship. I knew that he was not observing protocol; Jivaro etiquette dictated that he should have greeted the Sepa *curaka* first. Like Peruche he was an individualist, and thoroughly able to make his own rules when it suited him.

Utitiaja confirmed that he had taken fifty-eight heads in his lifetime. For a Jivaro, the taking of heads is only partly a matter of pride and a measure of one's manhood. Because Jivaro settlements live under constant threat of attack, those who have demonstrated their ability to fight and to kill are accorded much respect. But there are other factors which have their roots in Jivaro philosophy. When Utitiaja went on his first raid, for example, he avenged the death of his father. He was only thirteen when his father died, and he swore then to kill his slayer. It took him four years to bring peace to the soul of his father; during that period his father's soul was restless and unhappy.

A young Jivaro is taught at frequent intervals that if he succeeds in bringing peace to the souls of his relatives not only will he himself enjoy happiness, many wives and the respect of his fellows, but he will be avenged if necessary, and his own soul will find rest. If he fails to do this he will be miserable. I recorded such an indoctrination on one of my recent visits to the Jivaro territory. Yangora, a *curaka*, told his nephews with much fervor: "Your father's head was taken by Papue of the Camboca group, who also captured your two aunts. When you grow up it will be your sacred duty to seek blood vengeance so that the souls of your murdered relatives may rest in peace. Their spirits now are unhappy. If you succeed you will be blessed with fine wives and you will be happy men. If you fail in your sacred obligation, you will be cursed with nagging wives who will bear you no children, the game in the forest will elude you, and your crops will fail."

While Utitiaja, his family and warriors were camped with the Sepa clan I asked him what he thought about "taking the law into his own hands" when he killed those who were responsible for the death of his kin.

"Who else should kill your enemies?" Utitiaja responded. "I hear that you pay certain people to do that for you in your country. I think that is wrong. I am the one who has the right and the duty to kill them. And I have always fulfilled my duties, rather than trying to get someone else to take care of them for me."

After a successful raid, when enemy heads have been taken and then reduced,* the *tsantsa* feast is held. In a sense, this victory dance represents the climax of a Jivaro's life; it is the

---

* The entire headshrinking operation takes about five hours. First a cut is made from the crown to the base of the head, and the skin and hair are peeled off almost as easily as a skin is removed from a rabbit. After the cut is sewn, the scalp is immersed in a boiling solution made from the chinchipi vine, which has astringent qualities. Hot stones are placed through the neck opening. Next the head is repeatedly filled with hot sand and whirled about. The *tsantsa* is both shrunken and hardened by these successive operations. Finally, the hair is tied to a vine, and the head is left hanging. Smoke will dry out any remaining oil in the skin and complete the hardening process.

supreme moment of fulfillment. An important debt has been paid. The Jivaro has justified his existence. First, the heroic Jivaro is washed in chicken blood and painted with black *sua*. The *tsantsa* is impaled on a lance, and at peak moments of the ritual the Jivaros dance about the head, brandishing their spears, reenacting the kill.

Utitiaja was almost lyrical when he described his emotions during the *tsantsa* feast. "It is a wonderful thing," he said. "You feel that you are good, that you have done what you are supposed to do in this world. You have triumphed over your enemy by killing him. Now you triumph over his evil spirit and make it a good spirit that will help you. Until you have taken the soul of an enemy you are not truly a man. And now you can tell the souls of the people you loved that they can stop their unhappy wandering. These are splendid things to feel. It is almost like soaring as high as a condor."

Tsantsa feasts are time-consuming and expensive. Utitiaja, despite his fifty-eight conquests, could remember being able to afford only nine or ten celebrations. Yet he, like Peruche, embodied the supreme self-confidence that distinguishes the true Jivaro from other primitive peoples surviving in this hemisphere. It wasn't merely the feast or even the taking of heads that confirmed Utitiaja's strong sense of himself. His confidence lay in his certainty that the Jivaro way of life was the correct way and that no one had ever challenged it successfully. Few outsiders have penetrated Jivaro territory in sufficient numbers and with enough weapons or their own brand of moral courage and self-confidence to convince these people that they should submit.

The self-confidence of men like Utitiaja, however, is built into them from childhood. They are encouraged to believe that their capacities, inherited from father and grandfather, are equal to life's clear-cut challenge. Moreover, before each raid the Jivaro will drink *nateema* or *maikoa*, powerful hallucinogenic drugs that produce visions. These visions, interpreted by the *wishinu*, foretell whether or not the raid will be successful. A raid is carried out only if the visions presage success.

As increasing numbers of Jivaros have been indoctrinated in

the Christian missions of Ecuador and Peru, it is questionable whether the peculiar kind of self-confidence, the backbone of Jivaro culture, can endure. What happens when Jivaros lose their traditional orientation and must at the same time come to terms with the inevitable thrust of civilization? Will they continue to be *Jivaros*? If so, in what sense? Can you take from a culture its beliefs and rituals and expect it to hold together? Can we, as outsiders, even with the best intentions, pick and choose those qualities of a people we would like to see endure or vanish —as if we were cultural eugenicists?

Questions like these have troubled the friends of primitive or preliterate peoples the world over. In the case of the Jivaros it is particularly saddening because they are, by common agreement of anthropologists, missionaries, teachers, traders and others who have observed them, still a very vigorous people. And unlike other South American Indians, their numbers have not yet declined. In fact there is some evidence that, despite the costly feuding, their population may actually be on the increase. The most conservative estimates of their present numbers range above 20,000.

Yet the questions persist. When there are no longer men like Utitiaja, when the Jivaro concepts of the soul and blood revenge are gone, when Jivaro polygamy and the *tsantsa* celebration vanish, what will be left of their culture? What will become of the self-assurance with which the Jivaros have traditionally confronted the outsider?

Take, for example, Utitiaja's son, Esteban Gacepa, a Christian, a schoolteacher and a farmer. I was fortunate enough to meet him in 1968 in Limoncocha, where he was studying. I learned from him that he and his father had experienced probably the first "generation gap" in the traditional life of the Jivaro people.

In 1949 Utitiaja told me that his son-in-law had been killed and his daughter abducted in a raid by an enemy clan. He assured me that he would avenge this death and recover his daughter. A few months after I returned to New York I received a newspaper clipping from a friend in Quito. It reported that the notorious Jivaro chief Utitiaja had murdered a man from the Tutanangosa tribe, and as he was returning to his *jivaria* he had been captured by a detachment of soldiers flown in from Sucua to put down the recent wave of murders. There was much clamor in Ecuador over Utitiaja; he was regarded by the authorities as a gangster, a sort of kingpin of a jungle Mafia. They were insisting that he be brought to Quito to be tried for murder. But the government later decided to release Utitiaja in accordance with a law providing that no Indian could be punished for crimes against his own people.

What I did not know until almost twenty years later was how Utitiaja's arrest had affected him and the traditional father-son relationship. My first knowledge of a significant change among the Jivaros came in a letter from missionary Mike Ficke in Sucua in January, 1964, informing me of Utitiaja's death.

"In regard to Utitiaja," the letter read, "he quit fighting and killing after his arrest, due to the influence of his son, a Christian schoolteacher in Chupientsa. A tree fell on him, breaking his leg, and as he was so far in the forest at the time, they had quite a time trying to care for him. He died of the broken leg, and possibly from the infection, although the missionaries cared for him as much as they could."

It struck me at the time that not many Jivaros would have given up a life style at the prodding of a missionized son. As closely knit as I found the Jivaro father-son relationship, I would have expected the older man to have written off his son as some sort of perplexing aberration, at the least.

3 Jivaros: Lessons in Survival

AT LIMONCOCHA IN 1968, I relied upon Gacepa to fill in the events of the years between. He was huskier and taller than his father, with fine broad shoulders, high cheek bones, a rather stern face that now and then warmed into a smile displaying teeth unusually white for a Jivaro. He had some of his father's flair for gesticulation and, all in all, he cut an even more dramatic figure; if anything he, rather than Utitiaja, would have made the more convincing headhunter. The father, with his quiet poise, had a bearing reminiscent of a business executive.

The differences between father and son sharpened the longer I spoke to Gacepa. Taken as men, rather than as Jivaros, or as headhunters, the father had the qualities of a realized person, a man who had won the respect of his people and had fulfilled his life purpose. Nothing, at least when I met Utitiaja, could remove a jot of his conviction that he had completed himself. He was not a striver, a seeker after the pot of gold at the end of the rainbow

—he was there. His son, however, had lost his footing in the old way of life and had not yet grasped the elusive prize held out by civilization. He was a striver—for economic security, for a better life for his family, for a better job.

Gacepa's life had begun in traditional Jivaro style; at the age of six he already knew the forest, its dangers and its bounties. He also knew the enemies of his family and owned his own small blowgun. Later he was given an adult-sized blowgun and learned how to use it expertly. Yet, he recalls, the traditional indoctrination somehow failed to convince him that the Jivaro system of blood revenge was an appealing way of life. He remembers the wailing of women whose husbands went off to fight and be killed, the five days of drunkenness that often preceded a raid on an enemy clan—what he calls the false courage. He had heard of other ways of life and when he met his first missionaries he was easily won over.

By the time Gacepa was ten years of age he had learned from Utitiaja how to hunt and fish and work with the plants and forest materials that had male souls, but he was an unwilling pupil in the arts of war, headhunting and revenge. Gacepa remembers that his father attempted to convince him that he must follow in the footsteps of generations of Jivaro warrior heroes. There were beatings, threats, even pleas. "If you don't want to remain in the tradition of my life," Utitiaja warned him, "you will only have misery all your days." The father, however, gave way at last when he saw that his son was as immovable as he.

Although few Jivaro fathers would have been as tolerant of such resistance to the traditions of their people, I believe that Utitiaja's forbearance was not only a mark of his own individuality; in a way it confirms the Jivaro belief that for good or ill each man is responsible for his own destiny. Gacepa had been well instructed; Utitiaja could do no more.

Yet how was the son able to influence the father? The debate must have gone on over a period of years. Today, Gacepa regards his father with a certain grudging admiration. "My father, I suppose, was a happy man," Gacepa told me. "That is, according to his thinking. He knew no other life. He was trained in childhood for what he was to become—a great warrior. He felt he was a man of destiny."

Gacepa married when he reached manhood, set up his own *jivaria*, and, thanks to the training he received at the Salesian mission in Sucua, began his teaching career. His home was immune from attack by his father's enemies because he had made it clear that he would have nothing to do with the traditional Jivaro way of settling scores, even though nearby homes were raided by rival clans. "Yet," he told me, "I could never undertake a long journey without fear of an ambush, since my father was known as a killer and his many enemies* might at any time try to avenge themselves on him through me. I was never able to live in complete peace."

I knew that Utitiaja had several sons. Adamain was cast in another mold and had no intention of stepping outside the bounds of Jivaro tradition. This must have consoled the chieftain for the loss of Gacepa to civilization. Adamain like his father, and in some ways like his brother Gacepa, was an ambitious man. He grew up wanting to become a shaman, the prestigious and powerful *wishinu* who not only cures the sick, but also determines by occult means the enemies of the clan who are to be marked for revenge. Naturally, the *wishinu*, since he is also able to cast spells that will inflict injury or death upon foes at a long distance, is himself a frequent target of enemy vengeance. Adamain, however, never became a full-fledged shaman. He and his wife were killed at Cuchantsa, where he had gone to study with a *wishinu*. The killers had avenged themselves on Adamain whose brother-in-law had slain one of their people years before.

When Gacepa told me about his brother's fate, I remembered that Adamain, his wife Chupa and infant child had been present with Utitiaja at the meeting of the clans in 1949. I had photographed the mother breast-feeding both her child and a puppy

---

* Utitiaja's enemies were legion. They included members of the Yuriyasa, Yaupi, Santiago, Sepa, Tutanangossa, Cambanaca, and Macuma groups.

whose mother had been killed by a jaguar. (Domestic animals are precious to the Jivaros, as they are to most primitive peoples.) Adamain's child had since grown up and, with eight years of grade school behind him, he too has departed from Jivaro tradition. Gacepa told me that the young man wanted to come to Limoncocha and prepare for a career as a teacher in emulation of his uncle. It seemed to me that for a child who had shared his mother's bosom with an animal to want to become a teacher, even a rural teacher, was suggestive of the rapid changes taking place in Jivaro territory and elsewhere.

Recalling that meeting of the clans now, I wonder whether Utitiaja was of a mind to show his son that his "old-fashioned" father was a celebrity so far as the outside world was concerned. And what if his picture should appear, like that of Peruche, in an issue of *Life* magazine? There was a bitter irony in the thought that this pillar of modern communication and advertising might have served to reinforce traditional warrior values in the remote Jivaro forests and valleys of Ecuador.

It is not likely, however, that anything short of a miracle could have moved Gacepa to take up the life of a Jivaro head-hunter, especially after he learned of his brother's death and conjured up the vision of Adamain's head thrust on the end of a chonta lance. The killings that had led to his father's arrest had already given Gacepa ample evidence that he would be foolish to return to the old Jivaro ways—in Yaupi alone, the Jivaro population had already been reduced from 800 to 500. So Gacepa was determined to do all he could to change those ways—beginning with his father.

"I realized more than ever," Gacepa explained, "that although my father was a great warrior, his whole life was built upon fear and hatred. It was a terrible way to live, not only for him but for the entire Jivaro people. After he had been arrested and released I tried very hard to make him understand that he must change, that we all must change."

Gacepa was uncertain why Utitiaja had at last given in to his entreaties. Perhaps he didn't really change his fundamental beliefs; he simply retired or, like the proverbial old soldier, he just faded away, leaving a reputation that will live for a long time in Jivaro memories. As for Gacepa, he was forty years old when I met him in 1968; his eyes seemed rather sad. His face would occasionally become a shade grimmer as he told me of the limited opportunities for a Jivaro, especially one with a sketchy education. I asked him if he was happy in the life he had chosen.

"I am living in a different world from the one I knew as a child," he said. "It is different from my father's world. Killing and revenge are not part of my life. I do not have to spend my days in fear and hiding. But that is not enough. I want to better myself and am doing everything I can. Yet I can only go so far. When I am able I come to Limoncocha for teacher training so that I can teach children in the six- to ten-year group. At home a friend looks after my little farm in Chupientsa where I teach. I must go home soon and take care of things and look after my wife and my six children. I try to become a better teacher, I farm; there is not much else I can do. It will be better for my children, especially if I work hard and stay out of trouble. My life has been a struggle. My father warned me it would be that way . . . For my children it will go better, that is my hope."

Gacepa has two surviving brothers and a sister. The brothers, although they completed the fourth grade in the mission school, live more or less in the tradition of their father in the Upano-Chupientsa area. They each have their own gardens, some cattle and they speak enough Spanish to help them in their dealings with the *civilizados*. Their sister has had no schooling.

When asked about the concept of the soul that motivated the Jivaro headhunter, Gacepa thought for a bit, shrugged his shoulders, and replied: "The main thing was that we had to keep our honor and show the world that we were strong and proud."

"How do you feel about *your* honor?" I asked him.

"I don't feel that I have to show my pride as my ancestors did. The shamans, even today, are like this. They attempt to prove that they are worthy of trust. They try to carry on this tradition of pridefulness and insist that people notice how powerful they are. So they are obliged to advertise themselves and prove their high status. This is what my dead brother, Adamain, wanted. People still believe in the shamans and go to them with their jungle sicknesses. But if they are suffering from one of the white man's maladies, they go to a white doctor."

According to Gacepa, revenge killing is rapidly dying out among the Jivaros, although much bitterness prevails in the wake of past feuding. There are still unsettled scores in every clan. Could anything be found to replace the Jivaro expression of pride and rivalry in headhunting, I wondered. I asked Gacepa if competitive sports, or some other outlet for violent feelings, could ever replace the *tsantsa* raid. Gacepa responded with one of his rare slow, thoughtful smiles. "Yes," he answered, "I used to play soccer and volleyball. I'm a little too old for soccer now, though. But I really don't know if this is the answer. Has it worked in other countries? For example, in your country?"

Recalling the continuing American record of violence and the country's preoccupation with sports, particularly spectator sports, I shook my head. "Well, what is it that would make your life complete?" I asked and then volunteered, "You certainly have no taste for *tsantsa* raids."

Gacepa did not have to think for very long this time. "I'd like my teacher's certificate. Then I would be able to take better care of my children. Oh, yes, there is one other thing."

"And that is?"

"A sewing machine. I saw a beautiful one in a magazine the other day."

Whether Gacepa realizes it or not, his role as a catalyst in transforming the Jivaro way of life is essential. Unless the Jivaros can somehow maintain their splendid isolation (which no one with any knowledge of the situation really believes possible), they must learn to engage the Spanish-speaking people of Ecuador and Peru on more or less equal terms. The alternative is exploitation, whether open and bold-faced or insidious and covert makes little difference. The other alternative is resistance, a return to blood revenge, but this time on a broader and costlier

scale. In the end resistance will fail, too. The Christianized
Jivaros, like Gacepa, have no stomach for warfare, and there are
simply not enough of the old Utitiaja type to hold out indefinitely against submachine guns and low-flying aircraft.

Although everyone agrees that acculturation is both inevitable
and necessary, the Jivaros find themselves caught between opposing forces. On the one hand if they assimilate the white man's
ways too slowly they may have to choose between a destructive
exploitation and an equally destructive resistance. If, on the
other hand, they change their way of life too quickly they face a
socially dislocating loss of identity without any assurance that
they will be integrated into the white community. In fact, the
opposite is more likely to be the case, as witness what happened
to the North American Indians.

The Salesian missionary, Father Raul, predicts that oil will
soon be found in northern Oriente province. It has already been
discovered in Jivaro country. The Salesians, who have worked
among the Jivaros for seventy-five years, believe they know why
the process of Christianization has gone so slowly. The efforts
of the early missionaries were nullified by the conquistadores,
whose hunger for material wealth offset their own pious teach-
ings. Later the Jivaros, like other Indian groups on the upper
Amazon, were the victims of the rubber boom, and still more
recently they have faced the guns of Ecuadorian soldiers—difficult competition for men who talk peace. Before the missionaries
can convince the Jivaros to end their bellicose ways they must
teach them to confront the *civilizado* with more effective political means, as the Salesians know. Soon roads will be constructed
and their initial high costs will be paid back in the rich resources
of the Jivaro territories. Oil companies already employ Jivaro
men who, ignorant of the fair market value of their labor, sometimes find themselves working for months in order to pay for a
pair of pants.

One religious group called the Summer Institute of Linguistics
has penetrated several Jivaro areas with the intention of teaching
them to read and write their native language. A nondenomina-

tional Christian organization, the Institute has translated the Bible into the Jivaro's own tongue with the idea that if it is made available to the Indians they will find the gold it contains. (All told the Institute has made such translations into more than 400 primitive languages.) The Institute is aware, however, that the survival of Jivaro dignity must go hand in hand with their Christian salvation.

Dale Keitzman, an anthropologist connected with the Institute who specializes in South American preliterate peoples, points out that the Jivaro must become bilingual to deal effectively with the white man; the Jivaro who speaks Spanish is less liable to exploitation or intimidation by white merchants, traders, employers or government officials. But he must at the same time preserve his ability to communicate within his own society in his traditional language.

The Jivaro must also learn enough simple business arithmetic and elementary accounting to avoid being cheated in the wages he earns as well as in the goods or money he receives for the personal services he performs or the forest products he turns over to the white man. With such knowledge in Jivaro hands, Keitzman believes that the insidious patron system will soon become outmoded. A Jivaro will no longer settle for whimsically accounted trade goods in return for his labors; he will understand the debts that once chained him and many other South American Indian peoples to an unending obligation.

According to Father Bolla, head of the Salesian mission at Taisha, the Jivaros must be carefully schooled for the coming contact with civilization if they are to avoid the fate that has overtaken other indigenous peoples in South America. The schooling, however, must not only advance the pace of acculturation, he believes, it must also take into account both the capacities and the limitations of the Jivaros.

"Jivaro customs and psychology," Father Bolla said, "are different from those of the white man. You cannot force our educational approach upon him. His values and traditions, the things he loves, for example, his music—these must all be respected or it will not work. The Jivaro has a mind for concrete matters; he is confused by abstractions like mathematics. Things he can see, feel, or listen to, he understands. It does no good to make him feel inadequate or stupid. You raise the Jivaro by emphasizing his strengths, not his weaknesses."

But the Jivaro needs more than education, as important as schooling tailored to his needs may be. If he is to cope with powerful economic interests, if he is to have a fair shake in his dealings with agricultural, industrial and mining negotiators, if he is ever to chip his way into the iron fortress of government bureaucracy, he must develop his own sources of unified and sophisticated political power. Can the Jivaro achieve this power without undermining his essential identity?

To date, the most promising and probably the most challenging avenue of constructive change in Jivaro life lies in the hope offered by the Jivaro, or Shuar, Federation. This organization, which aims at strengthening and unifying Jivaro society without in any way destroying its traditional identity, was guided into existence by the Salesian missionaries in 1964. The Salesians, believing that permanent isolation was neither feasible nor morally justifiable, saw the Federation as the best way to erect a barrier against the all too familiar pattern of exploitation by the white settler, prospector or speculator.

There are many isolated pockets of Jivaros on the disputed Ecuador-Peru border; the majority are still protected, as in centuries past, by natural barriers and the hazardous uncertainties of transportation—the Andes and the Amazon forests are as formidable as ever. Yet many Jivaros, especially among the younger generation, are leaving their *jivarias* for jungle towns and government posts seeking the goods, the education and the jobs they have heard about from Christianized Jivaros or from the missionaries.

So with a sense of urgency the Salesians are preparing the Jivaros economically, politically and culturally for the inevitable head-on encounter with the white man. The Federation may or may not succeed in the long run; right now it is testing itself

43

against the stresses of internal disharmony and threats of external enmity and indifference. Should it succeed, the native organization might very well offer a blueprint for relatively painless assimilation that could be followed by peoples with similar problems in other remote parts of the world.

The real challenge of such a native organization can be put simply enough. How does a group of indigenous people become politically and technically sophisticated without seriously damaging the traditional customs and philosophies which define and support their sense of identity? Or, to put it another way, how can they play the white man's game without forgetting their own? Moreover, if the initiative and guidance for structuring the organization come from outside, from even the most well-intentioned sources such as the Salesians, how much pride and identification will the native peoples derive from the association? This is not a hair-splitting subtlety. Haven't we enough evidence already from militant black movements in America as well as from nativist movements in Africa and elsewhere that no amount of big-brother support and guidance from private or governmental "white" agencies can replace the incentives that come from within a people? As wrongheaded as many militant groups and their leaders might seem, are they not really saying, "We want to do it our way, make our own mistakes, take our own chances"?

As for the Jivaros, the very idea of their linking arms in a common purpose, without the unifying effect of a clearly outlined "enemy" threat, is enough to boggle the mind. Will they still be Jivaros, as we once knew them, when they no longer live by their code of feud and revenge? The existence of a successful Jivaro federation would itself be evidence of important changes in attitude. Their feelings about the soul as something to be gained or lost in combat, for instance, will have no place in organizational politics, nor will the witch doctor—and that, of course, will not displease the Salesians. And the complexity of the Federation, with its rules, its elaborate committee system and its representational base, is a far cry from the clan style of life in the old *jivarias*. The Salesians know that those converted

Jivaros who have given up the polygamous clan life, and the traditional basis of power and land-ownership in the *jivaria*, have been most vulnerable to the new mountain settlers and the patron landlords arrived from over the Andes. These Christianized Jivaros are most desperately in need of the protective shield of an organization like the Salesian-sponsored Federation. In short, as the Salesians see it, modern trends will function together beneficially, so that Christianized Jivaro families, educated to hold and plow their lands like Western farmers, will be unified in a cooperative fellowship and will use modern techniques of politics and communications to express their interests and concerns. But, at the same time, they will remain, by persistent self-indoctrination, cultural Jivaros.

According to a 1968 Salesian report, the Federation comprises 70 Shuar centers with approximately 14,000 bona fide members and a growing number of honorary members. There is a president, but the power of the Federation is chiefly in the hands of the General Assembly, which meets once a year, and the Directorio, whose members are represented in the Assembly along with representatives from each of the Shuar centers. The Directorio formulates the by-laws of the organization, imposes sanctions upon individual members and on centers guilty of infractions of its rules. It also secures student loans, sets up health centers and represents Jivaro health and welfare needs to the government.

The work of the Federation falls largely within the scope of five commissions. A Commission on Arbitrage and Colonization intervenes in disputes and deals with the complaints of members, and so has the burden of substituting reasoned discourse for the more traditional style of score-settling. It is also responsible for selecting and acquiring new lands for Jivaro communities. The Commission on Work and Artisans stimulates individual and collective labor and supervises the production and marketing of Jivaro goods—for example, the folkloric objects which are expected to enhance both Jivaro income and cultural identity. But the problem of dealing with the overall economic health of the

Jivaros belongs to the Commission on Cooperatives and Warehouse [sic]. This body is responsible for welding Jivaro communities into cooperative centers for the common good, supervising the warehouses where the commodities will be stored and marketed, and obtaining the best markets and the most favorable prices for Jivaro farm produce and artifacts. Here the work of the Federation could be especially important. Not only is there a great need for the protection of the native worker against unfair prices for his labor, but the very land he works can be taken from him unless forceful measures are employed to ensure his legal title.

Governments have been notoriously lax in supporting the rights of indigenous peoples, who usually have no more than the oral history of the tribe as proof that the land they regard as their own has been in their possession for countless generations. And white settlers and land speculators are well schooled in the means of acquiring title to native lands. The Jivaro Federation cooperatives may provide at least some protection. The Federation has gotten the support of the Ecuadorian Institute for Agrarian Reform and Colonization (IERAC). This agency, of strategic importance for Jivaro hopes, has accepted the Federation proposal to appropriate lands for Shuar centers, and has set up a subsection to deal exclusively with Jivaro land acquisition.

The Commission on Educational and Religious Culture was apparently created to make sure that the Jivaro would steer the proper philosophical course, giving up only those old ways which conflict with Western and Christian morality while maintaining pride in the "good" aspects of his traditional identity. This group plans educational courses for Jivaro leaders, and designs and encourages studies in religion and morality. It also obtains scholarships for members' children and is responsible for setting up schools and programs directed at intensifying Jivaro interest in sports and folk music. Finally, there is a Health Commission which will undoubtedly find itself increasingly busy as Jivaros and outsiders meet in growing numbers.

The headquarters building of the Federation, located in Sucua, had been only recently completed when I arrived there in 1968. It was the achievement of the combined efforts of volunteer Jivaro laborers, who contributed 1,400 work days, a group of Italian volunteers and the Salesians. Here the Assembly meetings take place, but it is also used as an educational center and as a hostel for Jivaros who are looking for a temporary roof in Sucua.

Perhaps the most interesting bit of news about the Federation during my 1968 stay in Sucua was the recent addition to Jivaro culture of a broadcasting station. I could not help thinking of how impressed Utitiaja had been with the pictures of Jivaros in *Life* magazine. Now, in a way, the Jivaros could do it themselves. Of course, they weren't ready to compete with mass-circulation media, for the Jivaros are still talking, as it were, among themselves. They are still "the people" and the outside world will have to use its own resources for learning about them, at least for a while yet. The station, built with money supplied by the Point IV Program and by the Salesians, operates with a slogan that might well be the motto of the Federation itself: Faith and Work: A Better Tomorrow.

The station, broadcasting in both Castilian Spanish and the Shuar dialect, was set up primarily to serve and stimulate the activities of the Federation. Among its aims is the dissemination of educational courses intended to benefit the Jivaro tenant farmer and his community, the leaders, the teachers and the local authorities. Its programming is also designed to promote Jivaro cultural self-consciousness, to make the Jivaro proud of his educated brethren who participate in the programs and who will be given air time to discuss and promote cultural activities such as musical, artistic and sports events. I found myself wondering what Peruche might say to his listeners if he and Utitiaja could have joined in a kind of nightly Jivaro-style panel show.

4 Mato Grosso:
"Die if you must . . ."

MOST OF THE MATO GROSSO, one of the great remaining hearts of darkness, has become the Brazilian mecca of the adventurer, the fortune seeker,
the land grabber, the planter, the miner and the
corporate agent. But the northern half of the
Mato Grosso is still one of the least-known and least-charted
territories on earth. There in the heart of the South American
continent, this vast piece of real estate of incalculable value is
the second-largest Brazilian state—more than twice the size of
France. On a physical map of Brazil it is mainly a sprawling blot
of tan plateau which merges into the green Amazonian canopy.
Its people conform to no single cultural pattern.

Some, like the nomadic Chavantes, are fierce fighters, resentful
of intruders to the point of murderous ferocity. Others, like the
Camayuras, are docile and trusting. The Xinguanos—the remaining nine or so tribes left along the upper Xingu River—love
nothing more than to compete in wrestling matches. The Bororos

devote much of their tribal energies to elaborate funeral ceremonies.

It is possible to encounter natives living in still-unexplored parts of Mato Grosso as they have lived since the Stone Age; or to see Indians working on ranches or operating farm machinery, going to mission schools and wearing the first true garments in the history of their people. For the most part these people share the knowledge, or at least the intimation, that their end is approaching, that they are people without a future.

The wealth of Mato Grosso cannot be calculated because it has only begun to reveal itself. There are, to begin with, thriving cattle ranches. The area is well endowed with precious metals and gems—but prospectors and Indians make notoriously poor mixers. In 1966 more than a thousand diamond hunters descended the Jatoba River from Cuiabá, the state capital, and clashed with the Tchikao Indians who are already in the same category as the whooping crane. How many were ruthlessly killed by the *garimpeiros*, as the diamond seekers are called, is not known. There were fifty-three Tchikaos left in 1968, as compared with about 400 only a few years before. Skin hunters too have gunned down or chased off various other Indian populations in this region. It is well known in Cuiabá that a certain entrepreneur regularly hires killers equipped with machine guns and rifles to clear out troublesome Indians who encroach upon his lands rich in rubber and Brazil nuts.

A land of one-half million square miles with an approximate population density of one person per square mile could not possibly have escaped attention indefinitely, considering the land and resource needs of the expanding Brazilian economy. The neighboring state of Goias, still largely undeveloped, has more than twice the population of Mato Grosso in less than half the area. They share much of the same landlocked tableland, and both states are attracting land developers, agricultural, mining and industrial interests who have the encouragement of the government. But Mato Grosso remains the frontier state, the great unknown beckoning the *civilizado* in much the same way that El Dorado lured earlier explorers.

The region has long been bathed in the glow of legend. An ill-fated gold rush petered out in the eighteenth century because the cost in lives was too great. Angry Indian tribes, some of whom had been driven into this territory by earlier conquistadores, massacred the prospectors. The Rio das Mortes, or River of Deaths, in Chavante territory, is said to have run red with blood for two days when a party of gold and diamond seekers was cut down attempting to cross it during this gold rush. Missionaries and scientific explorers have also met untimely ends here.

In the mid-twenties Colonel Percy H. Fawcett set out to find the fabled "lost city" with his son, Jack, and a friend, Raleigh Rimmel, and they all vanished mysteriously. Probably the British explorer and his party were beaten to death by the club-wielding Calapalos Indians whom he had recruited to assist him in his mission. Apparently he had dealt insensitively with the Calapalos, and he may have been "condemned" to death. But precise information about Fawcett was sparse and long in coming. A number of rescue expeditions were sent to the upper Xingu area, some of them launched under the delusion that Fawcett might indeed have found his city of gold and was unable to remove himself from so regal a setting. One attempt claimed the life of an American, Albert de Winton, who was poisoned with bitter manioc by the Calapalos Indians.

Accounts of unsuccessful attempts to pacify the Mato Grosso Indians, especially the warlike Chavantes, helped to deter the *civilizado* from penetrating this region. In the early thirties, two priests came to the Rio das Mortes hoping to Christianize the Chavantes. They were later found in the river, clubbed to death; their hands, pierced by arrows, were holding crucifixes. Another time six missionaries went deep into the forest intending to pacify the Chavantes with gifts and acts of love; they too were massacred. Then, in 1941, the Indian Protective Service sent an advance scouting party into Chavante territory under Dr. Genesio Pimentel Barbosa.

Pimental Barbosa, heading a team of seven men, actually communicated with the Chavantes through his Sherente-speak-

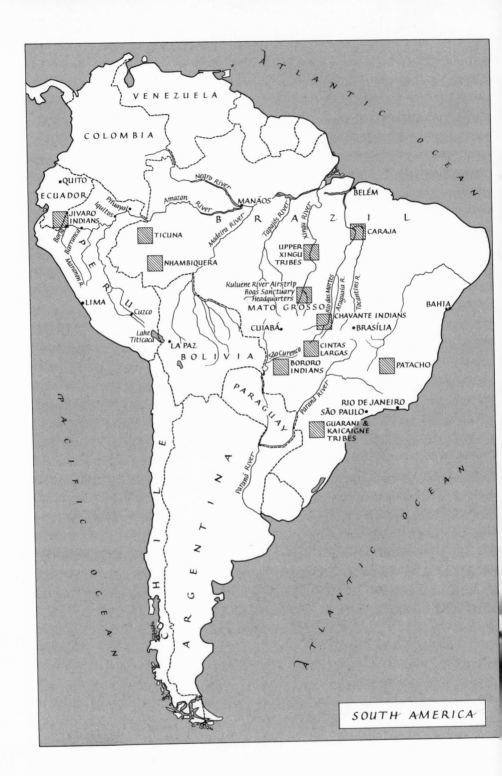

VENEZUELA

COLOMBIA

ATLANTIC OCEAN

•QUITO
ECUADOR
Piñuaya•
Iquitos•
JIVARO
INDIANS
Bobonaza
Barranca
Marañon R.

Negro River
Amazon River
MANÁOS
Madeira River
Tapajós River
Xingu River
BELÉM

B R A Z I L

TICUNA

NHAMBIQUERA

CARAJA

UPPER
XINGU
TRIBES

•LIMA
Cuzco
Lake
Titicaca
•LA PAZ
BOLIVIA

Kuluene River Airstrip
Boas Sanctuary
Headquarters
MATO GROSSO
CUIABÁ•
São Curenço
BORORO
INDIANS
CINTAS
LARGAS

P E R U

Rio das Mortes
Araguaia R.
Tocantins R.

CHAVANTE INDIANS
•BRASÍLIA

BAHIA

PATACHO

PACIFIC OCEAN

PARAGUAY

Paraná River
RIO DE JANEIRO
SÃO PAULO•
GUARANI &
KAICAIGNE
TRIBES

Paraná River

C H I L E

A R G E N T I N A

ATLANTIC OCEAN

SOUTH AMERICA

52

ing guides—in itself a major achievement. The Indians, however, spurned the gifts and offers of friendship in stony silence. When the seven scouts had left their gifts and turned to go they were attacked. Only one man survived to tell what had happened. Pimentel Barbosa and his men had died without firing back at the Chavantes in absolute obedience to the creed of the man who had founded the Indian Protective Service: Die if you must, but never kill an Indian.

General Candido Rondon, the original head of Brazil's Indian Protective Service, insisted that the *civilizado* must set an example as peacemaker, must even die, if necessary, rather than shoot down Indians who were determined to protect their territories. By and large, where Rondon's method has been practiced consistently and patiently it has worked. It has made the inevitable conquest of interior Brazil much less painful and costly for both Indian and *civilizado*. But whenever Rondon's ideals have been abandoned the Indians have suffered as a result, and so, perhaps, has Brazil's conscience.

Born in 1865 in Cuiabá, Rondon lived until 1957, and during that span his influence or direct intervention was responsible for the nearly complete pacification of Brazil's Indian population. Even before the establishment of the IPS in 1910, he had already won over the Bororos, Umutinas, Nhambikuaras and other tribes; and his work continued until the last years of his life, when he learned of the hard-won triumphs of Francisco Meireles, Colonel Vanique and the legendary Villas Boas brothers.

Without the work of Rondon, one of the plans for opening up this area might have failed. The epic Roncador-Xingu expedition was begun more than twenty-five years ago by the Central Brazil Foundation under the urging and direction of the dynamic Joao Alberto Lins de Barros, then minister of immigration under Getulio Vargas. This was the historic counterpart of Lewis and Clark's trek, the opening wedge for the large-scale—and inevitable—development of the Mato Grosso lands. It is quite possible that future historians will divide the history of central Brazil into two distinct periods—pre- and post-Roncador-Xingu expedition.

Vanique took on the leadership of the Roncador-Xingu expedition, which set out in 1943 on a six-year trek through dangerous Chavante country to Roncador (snoring) Mountain. One of the main purposes of the expedition was to establish a series of jungle airstrips for refueling and emergency landings between Rio and Manáos. Brazilians called the newly established direct air route between Miami, Caracas and Rio "the Great Diagonal," representing—before the advent of jet planes—a saving of some 1,500 miles by comparison with the older route around the eastern hump of South America. Without these new bases it would have been impossible for commercial aircraft to cross the vast uncharted region between Rio and Caracas. But besides the establishing of a new route and the mapping of hitherto unknown large areas in Brazil's interior, the expedition inevitably brought Indians in the region drained by the Xingu, Tapajós and Araguaia Rivers face to face with civilization.

Following the urging of Rondon, Vanique and his men met Indian distrust with the white man's new-found patience. Because direct encounters with Chavantes were still impossible, Vanique left gifts along the trails, hoping that sooner or later he and other *civilizados* would be accepted in friendship. As late as 1947, Francisco Meireles of the IPS narrowly escaped the fate of Pimentel Barbosa during a peacemaking expedition near the Serra do Roncador. Yet he continued to cross the River of Deaths, leaving gifts of cloth and aluminum pots on the trails— as he had been doing since 1945—until at last the Chavantes began asking for gifts and accepting food with obvious signs of gratitude. Then, in 1950 Meireles became the first white man to be invited to meet a Chavante chief in his own village. It is said that Chief Apoena, whose men had killed Pimentel Barbosa and others, could no longer continue the one-sided fight and that when he greeted Meireles, the chief broke down and wept on the white man's shoulder. When Rondon heard the dramatic news of the truce he pronounced it "a victory of patience, suffering, and love."

Rondon believed, until perhaps the last few years of his life, that the Indian's interests would best be served by teaching him to live with white men. His integrationist philosophy is not shared by the man who earned his mantle and who moves with the same aura of charismatic leadership and influence. That man is Orlando Villas Boas who, with his two younger brothers, Leonardo and Claudio, quit routine jobs in São Paulo to join the Roncador-Xingu expedition. When Colonel Vanique gave up the leadership of the expedition because of failing health, he was succeeded by Orlando Villas Boas. Since then, Orlando has been without equal in his ability to win the trust of Indians, and he has helped to shape policies that may very well provide the pattern for the rescue of what remains of Indian culture in Brazil.

When I first met Orlando in 1949 at the Rio das Mortes airstrip, I was prepared to find a jungle titan of imposing frame and manner—something of a Frank Buck and a Conrad hero rolled into one. But I found instead a slight man about five feet six inches tall who wore only a pair of faded pants and a battered cloth hat. His face was darkened to the same mellow tan of his Indian friends. It was a face, however, that one does not easily forget—hawklike, with a short, fierce beard and wise yet gentle eyes. It was typical of Orlando that I should find him surrounded by a group of clinging Indian children whom he treated with as much affection as if they had been his own.

It was Orlando's belief then, and when I found him again in 1963, that the Mato Grosso Indians were "doomed." For Orlando the Mato Grosso and especially the upper Xingu are among the last fastnesses of primitive man. Orlando has made it his responsibility to slow the pace of assimilation. So far as the government's Central Brazilian Foundation is concerned, Orlando and Claudio Villas Boas are making it possible for construction crews to build new airstrips and extract precious stones and metals from the interior. But for Orlando and Claudio the Indian tribes which are on the verge of extinction come first.

In 1968 Orlando told me that General Rondon, four years before his death, had agreed with the Villas Boas brothers that isolation of Indian cultures was a better idea than rapid pacification and assimilation. And so, Rondon, Orlando and Claudio went to the then president of Brazil, Getulio Vargas, and asked him to create a national park where Indians could live in their traditional way, undisturbed by gold and diamond prospectors, rubber men and assorted land grabbers. How long such an artificial Eden can survive is a moot question, but Orlando believes that the more time the Indian can have the better.

The 8,500-square-mile Xingu National Park was founded in 1961, the same year that tropical fever claimed the life of Leonardo Villas Boas. Today, Orlando and Claudio, based at Posto Leonardo Villas Boas, the Park headquarters, administer this sanctuary for the National Indian Foundation, a department of the Ministry of the Interior and successor to Brazil's scandal-ridden Indian Protective Service, which became defunct in 1967.

I asked Orlando about the old organization, which for so long had embodied the ideals of General Rondon. He told me that it was not the Indian Protective Service itself, but officials lured by larger sums than they were accustomed to earning who were corrupted. They wound up protecting the exploiters and persecutors of Brazil's Indians rather than the primitives entrusted to their care. There was, however, at least one positive result from the scandal. It eventually drew the attention of the world press to the plight of the Brazilian Indian (and, by the way, brought me back to the Mato Grosso in 1968). Orlando explained what had happened.

"The world is learning that the Indians belong to the whole of humanity. We here have the duty to defend and protect their culture. When a people becomes extinct, a language disappears, economic principles disappear, cultural principles disappear— and we have the obligation to see that they do not disappear. When the uproar about the Indian Protective Service reached the ears of the outside world, journalists from all over Europe came to Xingu after stopping off at the Ministry. They would ask us how a thing like this could happen. They said, 'It is your

privilege to have Indians in your country, but their culture belongs to everybody—Europeans, too. You have the obligation to
protect them—their culture belongs to all humanity, not to one
nation in particular.' "

The combined population of the tribes now in the Xingu National Park numbered an estimated 3,000 before the turn of the
century. Today, fewer than 1,000 survive. There are less than 30
members of the Yawalpiti and Trumai peoples left. Orlando and
Claudio have gotten to some groups in the eleventh hour of their
cultural life. In the sixties, for example, the Villas Boas brothers
searched out the warlike and mistrustful Tchikaos, about 400 of
whom had survived white invaders, their guns and their diseases.
By the time they were located and brought to the Park there
were only fifty-three.

5 Xinguanos:
A Last Look at Eden

XINGUANO is the collective name given to the remaining tribes* in the upper Xingu, the major part of the Villas Boas refuge. When you meet many of the Xinguanos, it is not difficult to understand Orlando's personal involvement in their destiny. My own first meeting with the Camayura people was like a visit to an unspoiled primitive paradise. I couldn't help wondering if the lost cities of gold sought by men like Fawcett were not really there before their eyes all along—not in temples or palaces, but in the golden people themselves.

The Camayuras were living then in 1949 much as they had lived for centuries. I had flown over Chavante territory where not long before low-flying aircraft had been showered with

---

* These include the following peoples: the Camayura, Aweti, Mehinaku, Yawalpiti, Trumai, Kuikuru, Calapalos, Waura and the Matipu. The peoples of this region have a fairly homogeneous culture; they trade and compete in games with one another, but represent five different language groups.

arrows; my destination was the Kuluene River from where it was possible to hike to Camayura territory. Before air travel, this area was isolated not only by geography but by the formidable Chavantes as well. Just as I caught a glimpse of the Camayura thatched huts I was greeted by a group of superb-looking Indians, statuesque, graceful, with tranquilly smiling faces. The men wore the typical Xinguano "sugar bowl" bob and nothing else; the women sported an *uluri*, a barely discernible bark triangle (about the size of a postage stamp) attached to the cord which encircles the waist and is tucked into the crotch.

Both my friend Major Luis Sampaio, the daring pilot of the Roncador-Xingu expedition, and I were welcomed with warm embraces. Two young girls, one seventeen, the other a little older, bubbled over with laughter as they toyed with my earlobes, wriggled against me and took my hand, encouraging me to stroke them as I would a pet animal. Although I would not again find a people quite as free of care as the Camayuras with their uninhibited life style and their innocence—if one can call it that —they were typical of many of the Xinguanos.

One of the reasons that the Villas Boas brothers are so careful to keep intruders away from the Xingu National Park is, in fact, to preserve that very innocence. Orlando, while friendly and gentle in every other respect, can be as hard as nails when given reason to suspect the motives of an outsider. Once a young newspaperwoman flew in to the Park with a small party of journalists and other observers; something about her manner struck Orlando the wrong way, and he packed her off in the same plane.

To some outsiders the Xinguanos may seem too good to be true. Their natural warmth and openness disarm the visitor, and they do not have the feeling of guilt about their sexual relationships that has plagued Western man. The nudity of the Indians is wholly lacking in prurient appeal. I am partial to the theory that many of the outsiders who want to cover them up with clothes are only envious of their naturalness and beauty—a beauty with no sense of sin attached.

"The Xinguano is modest—exaggeratedly so, in fact," Orlando told me in 1968. We were discussing Indian customs. The Txukahamei, for example, enlarge their lips with progressively larger lip-disks as they mature. By the age of fifteen, a Txukahamei may wear a disk up to five and a half inches in diameter as an indication of prestige and manliness. How do they kiss?

"Indians, in general, do not kiss on the mouth," Orlando said. "Even the ones without lip-disks. They think it is terribly unclean. A male Indian will not kiss his wife at all. He will kiss his fiancée—and then only on the face, forehead, or near the ear. And, of course, he is very shy about it."

Orlando's Xinguanos are deeply disturbed by *civilizados* who are sexually frustrated; they cannot understand how a man can become aroused at the sight of a nude woman. In his twenty-five years of daily life with Indians, Orlando told me, he had never seen an Indian with an erection. It would be absurd to them. Nor has Orlando seen or heard of any instances of sexual deviation among the Indians. They did not know what masturbation was until they saw a *civilizado* telegraph operator doing it.

From then on the telegraph operator was a problem to Orlando and his colleagues at the Park. The Indians despised him because, in their eyes, he had done something reprehensible. There was nothing to do but remove him from the Park.

On the other hand, sexual intercourse among the Xinguanos is as casual as any other natural act. The Indian's sexual activity usually takes place in the hut where several Indian families live. At one time, Orlando explained, the Indians copulated openly at the Post when they came to visit the Villas Boas brothers. Orlando had to put an end to this freedom because of the effect it had on the *civilizados* who came to the Post. There was, for example, a well-known Brazilian who had coerced an Indian couple to have sexual relations so that he could photograph them, no doubt for the amusement of his friends back home. Orlando was, of course, furious with the amateur pornographer, not only for the coercion but for his coarseness in reducing an act of love to the level of a tasteless joke.

Indians are no longer free (nor do they feel free) to have sexual intercourse at Posto Leonardo or in the villages when outsiders are present. They have learned that their attitudes toward lovemaking are not those of the *civilizados*. They do, however, trust the Villas Boas brothers, and when Orlando or Claudio visits them the Indians continue to act as they do among their own people. "No one stares," Orlando explained. "No one is bothered by it."

In a typical Xinguano hut the husband's hammock is placed above the wife's. It is the wife's obligation to keep the fire going; if it should burn down during the night, the husband will awaken the wife to relight it. When he wants to make love, he summons her to his hammock; he will not go to her. I asked Orlando why this was so.

"It is because she wears the chastity belt, and this belt regulates their sexual relations." (The chastity belt is the *uluri*, a thin, hardly noticeable strip of fiber.) "A man will not touch that belt under any circumstances whatsoever," Orlando continued. "If he does, he knows for sure that his culture hero will punish him; his arrows will never reach their mark; he will meet with misfortune."

An Indian will never take a woman by force. If she does not want to remove her *uluri*, there will be no lovemaking. Although her husband rules the roost in that he can "command" her to remove the belt, she retains the right of refusal, and she may refuse him if she is angry with him. However, the outlook for the husband is not totally bleak in this event—many Xinguanos have two wives, and some have three.

Often, if the family head likes his son-in-law he will offer him a second daughter. The husband must accept the gift or he will not be permitted to take a third wife. It is in the father-in-law's best interest that his daughter's husband be happy with his bride because the older man will be reincarnated in his grandson, who must therefore be wanted and loved by his father. And this is also why any infidelity on the part of the daughter is discouraged. Her father wants to be sure that he will return in the form of a child who is accepted by both parents. If his daughter should have relations with another man, he stands in danger of returning as the son of someone who will resent him. In cases of wifely infidelity (which are rare), the father-in-law will insist that the husband administer a beating to the guilty wife. The beating is more symbolic than painful; she is spanked much as a child would be—on the buttocks or shoulders, never on the face or breasts or head. The tears she sheds are mainly out of humiliation.

If the husband should stray (and with three wives adultery committed by the husband is also a rarity), he too is beaten— always by the first wife. He does not defend himself, but merely laughs during the hair-pulling. Among wives there is remarkably little jealousy. When a new wife enters the family there may be some initial rivalry, but when the second and third wives bear children the jealousy ends. The first wife remains responsible for the cooking and housekeeping, with the others assisting her. There are usually no favorites.

The harmony in the Indian hut comes from many centuries of traditional life. But when Indian village life is destroyed, or when the Indian is made to feel that his customs are inferior to those of the white man the culture shock reaches deep into his personality. It can be read on his face. He even learns to distrust his own instincts.

When I visited the Camayuras in 1963 the women were as lovely as I had remembered them, and they were still wearing their minuscule "fig leaves"; the men were still fine specimens, too. Yet something had gone out of them. They were not as freely affectionate as they had been fourteen years before and did not greet me with bear hugs. They were down to about half of their previous number—approximately ninety—and instead of occupying four villages, only one community was left.

In 1968 I reached the Camayuras after a short Jeep ride from Posto Leonardo. (It's a two-hour walk.) What remains of this tribe is now gathered on the shores of Lake Ipavu, under the protection of Orlando and Claudio. Many had died of pneumonia, influenza, smallpox and tuberculosis. Yet it seemed to me that with improved medical care and their proximity to the Post and the watchful eyes of the Villas Boas brothers, they were in better condition than in 1963. There were about 110 in 1968, a gain of perhaps twenty. On my earlier visit I had pitched a hammock in an unused hut near the edge of the village square, and all through the night I was kept awake by coughing, hacking and spitting. Five years later they seemed to be in better health; the village was clean, the women and children were happy. Progress had to be measured here with a different set of values, I realized—not by the pace of innovation, but by the fact that life remains the same, by the numbers of people who do not die off, by the customs that do not vanish.

The *guarup*, or annual feast of the dead, is the outstanding ritual among the Xinguanos. In 1963 I attended the feast given by the Kuikuru tribe. (A rotation system gives each tribe a chance to play host.) The men carry in from the forest huge logs, about six to eight feet long and up to a foot and a half in diameter; there is a log for each member of the tribe who has died since the last *guarup*. These logs are buried with about four feet showing above the level of the ground. This part of the log is decorated with red and black paints, cotton waistbands and feather headdresses. Another feature of the *guarup* is the dance called the *urua*. The music and dance rhythm are supplied by two men with double-tubed bamboo flutes; one tube is about seven feet long, the other about five. The music is lively and the dance is a spirited trot with a rapid emphatic beat of the right foot. The men dance around the open area of the village, which in the upper Xingu region is typically encircled by long thatched huts. They duck into one of the huts and reappear seconds later still playing their flutes, followed by the girls who trot behind the male dancers in perfect tempo, right hands on the right shoulders of their partners.

It is possible that the Xinguanos have been able to sublimate their aggressions in competitive wrestling—in intertribal contests which take place at weddings and spearthrowing ceremonies. The championship of the entire upper Xingu, however, is dedicated at the annual *guarup*.

Wrestling in upper Xingu takes place in the villages throughout the year, but there are weeks of training and preparation before an intertribal match. Members of the teams selected to represent the individual villages must abstain from sexual intercourse, must observe certain dietary restrictions and must live in the forest until the match is held. Victory is won not by the contestant who can pin down the shoulders of his adversary, but by the first man who can grab the back of the upper thigh of the other. It is mainly a question of agile footwork.

Although the Xinguanos place a great deal of importance on their ceremony of the dead, they are not preoccupied with the idea of death to the same extent as the Bororos, a tribe 500 miles south of the Xinguano area, who are not under the protection of the Villas Boas brothers. On my several visits to the Bororos I realized that these people, perhaps more than any other in the Mato Grosso, epitomize the surrender of tribal vitality and the sense of defeat. Only a few decades ago the Bororos were a brave and proud warrior tribe numbering over 5,000. When I saw them in 1949, their numbers had dwindled to about 2,000. In 1963 they were down to about 200, and when I returned in 1968 there were less than 150.

The Bororos were unlucky enough to have been in the path of intensive Brazilian penetration of the interior. They were partly victims of civilization's diseases, partly of their own loss of confidence. Their tribal traditions, centering largely on their warrior pride, fell to pieces. Many individual members of the tribe left their villages and lived as beggars and outcasts on the rundown fringes of towns in the surrounding areas.

I saw much evidence that the Bororos were committing racial suicide. There were few children in the villages. Like many other primitive peoples, the Bororos kill all children who do not appear healthy at birth. I couldn't help wondering whether the Bororos were not unconsciously applying increasingly stringent standards to their infants. Moreover, I have heard Bororo parents maintain that they have no wish to bring children into the world as it is now, echoing a sentiment often heard in our own culture. While many Mato Grosso Indians are aware of and use birth-control preparations obtained in the forest, the dread of childbirth itself is, as psychologists have pointed out, an effective contraceptive.

The Bororo sense of defeat when faced with civilization may stem from their own preoccupation with death and its rituals, and from their conviction that man is basically evil. The Bororo funeral ceremony, an eight-day affair, culminates in a ritual drama during which members of the tribe impersonate the *bope*, or evil spirits, who prevail against the dead. The ritual concludes when a member of the tribe secretly removes the body and takes it to the river where he scrapes off the flesh and washes the bones clean. The soul of the dead thereafter wanders unhappily, embodied in a frog, a bird or, most desirably, a deer.

When I returned to Bororo territory in 1968, I became convinced that they were on the road to extinction. The most telling sign came during a meeting with a Bororo chief. After my earlier visits, I had expected to find a man of bearing and great poise. A Bororo chief may never have been surrounded with the pomp of a pharaoh, but he was nothing if not proud.

Chief Macha was a defeated man. His eyes swept the ground, but when he looked up and saw me coming with a bundle under my arm some of the dullness disappeared from his face; despair gave way to expectation. Had I anything to give him, he wanted to know. He didn't care what it was—something of value. Perhaps some food. He begged me to open my bag and begin to dispense my gifts. I was stunned, but even as I opened my pack and searched my mind for a suggestion of what to give him, he continued to beg and whine. He was no longer a Bororo.

The Chavantes, too, are losing ground in their struggle to survive. Despite the good intentions of the pacifiers of a decade ago, this tribe—so long a symbol of Indian resistance to civilization's intrusion—may be going the way of the Bororos. Twenty years earlier I never would have believed that I could have met

Chavantes and lived to tell of it. In 1968 I was not only able to meet Chavantes, but I was able to see the bitterness of their fate in the silent language of their faces. It was not that I was unwelcome. In the faces of the older ones was a message that I could clearly read: We have had our day. We were great once . . . too bad you couldn't have seen us then. It was a look of profound resentment, not for me as an individual, but for everything I represented.

At Orlando's headquarters I met Adrian Cowell, author of *The Heart of the Forest*, who had accompanied the Villas Boas brothers on several of their expeditions. This young Englishman told me that the Chavantes were rapidly dying out. The causes of death, he said, were influenza, measles, tuberculosis and venereal diseases, as well as the effects of the psychological and cultural shock they had experienced in the past fifteen or twenty years. (Incidentally, he himself had contracted the dreaded tropical disease, leishmaniasis.) He believes that outside the Xingu National Park 95 percent of the Indians must be dying. As soon as they come into contact with the whites, he said, the Indians not only pick up the white man's diseases, but because medicine is expensive they do not get proper treatment.

National parks of the type championed by Orlando Villas Boas may represent the Indians' last hope for the future. Not everyone in Brazil, however, is in favor of such parks. Large corporations in Rio and São Paulo have been buying extensive tracts of land in the Mato Grosso, and during the last few years they have been more successful in clearing out both the early settlers and the Indians. Many businessmen in South America have the attitude that the parks are holding back the pace of economic development and progress.

"Do you have any idea," a Brazilian mineralogist asked me during my return flight to New York, "how many millions of dollars, how many jobs, how much trade is being lost to us because of just several hundred Indians who aren't going to be around in another few years anyway?"

Fortunately for the Xinguanos, the Xingu National Park had

been firmly established well before these companies could move in. Other culture groups, including the Chavantes, Sherentes and Bororos, are not so lucky. For Orlando's park concept to survive, he will need the continued support of the Brazilian government and people. As we shall see, not even all of the friends of the Indians favor Orlando's approach.

There are two basic policies for dealing with the Indians: bring them into Brazilian society or keep them out, integration or isolation. Of course, it is not quite that simple. Those who support integration generally recognize that the pace at which the Indians are brought into civilization is all important. A too-rapid integration can lead to a cultural disaster, as in the case of the Bororos. On the other hand, those who favor isolation know that sooner or later the Indians of Brazil will be confronted by the inexorable thrust of civilization; understandably, they hope it will be later, much later.

At Posto Leonardo I asked Orlando about the merits of his policy of isolation. He was insistent. "For the first four hundred years of contact in Brazil the policy of integration was followed. Obviously it hasn't worked. The Indian in our world is only a marginal person. You cannot jump from one society to another without losing the cultural, economic, and tribal structure that gives the Indian his identity. This is why we believe in preserving the Indian culture in its pure state."

Looking at the Indian families that trooped to Posto Leonardo, I had to admit that they were among the happiest and healthiest I had seen in Brazil. Orlando was quick to illustrate his point with examples of less-fortunate Indians.

"Take the economically favored state of São Paulo," he said. "For four hundred years Indians along the coast were in contact with the economy of the state. What have they gotten out of it? Today they are the marginals. They are the lowest of the low.

"In the interior of Brazil it has been no better. There the representatives of civilization are the pioneering vanguards. And who comprises these vanguards that the Indian assumes are typical of the world outside? They are the *seringueiros*, the *garimpeiros*—rubber gatherers and prospectors to whom integration of the Indian means his peonage and servitude at best. These men are called 'civilized' because they speak Portuguese—for no other reason. To adjust to their way of life would be fatal for the Indian."

The difference between Indians who have been in touch with civilization—whatever its forms—and those who have remained isolated seemed to Orlando to be proof enough: there was only one practical method of survival.

"Speaking of people who live closer to our area, look at the population along the Araguaia River," he continued. "Compare them with the Chavantes—I mean the Chavantes who have not grown up among white men. In the Cocalinho settlement along the Araguaia, 92 percent suffer from leishmaniasis. But only a hundred kilometers to the west there is a group of healthy Chavantes. Almost six feet tall and with perfect teeth, they live to eighty and ninety years of age and are in fine condition. The Araguaia settlement is directly in the path of civilization.

"But we are watching the extinction of the Chavantes, too. When we crossed the Roncador area in 1946, there were about 4,000 Chavantes there. Today there is only a small nucleus surviving at Pimentel Barbosa [the post ironically named after the celebrated victim of the Chavantes in the period of their fiercest resistance]. The greatest portion of the Chavantes—those big, beautiful people, those happy people—have disappeared. Today the Chavante is a suffering man because of the contact he has had with the 'vanguard' of civilization. Nowadays the Chavantes only laugh for the sake of tradition, not because they are happy, not because they are living a free life as they would if they were living in an environment of their own, a culture of their own."

I recalled the fine words of the early pacifiers, the patience they had demonstrated and the suffering they had endured in order to achieve a peaceful relationship with the Chavantes. Was it all for this? One still had to admire men like Pimentel Barbosa, Vanique and Meireles for their indomitable courage and dogged persistence—but if the result of their efforts (however indirectly and even though it was not their intention) turned out to mean the destruction of a people, then one would have to take a new look at "pacification."

Most of the friends of the Brazilian Indians, however, recognize that rapid "pacification" or assimilation can be catastrophic. Those who are urging a quick absorption of the Indian into the national life merely want to have the problem resolved with a minimum of discomfort—to themselves. They would like the Indian to disappear so that economic development can proceed unimpeded. They do not like to be quoted, of course. They speak in positive terms: of building more Brasílias, of "opening up the West" and of providing more living space, jobs and incentives for the entrepreneur. There are others who, rejecting the idea of rapid assimilation, still believe that it is necessary to prepare the Indian with deliberate speed for his eventual confrontation with civilization. For them the Villas Boas goals, albeit noble enough, appear to be unrealistic.

Padre Mario is the director of the Salesian mission in San Marco, Mato Grosso. He believes that he can serve the best interests of the Chavante by preparing him in his own tribal setting for his inevitable meeting with the fast-expanding Brazilian society. "We must save the Indian," he said in 1968, "according to the conditions of our times. We cannot build a barrier between the Indian and civilization, but we can prepare him so that he will not be crushed when the world outside does overtake him. Meanwhile we must keep the Indian in his setting for as long as it is possible."

The Salesian missionaries do their best to prevent the Chavantes from straying into urban areas. Frontier towns, according to Padre Mario, have a fatal fascination for them. Here they quickly become "marginals"—drifters and derelicts. They are unable to do the work of an urban environment, and when they return to their people they bring diseases that threaten the existence of their entire clan. (This is precisely the same condition which is occurring among primitive peoples in places as distant as Australia, New Guinea, Alaska and East Africa.) In Padre

Mario's words, "we simply don't allow them to go into the towns, just as we do not permit the Indian to work for the *civilizado*, who not only exploits him shamelessly, but cuts the ties which bind him to his people and his culture."

How were the Salesians able to keep the Indians isolated? After all, they did not have the benefit of the natural barriers of the National Park. "It so happens," Padre Mario told me, "that we have prepared them for this situation. A number of Chavantes have already had some contact with the *civilizado*, and in most cases they have caught the *civilizado's* diseases. Now we equate town life with the diseases he fears. But there is another, more positive approach perhaps. The Indian, until he is entirely defeated by life in the town, is a rather proud man. He may be at a loss in the environment of an advanced civilization, but he does have his own culture and there he regards himself as an expert, which of course he is. We tell him that in town he will be reduced to the role of a beggar, a person of no worth who goes from house to house begging for food. We let him know what it is to become a member of a minority group, to be looked down upon as an inferior being, to be humiliated. We say to him, 'Don't ever beg. The day you do you are no longer a man but a child again.' We encourage him to stay in his own village, to adhere to his own traditions, his feasts and ceremonies."

Under the Salesians, the Indians of the Mato Grosso are permitted to perform their own wedding and death rites, but Roman Catholic ceremonies are added by the missionaries. Padre Mario insists that the missionaries have no intention of destroying Indian customs. "We want them to be good men, and that means being good Indians," he says.

Aside from the example of Catholic ritual, the Salesians believe that the Indians cannot be left in a totally "pure" state as the Villas Boas brothers advocate. Padre Mario believes that it is necessary to introduce the Indian to some of the advantages of civilization such as medicines and adequate diets for their children. The Chavante infant mortality rate was staggeringly high, he said, when they lived in the forest. "One shouldn't forget that an adult can be happy eating roots, but a child cannot," he said. "We keep hammering at this idea. The Indian can maintain his nobility, his beauty, and his health when he lives in his own environment. But he needs discipline.

"Our Chavantes are healthy and strong, but that did not happen by itself. We keep their traditions, and at the same time we cultivate their love of work, their interest in farming. And we do what we can to alienate the aggressiveness that the Chavante is best known for. A mission near Chavantina was closed not long ago because of a vengeful attack by another Chavante group. On the other hand, several years have gone by here without a single fight among our Indians."

According to Padre Mario, it has already become virtually impossible to keep the Indian in his natural state. There are those who criticize the Salesians for introducing the Indian to *civilizado* culture at all. I recalled that Orlando Villas Boas had insisted that this "pure" state should be maintained as long as possible. For him it was a duty not only to the Indian, but to the world—a sacred obligation. Padre Mario summed up his side of the argument in this way:

"It is really a very baffling question, but there seems to be no other answer. We cannot leave the Indians in their natural state. The truth is that they don't want it anymore. They have all had some contact with the *civilizado*, and they feel inferior. This is the situation we must deal with. We tell them, 'You should not feel ashamed that you are Indians. On the contrary, it was very brave of you to have conquered this land that only now the civilized man dares to enter. It is rather a title of nobility to have lived on these lands and to have mastered them for so many centuries.'

"No, it is not possible to keep the Indian in his natural state any longer. Civilization is on its way, and that is an irreversible process. We can only help to minimize the shock. We can teach them how to accept civilization without feeling like second-rate human beings. We try to show them that our mission at least offers something better than the other people they are likely to meet around here. For the most part they are little more than bandits who are morally unfit to serve as examples for the Indians. There is a nearby settlement composed of about twenty white families; half of them, I am told, are hiding from the police. These *civilizados* can offer them no progress, just a lot of misery. Here we encourage them to work, to plan for the future; we give them care for their sick. Our pharmacy is a hundred yards away from their village. It is an ideal life for them."

Padre Mario believes that when it comes to saving the Indians from extinction there is no one to say, "Do it this way because it has worked before." His mission is one of a number of sanctuaries operating on the principle that it is best to keep the *civilizado* out for as long as possible. The differences between the mission approach and that of the National Park come down to this: "More than isolating the Indian physically from the effects of civilization," Padre Mario puts it, "we try to isolate him morally." For Orlando Villas Boas and his National Park it is important to isolate the Indian both morally and physically. There can be no other course, as Orlando views the situation. "The Indian cannot survive in civilized society. He must be kept in his natural state."

Difficult and perhaps pointless as it is to choose sides in this dispute, I can only add that the mission approach seems best in cases where the Indian populations have already had or are threatened by imminent contact with the *civilizados*. By then it is too late, as Padre Mario points out, to isolate them physically from the effects of civilization. But the National Park offers the best hope to Indians who have had relatively little contact with white men and who are capable of living together on an intertribal basis—which is happily the case among the Xinguanos.

There is, however, an unsettling question or two about the future of the National Park approach. Living space like the 8,500-square-mile Xingu Park cannot be carved out of a growing Brazil without the generosity and farsightedness of society at large, as well as the cooperation of powerful industrial and agricultural interests. Moreover, the success of the National Park is largely the result of the selfless service of Orlando and Claudio Villas Boas. Who will look after the Xinguanos after they are gone?

I asked Orlando that question, and his reply was hopeful; someone else would carry on the work that he and his brothers had begun. I told him that I somehow doubted that anyone could be found to keep out the rubber and diamond hunters, the curiosity seekers and the hired pacifiers. I did not see who could be enlisted in the service of a difficult and perhaps inevitably lost cause, when it could be both lucrative and adventurous to enlist on the side of progress. It would take more than an anthropologist or a man of good will; it would take another Villas Boas with that peculiar combination of guts, charisma and stubbornness that has succeeded in winning time for the Indian—time to go on living as he has always lived.

Orlando could only shrug his shoulders, and move back to the subject he preferred. "Come on," he said, a twinkle in his eye again, "let me show you some wonderful people."

6 The High Arctic: Sled Dogs and Snowmobiles

THE NATIVE PEOPLES of the Arctic had held no particular fascination for me until rather late in the game. I was what you might call a "tropics man." Ever since the mid-1930s I had been filming with an eye to color, literally and figuratively. The unrelieved whiteness that I thought covered the top of the world discouraged me from visiting Eskimo societies. Besides, I never really cared for subzero temperatures. I preferred to slog my way through steaming, bug-haunted rain forests just for a sight of tribal dancers ablaze with colorful feathers and paint. But if my life has had one pervasive theme, it is that I quite often find myself where I do not expect to be, doing things I have never done before.

At a dinner in Ottawa, where I was showing a film that I had made on New Guinea, I met the commissioner of the Royal Canadian Mounted Police, C. W. Harvison. He took me aside after the screening and began to break down my resistance to

Arctic exploration—and he knew how to do it, too. He had in mind that I should visit the northernmost settlement of Canadian Eskimos on Ellesmere Island. He assured me that I would find people hunting, fishing, carrying on their everyday life, as they had for centuries, perhaps thousands of years. This would be, he insisted, my last chance to see them before they stepped abruptly out of the Paleolithic life of their ancestors and into whatever compromise they could make with the twentieth century.

That, of course, did it. "Go to the High Arctic before it is too late," Harvison said. I didn't want it to be too late. Twenty-five years earlier I had gone on my first expedition because I had heard Jan Smuts say almost the same thing about Africa. Convinced that it was my destiny to be racing off to witness the last act in the drama of one or another people's history, I made for the bottom fringe of Ellesmere Island in the spring of 1962. When I returned, a few months later, I knew quite well what I had been missing in not visiting the Arctic, for I had seen a community of the happiest people I had ever known. And it was all about to change.

In 1969 I took off again for Eskimo country, this time to the North Slope of Alaska, and I was even more thankful then that I had gotten to Ellesmere Island when I did. The Alaskan natives were experiencing some of the more advanced stages of cultural disintegration. It was a preview of what is now happening to the most remote Eskimo communities in Canada's High Arctic.

My specific destination on Ellesmere was the small community at Grise Fiord. I had been promised "unspoiled Eskimos," and that was what I found. No missionaries. No schools. No Hudson's Bay Company store. No radar installation or nearby military post. Just seventy-two Eskimos and two RCMP constables.

The constables, one might say, were a relatively minor intrusion into the otherwise unspoiled existence of the Grise Fiord Eskimos. They were there partly to introduce to the natives some of the minimal benefits of modern life—health services, trading assistance and a small degree of social guidance—but they were also there as a kind of two-man diplomatic DEW Line.

Grise Fiord, well above the Arctic Circle and 3,000 miles to the north of the United States, epitomizes the attempts of the Canadian and United States governments to shepherd their remaining primitive peoples into the Industrial Age. These Eskimos were not the first to live on Ellesmere Island. They were preceded by an earlier culture, the Pre-Dorset Eskimos who inhabited the island as much as 3,000 years ago. The Dorset and Thule Eskimos succeeded them as inhabitants of Ellesmere. Then, early in the seventeenth century, it is believed that worsening weather conditions created a massive Arctic ice jam and blocked the migration of the great bowhead whales which were hunted by the daring Thule people. In any event, Ellesmere Island, a land mass of over 77,000 square miles, was abandoned by its inhabitants, and not until 1953 were Eskimos living there again. This time they were not quite alone.

They were there, in part, for the same reasons which prompted the Villas Boas brothers to set up the Xingu National Park in Brazil's Mato Grosso. The first few families were brought to the RCMP post at Craig Harbor, on the southeast coast of Ellesmere, aboard the Canadian icebreaker *C. D. Howe*. But by 1956 they had gradually shifted to Grise Fiord, where a high mountain ridge offered protection from the icy winds. They had come to Ellesmere as volunteers from Port Harrison in Quebec and from Pond Inlet on Baffin Island. Canada's Department of Indian Affairs (then called the Department of Northern Affairs and Northern Development) had observed with increasing concern the drop in game reserves in those areas of relatively high Eskimo density. The Department, of course, wanted to preserve the game, but they were more interested in the Eskimos. And, for the Eskimos, Ellesmere Island represented an opportunity to carry on their traditional life in an environment admittedly harsh but mercifully remote from what was by their standards a veritable population explosion. (When I arrived at Grise Fiord I learned what the Eskimo concept of a crowd was. For them a group of 75 or 100 was like New Year's Eve in Times Square.)

The difference between the Ellesmere settlement and Xingu Park has become quite clear in the few years that have passed

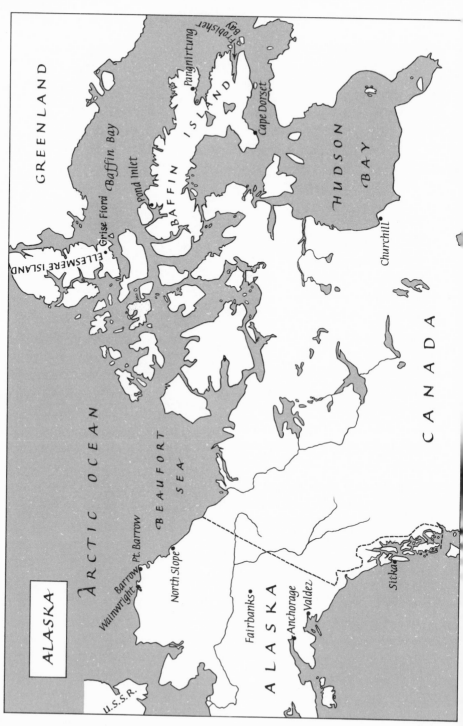

since I visited Grise Fiord. The Villas Boas brothers never intended anything but a last-ditch defense of the South American Indian against the intrusion of Western culture. The Eskimos in Grise Fiord, however, were going to be taught how to survive in the modern world. And these were indeed the same policy alternatives I had encountered wherever enlightened governments attempted to deal justly with their indigenous peoples: isolation or assimilation. All the rest—the in-betweens—were variations on one theme or the other.

There was another reason why the Eskimos and the two constables were living at Grise Fiord. Ellesmere Island had been of considerable interest to white explorers, hunters and whalers ever since the first European, William Baffin, entered Jones Sound (which he named) in 1616. But from the late nineteenth century on, the island had attracted a number of Danish and Norwegian explorers, and in 1919 Knud Rasmussen of Denmark disconcerted the Canadian government by landing on Ellesmere Island and shooting a number of musk-oxen. Ottawa's complaint was rejected by Rasmussen on the grounds that the High Arctic islands constituted a *terra nullius*: they belonged to no one. Determined to establish its territorial claims to Ellesmere and the surrounding islands, Canada sent its first detachment of Royal Canadian Mounted Police to Craig Harbor in 1922. An outpost was set up, and some thirty years later the Grise Fiord Eskimo community gave *de facto* as well as *de jure* status to Canadian claims. Ellesmere was no longer an uninhabited island.

Under these circumstances I suppose it was inevitable that the community of "unspoiled" Eskimos I lived with at Grise Fiord in 1962 would undergo rapid changes. And it is not easy to blame the government. If a national government "sponsors" a native village, it is likely to invest in a school, a post office, a police force and so on. It will naturally expect its citizens to make use of these facilities in order to justify them. A school, for instance, places a number of restrictions on the comings and goings of the members of a community—as any suburban mother who must get her child up in the morning, perhaps deliver him to school and pick him up at the end of the day, will tell you. And a constabulary force adds new kinds of authority to a community. They supercede the older authority of nature—the seasons, the frequency and type of snow, the periodic abundance or paucity of game. Aside from what the Eskimo child might learn in school, the very fact of its existence makes it difficult for the child to be close to its mother and father at the early age when indoctrination in the traditional life is so important. But when I reached Grise Fiord the schoolhouse had not yet been built.

Once at this settlement with my cameraman, Doug Sinclair, I had only the vaguest notion of what sort of motion picture would result. There were only three small shacks, two fur-clad constables—and not an Eskimo in sight. They were off seal hunting, and their nearest camp was a five-hour trip by dog sled. Since the plane that had brought us was still available, I decided to forgo the five-hour ride on the *komatik*, or dog sled, this time. Today, if you were to visit Grise Fiord, there would be no difficulty in finding Eskimos. They live in permanent, well-heated homes with modern kitchens, and many have washing machines. As it happens, they are all gathered about the original few shacks I found there in 1962.

So it wasn't until the morning after my arrival that I first saw real Eskimos. It took our plane about fifteen minutes to cross the frozen waters of Jones Sound and arrive at the camp that had been suggested by one of the constables, Terry Jenkin. He told me that there I would find the two best hunters in the community. (They were not difficult to spot, either.) Soon after we landed near a group of five igloos on the ice we were surrounded by Eskimos, their eager faces aglow with life.

I was looking for individuals with a certain indefinable quality or presence that comes through on film. Those individuals who have this—call it charisma, if you will—usually turn out to be the leaders of the group. Among the first to be selected for my documentary were the very men Constable Jenkin had wanted me to meet—the top-ranking hunters of the community, Akpaliapik and Markosie.

Akpaliapik was the acknowledged leader of the community for his skills in what Eskimos consider most important: hunting, fishing, providing food for the family and the community—which to the Eskimo is only an extension of his family. His superiority as a provider, of course, was the basis for Akpaliapik's self-confidence and for his respected position in the community. When Eskimos are employed for wages and there are general stores for their wives to spend the money in, their reliance upon leaders like Akpaliapik diminishes. That is why so many older Eskimos throughout the Arctic maintain their role as at least part-time hunters, even when wage work is available.

Constable Jenkin had told me that there was little or no wage work to be had around Grise Fiord. "But they like a chance to earn a little money, to buy a few of the products of civilization at our cooperative," he said. "I'm sure they'll want to work in the film."

I think now they might have been glad to work with me even if there had been no compensation. It wasn't long before I was fully convinced that cooperation is a deeply ingrained feature of the Eskimo life style. Unless they have been given good cause to distrust strangers they seem eager to treat outsiders as members of the family. To what lengths an Eskimo would go to be cooperative I discovered when I asked Jenkin to find out whether it would be possible to film the birth of a baby during my stay at Grise Fiord. The translated answer came back. "No babies are due now. One was born just a few weeks ago, but no more are expected for quite some time." Markosie must have noticed my obvious disappointment. He said something to Jenkin who turned to me, and without embarrassment explained, "Markosie says, 'Why don't you take my sister and make her pregnant? Then you will have your baby.'"

When there is very little to go around, it makes good sense to share and to cooperate. Eskimos offer anything and everything they have, and they feel that a man needs a woman or a woman needs a man in much the same way they need food. To an Eskimo brought up in traditional ways, a need is a need. It is only when he becomes assimilated that he inherits from our world the confusion between necessity and desire. He may find it difficult to recall what he once truly needed in his newfound possessiveness. Having things—a television set, property, a wristwatch, a woman of his own—becomes an end in itself.

Igloo is the Eskimo word for house, and it can be made of snow, sod, driftwood or anything he can get his hands on. Like almost everything else in the environment of the traditional Eskimo, it impresses you immediately with its limitations. There is obviously very little space or privacy in an Eskimo house. Father, mother and children sleep on the same platform along with perhaps a grandparent or two, a cousin, an adopted child or even any wayfarer who has happened along. Understandably, all that body heat generates a good deal of warmth, even in a snow house where the temperature may rise to a tolerable forty degrees. After you have spent a night cuddled up with an Eskimo family, it isn't necessary to make overt gestures of friendship the next day. And if you should go hunting together the comradeship that will see you through many dangers is as deeply felt as it is unspoken.

All this has been changing radically since my first visit to Grise Fiord. From Ellesmere and Baffin Island, across Canada's Northwest Territories to Alaska, the white man, or "southerner" as he is considered in the High Arctic, has made his presence felt, whether as DEW Line engineer, mineral prospector, oil geologist or government official with the mission of educating the Eskimo and providing warm, dry housing for him. Nevertheless, the pattern of change is generally the same, with only minor variations.

Men like Akpaliapik and Markosie, hunters of seal and walrus, are fast vanishing. Attracted by jobs on the DEW Line or in the newly discovered oil fields in Canada and Alaska, they have gathered in settlements ranging from 50 to 500 inhabitants. Once there they are assured of welfare payments and medical services, education for their children and year-round housing. The mortality rate, particularly among infants and children declines, and the population increases. The growth rate in the Canadian North

This Jivaro father-and-son team has made many raids into the territory of enemy clans over the years and have taken more than their share of heads. On the right, wearing the hat which was the gift of the author, is Chief Peruche; his son proudly carries an ancient shotgun.

Jivaro children from families still living in the traditional manner study in a mission school operated by the Salesian Fathers in Sucua. The parents of some of these children were killed in vengeance raids.

No generation gap here. A Jivaro warrior proudly displays a tsantsa for his son in order to impress upon him his sacred duty to follow the Jivaro tradition of vengeance. (*right*) After the head-shrinking process has been completed, the victorious clan participates in the tsantsa dance, whose purpose is to inform their avenged clansman that the score has been evened and his soul may now rest in peace. The warrior who has taken the enemy's head proudly wears it during the dance, after which it is discarded.

The tsantsa dance ceremony is not exclusively for the men. Women, too, dance around the shrunken head. Their waists and ankles are decorated with circlets of bones which help to keep up the rhythm of the dance.

The author tries to engage Orlando Villas Boas, the greatest friend of the Indians of Brazil, in conversation while an affectionate Indian child hugs him possessively. Villas Boas was the pathfinder of the remarkable Roncador-Xingu Expedition which successfully penetrated areas of Brazil never before seen by white men.

The renowned Chief Utitiaja (center), with 58 enemy heads to his credit, remains impassive as he views a copy of *Life* magazine containing the author's photograph of a shrunken human head.

Not all is sadness. After the mourning ceremonies of the *guarup*, men and women of the Xinguano tribe engage in a colorful dance that moves endlessly from hut to hut to the music of these 7-foot-long double flutes made of bamboo. The women dance in a stylized manner with their left hands on the right shoulders of the men. *John Moss, Camera Press, London.*

Although not as famous for their beauty as the Camayura woman of the Xingu, 500 miles to the northeast, these very attractive Bororo women are just as proud and even more independent. *University Museum, Philadelphia.*

When the author first visited these tall and superbly built Bororo warriors in 1949, the tribe numbered about 2,000. On his return 19 years later, they were almost extinct as a result of their disastrous confrontation with civilization.

This tough, proud, and suspicious Chavante is embittered and frustrated. Before his tribe permitted themselves to be pacified, they were the most feared tribe in Brazil and killed every explorer and missionary who tried to make contact with them. *PIX, Inc., New York.*

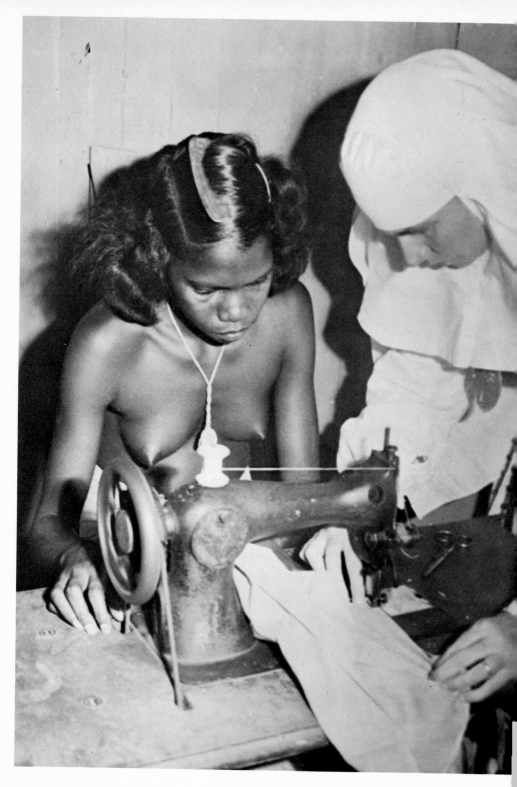

At a mission in North Arnhemland, nuns train aboriginal girls in home craft. At the age of 16, girls will leave the mission and attempt to make their transition into modern life. *PIX, Inc., New York.*

Whither the Aborigine? These spear-holding hunters seem to be pondering an uncertain future as they scan an empty landscape in quest of the ever-elusive game. *Australian News and Information Bureau.*

The dignity and independence of Aboriginal man is clearly mirrored in this group clustered around an outback campfire. *Australian News and Information Bureau.*

Clay-daubed Aboriginal spearmen rush forward to hurl their weapons at the accused during a ceremony (*corroboree*) at a government mission in Arnhemland. *PIX, Inc., New York*.

Papunya, 150 miles west of Alice Springs, is a government settlement for about 1,000 Aborigines of the Pintubi, Ngalia, Waibiri, and Aranda tribes. These primitives had never before seen water coming from a tap, canned food, or a cow or a horse. Many of them did not like the closed-in feeling of the houses built especially for them and camped in the open in rude shelters on the fringes of the settlement, shunning the members of other tribes. *Australian News and Information Bureau.*

Happiness was a natural characteristic of the Aborigines but this group of Pintubi women at the government settlement of Papunya in central Australia has little to smile about now that their former way of life has almost disappeared. *Australian News and Information Bureau.*

Discarded European clothes and a few tentative smiles cannot conceal the essential bewilderment of these Aborigines who are trying to adjust to a new and unfamiliar life style at the Oenpelli Mission in Arnhemland. *PIX, Inc., New York.*

An Aboriginal stockman on a cattle station near Alice Springs in Central Australia. From viewing Westerns they have learned to affect the style and dress of the American cowboy. *Australian News and Information Bureau.*

In 1968, Lionel Rose, an Aboriginal boxer, received a hero's welcome when he returned to his home in a Melbourne suburb after winning the world bantamweight championship by defeating the Japanese titleholder.

A classroom in the far west of Alice Springs. Population is sparse in Australia's arid inland, where the main economic activities are sheep and cattle raising and mining. Schools are established where there are enough children, but many of the children, in widely scattered settlements, receive lessons by radio from the School of the Air, operated from Broken Hill. *Australian News and Information Bureau.*

To the uninitiated the varied decorations of the participants at a *corroboree* have no meaning. These Aborigines are performing a traditional ritual dance at the government settlement at Mangrida, Arnhemland. *Australian News and Information Bureau.*

is about three times that of the southern provinces. Alaska's rate of population increase, thanks to immigration as well as the growing native birth rate, is the highest of any of the fifty states. Perhaps this doesn't sound particularly threatening, but it is only one part of a vicious circle. The new Eskimo settlements have grown too rapidly to keep up with the available jobs, and there is not enough land and sea life in the surrounding regions to accommodate the larger population.

Perhaps one of the most vexing aspects of the Eskimo problem is the social disorganization often brought by the new schools. Without education the Eskimo could be destined to the kind of second-class citizenship that has been the lot of so many native peoples around the world. Too often in the Arctic schooling brings with it a host of attendant social changes. First, as previously mentioned, the addition of a schoolhouse to the community limits the mobility of traditionally nomadic parents. Not only are sons unable to accompany their fathers on hunts, but mothers are reluctant to join husbands at the trap lines, and without them to perform the "women's" tasks—cooking, skinning and butchering animal carcasses—there is little that the men can do except remain close to home.

Among Eskimos there is a rather strict division of labor, as there is in most primitive societies. Such a system worked well when men and women were dependent upon each other for their survival, and it is still regarded as demeaning for a man to do woman's work. Women are needed to scrape, clean and dry the skins of foxes, bears, caribou and seals. There is even a "women's tool," a half-moon-shaped knife called an *ulu*. A woman is needed to chew leather to make it moist and pliable so that it can be worked. I had seen Akpaliapik's wife and daughter chewing on leather for boots and mittens, and sinewy strips used in making and mending clothes. Sometimes this went on for the better part of an evening, while he regaled us with tales of memorable hunts. In many primitive societies hunting is strictly a man's activity, but among the traditional Eskimos it is (or was) a cooperative enterprise for the entire family group.

One of the saddening aspects of this pattern of rapid change is the generation gap that inevitably results when children of preliterate parents are sent to school. Once the Eskimo youngsters have learned to read and write they are not particularly anxious to partake with their parents in the traditional life. And like many American-born children of immigrant parents, these Eskimo children reject their ancient heritage. The difficulties of the Eskimo are compounded by the fact that there simply are not enough jobs to go around in the Arctic settlements. And what jobs are available do not usually pay enough for Eskimo parents to maintain the young in the new style of life to which they would like to become accustomed. The worst of it is the accompanying identity loss. They are Eskimos no longer, but neither are they "white men." And if they join the welfare rolls, the protective government agencies turn out to be a very inadequate substitute for either the families from which they have broken away, or the self-respect which accompanies employment in the new wage economy.

An Eskimo without pride, without roots, can neither survive in the snow fields nor in the villages. One day, toward the end of my visit to Grise Fiord, I saw Akpaliapik and Markosie take on a huge, lumbering polar bear, while Constable Jenkin, my cameraman and I stood by frozen with apprehension. Although the first harpoon thrusts hit their mark, the bear, in a frenzy of fury, bent the shafts as if they were plastic. As he advanced toward us, Akpaliapik, choosing his own moment, lunged with his spear and struck home. I knew then what made Markosie and Akpaliapik such great hunters. It was the same air of self-reliance and pride that had drawn my attention to them from the first moment we arrived at their camp. Beneath this pride there was a stubborn refusal to retreat in the face of any of nature's perils. Although it was not yet apparent at Grise Fiord in 1962, in much of the Arctic the Eskimo's pride was the first casualty of rapid assimilation.

Another casualty of modernization in the Arctic has been the storied Eskimo sled dog, now being replaced by the ubiquitous snowmobile, a more efficient means of locomotion perhaps, but in many ways a riskier one. In Alaska I heard accounts of snow-mobiles that had run out of fuel, stranding their passengers far beyond the reach of help. A few such tragedies have already occurred. Sled dogs have incredible endurance and are not likely to run out of fuel. In fact, dogs have served as a source of food when no other sustenance was available. The gasoline-powered snow scooters can attain a speed of thirty-five m.p.h., while the huskies cover ground at only five or ten m.p.h., at best. Admittedly, feeding and caring for the Eskimo dogs was a burdensome chore. Enormous amounts of food had to be carried, for sled dogs can consume as much food each day as does a human, and when they are fed it can be a frightening spectacle.

Once, while filming some dog feeding scenes at Grise Fiord, I was repelled by the sight of a dozen or more beasts, lunging with furious howls at a huge pile of meat, all the while attacking one another as they pulled and tugged at the larger pieces. When the feeding was over, it was obvious that the more ferocious dogs had gotten most of the food, while a few of the others had even received wounds, which they were licking busily. Markosie approved of the scene. "The big dogs get the most," he told me. "They work the hardest."

Eskimo dogs are utterly fearless—they will hold their ground against even a polar bear—and on a long trip they will press on when men are ready to drop from exhaustion. Without these remarkable animals, the Eskimo could never have survived as a hunter-trapper in his inhospitable environment. Mounties have been brought back, injured or ill, by their sled dogs. But in 1969 the Royal Canadian Mounted Police gave up their huskies in favor of snowmobiles, thus closing out another chapter in their history.

Now that their usefulness is coming to an end, Eskimo dogs are being killed in large numbers. They can no longer be supported, and turning them loose could have disastrous consequences. Completely wild, they would only add a new and senseless peril to life in the Arctic.

The Eskimos are not intimidated by technological innovations, but they like to adapt them to their traditional style of life. I have seen Eskimos hitch their old dog sled to the snow scooters, just as I have heard of Eskimos who have taken along a few dogs on their gasoline-powered journeys—just in case. Eskimos are genuinely fascinated by gadgets of all kinds, and they like to give the same care and attention to machines that they have always lavished on harpoons, knives, cooking and camping equipment. William Byler, director of the Association on American Indian Affairs, told me that he had once asked an Alaskan friend for a good, brief description of the Eskimo personality. After a little thought, his friend—an Eskimo himself—gave this definition: "An Eskimo is the kind of a person who will get a brand new outboard motor, study it carefully, then get a hammer and start banging away at the propeller until he can say to himself, 'Now it's really workin' good.'"

In 1963, Doug Sinclair and I decided to return to Grise Fiord to shoot some additional footage for our documentary film. When we arrived I spotted a small crowd waiting on the sea ice where our small Otter plane was to land. No sooner had I stepped out when I heard someone call my name. It was Markosie, and he was about to take a picture of me with a small box camera which Constable Jenkin had taught him to use. He was laughing too hard to get a sharp picture, but I knew that nothing could give him more pleasure· than to show me that he too could operate a camera. Perhaps behind the joke was Eskimo pride once more. Certainly if the Eskimo had his way he would master all of the innovations that came along.

The Eskimo's adaptability had always been the key to his survival in a harsh environment. Now he was ready and willing to master the new technology brought to the Arctic by the white man. He accepted the rifle, the explosive harpoon, the snowmobile and the outboard motor, because they could help him to survive, albeit at the price of some of his ancient beliefs. Anthropologist Norman Chance in *The Eskimo of North Alaska* puts it this way:

Although the use of the rifle made hunting easier, it reduced the need for sharing and cooperation among kin groups, lessened the prestige of the hunter, and brought into question the validity of the traditional religion by raising doubts about the importance of certain rituals and taboos connected with hunting.

Still, if the changes had come about more gradually, the Eskimo could have adjusted to the new life, as he had for many centuries adjusted to the harsh life of the Arctic, without any serious changes in his character. True, the fatalism which once enabled him to make a kind of sense out of an uncertain and hostile environment might have vanished. The taboos which once armed the primitive hunter with a not excessive caution, and which accounted for his sudden misfortunes, might have slowly faded. In short, his attitude toward nature would have become "Westernized" through the introduction of the implements and weapons of our world. But he could still have maintained intact his pride and his identity as an Eskimo. The most damaging blow to his self-esteem—to his understanding that the Eskimo way of life, challenging as it was, had glory and privilege in it—came not from technological change alone. It came from the rapid pile-up of demands upon his adaptability which perhaps no human beings could have survived without loss of self-esteem.

In only a few decades many an Eskimo was wrenched out of a subsistence economy and thrust into—or teased by—a cash system he was totally unprepared for. Education showed the Eskimo that he occupied a relatively small corner of the earth—and an unimportant one at that. Great events were taking place in an outside world that had largely passed him by. In school his children learned that his language was no longer adequate either for the interpretation of the universe around him or for the communication of the subtle feelings and knowledge which were beyond the interest or concern of the white man. The Eskimo learned, too, that he could no longer live by the ancient clock of the long days and nights, that another world existed where people worshipped time in quite a different way, where the day started at nine and stopped at five, regardless of what the sun was doing.

In this new world he discovered a sharp division between leisure and work; when it was time to work *everyone* worked, and when it was time to rest *everyone* rested. The individualism of the hunter's free life had given way to the conformity of the regimented work day. He discovered new dreams and new appetites he never knew he possessed when he saw movies and television and full-color advertisements in magazines. And he found new religions—sometimes one at a time, sometimes several—competing for his soul. As if he had not enough to bedevil him, he was introduced to alcohol by whalers and traders who would give him a bottle in exchange for pelts that could fetch up to $200 in the States. If he finished the bottle immediately, as he often did (it wasn't his way to think about tomorrow), he was pushed aside and further convinced that he was of little value to anyone. Finally, he discovered that the one thing on this earth that he thought was truly his—the land of his fathers—could, by the stroke of a pen in some strange and distant climate, be taken from him.

If all the forces of change are weighed—and they are being weighed at last—the unhappy situation of the once-proud and highly individualistic Eskimo can be approached with the resourcefulness and intelligence we should have used in treating the Indians a century and more ago.

In Alaska the opportunity still exists to apply that intelligence. And, judging by what I observed during my 1969 visit to the North Slope, we'll need all of that commodity we can get.

7 Alaska:
Grandma Was an Eskimo

I MUST CONFESS to having undertaken my Alaskan visit with mixed feelings. My memories of the Eskimos at Grise Fiord were still fresh in my mind. When I left there in 1963, the radio had just brought word that the *C. D. Howe* was ahead of schedule and would in a few weeks steam up Jones Sound with its complement of doctors, nurses, materials for a schoolhouse and the teacher to go with it. I knew that I had gotten to Ellesmere Island none too soon.

But Alaska would be different. For once I knew I would be arriving years, perhaps decades too late. Too late that is to see an indigenous people living in virtually untouched conditions. After all the first contacts with white men had taken place in 1740 and in 1826. Sir John Franklin and Captain F. W. Beachey of England had explored the region. The Alaskan native had long ago acquired a dispirited view of the *tannik*, or white man. By 1867, Alaska's Eskimos had learned about civilization from either the lawless and irresponsible crews of American whaling ships north of the Bering Strait or from the oppressive hirelings of Russia's fur-trading company to the south.

There was still another thought that I could not get out of my mind as I arrived at modern Fairbanks and prepared to head north for Barrow. I had visited aboriginal societies in many parts of the world where other advanced nations were mopping up the remnants of primitive cultures, sometimes carelessly, sometimes with compassion. I had witnessed traditions that had weathered thousands of years disappear overnight; I had seen tribes that were once proud and independent reduced to a handful of dejected and bewildered survivors by disease and psychological trauma, even genocide. But the Arctic peoples and especially the Alaskan natives, were *our* responsibility; since 1959, in fact, they had been citizens of our forty-ninth state. They had as much right to maintain their cultural identity as any other minority group in America. And so long as they desired to go on living as Eskimos they were a continuing challenge to the tolerance and understanding of other Americans.

For the Alaskan natives—the Aleuts, the Indians, and particularly the Arctic Eskimos—there were still alternatives. For the people of the lower states—the "southerners"—they provided a last chance to use compassion and sanity in our dealings with the indigenous people of this continent. I wondered how, when it was all over, it would be said that we had met that challenge.

These were some of my thoughts in Fairbanks as I prepared for the flight north. I was eager to get to Barrow, the northernmost town on the North American mainland, and the location of the largest single Eskimo community. While in Fairbanks, I decided to visit the local museum, and on the way I was able to learn something of the fate that awaits Eskimos who drift into the larger towns. I hailed a taxicab, and my Eskimo driver, as it turned out, didn't mind talking about himself. Our conversation really became animated when I mentioned that I had noticed the rows of shabby honky-tonk saloons, bars, pool halls, slot-machine arcades and hot dog stands on Fairbanks' main thoroughfare.

They were filled with native people, many of them derelicts. I wondered aloud how many Eskimos were destined for one skid row or another.

"The welfare checks all wind up in those bars," the driver told me. He was about thirty-eight, intelligent and articulate. Although born in Fairbanks, he remembered killing a polar bear with a .22 rifle while camping at about the age of eleven. The bear had caught the scent of an open can of sardines in his tent and wandered in for a meal. Both boy and bear must have been mutually surprised.

"I pick up about five drunks a day. Eskimos," he went on, "start drinking at about five in the morning, and once they open a bottle they don't quit until it's finished."

"Why are they on welfare?" I asked him. "Can't they get jobs?"

"They can get jobs and make money," he explained. "But in general they take jobs just to have the money to drink." After a brief silence he continued, "You wouldn't believe it when they are drunk. They're wild—not the same people at all. It's disgusting to see them. Naturally, when they're drunk that way the oil companies, who do a lot of the hiring around here, will have nothing to do with them. That makes the Eskimos feel even sorrier for themselves, and when they get another chance to get drunk they go at it even harder."

Before we reached the museum the driver told me he was in love with an Eskimo girl in Fairbanks. She was charming in every way, and he wanted to marry her and start raising a family. "But what can I do?" he asked plaintively. "She's fallen off the wagon twice, and when she goes on a drunk she's an entirely different person. Her father was an alcoholic. She had eight brothers and all of them are dead now. One of her four sisters was an alcoholic, and one day she hanged herself."

I asked him why it was so bad.

"Eskimos feel inferior," he replied. "They feel very inferior and sorry for themselves."

First-hand experiences like this are well supported by impersonal statistics. There is no shortage of data if that were all that was needed to dramatize the crisis facing the Alaskan native. For example, as high as the suicide rate is among Alaskan whites, it is twice as high among the native population. According to state Health and Welfare Department figures, the death rate of natives from influenza and pneumonia was ten times that of whites in 1966; the native accident rate resulting in death was three times higher. The average age at death of Alaskan natives is about half that of any other Americans. In 1966 the average native life span was 34.5 years. His children have one half the chance that white Alaskans have of surviving infancy. However, mental health, if alcoholism, child neglect, delinquency and a wide range of other behavioral problems are included, has become the number one problem of the Alaskan native.

The problem of mental illness among Alaskan natives is both a symptom and a cause of their frequent inability to cope with the new culture of the whites. When the Eskimo learns that his traditional identity not only fails to sustain him in a time of sudden change, but may actually cause his downfall, he experiences a deepening sense of worthlessness. And it is all the more unlikely that he will adjust to the new life that has been thrust upon him.

It wasn't the plight of the Eskimo in the larger towns and cities that drew me to the forty-ninth state in the spring of 1969; I was more concerned about the natives of the North Slope region. There, Eskimos were still clustered in small villages and were being forced to make a working compromise between past and present. This region, entirely within the Arctic Circle, extends north to the Arctic Ocean from the 600-mile-long Brooks Range, a towering glaciated wall that literally slices off the top of the state. A series of graduated declines leads down to a vast coastal plain once submerged and now covered by a tundra that provides food for lemmings and the remaining caribou and insulates the underlying permafrost in the warmer months. The geological features of this area have been of particular interest to oil companies—notably Humble and Atlantic-Richfield—who have in the last few years discovered reserves conservatively estimated in one field alone to be from five to ten billion barrels.

The Eskimos have traditionally lived off the sea mammals along the coast or have been nomadic hunters of the caribou inland. Before the white man arrived, the aboriginal Eskimos had grouped themselves into nomadic bands or in villages out of choice, and the size of each group was limited by the number of mouths that could be fed by the food sources in the environment. On occasion groups might meet for trading purposes or they might shift their location to suit the migratory pattern of the wildlife. For many, however, the *entire* area was—and still is—their home. Beginning with the Eskimo's first major contact with white civilization in the middle of the last century the migratory pattern of their life was to be radically altered.

The whalers eventually were instrumental in reducing the whale population upon which the coastal Eskimos were dependent. They introduced the Eskimos to whiskey and then bartered repeating rifles, tobacco, matches and molasses for highly prized whalebone, furs and caribou meat. Armed with rifles, the Eskimos soon reduced the population of sea and land mammals which were their subsistence. Before long the caribou were all but wiped out.

The United States Bureau of Education, given responsibility for Eskimo welfare, introduced reindeer herding in 1890 and made loans available to natives who had served an apprenticeship under Lapp and Chukchi herders. The growth of the reindeer population around Barrow helped the Eskimo to survive when his old subsistence economy had virtually disappeared. Unfortunately, poor herding practices, disease, wolves, overgrazing and new job opportunities had nearly put an end to reindeer herding by 1950.

The Eskimos had learned to become dependent upon the cash economy of the white man during the whaling periods, and their attempts to return to a subsistence economy were doomed. Nevertheless, without the introduction of the reindeer they might have faced a devastating period of starvation. The whalers and white traders were also largely responsible for the spread of diseases to which the Eskimos had developed no resistance; some communities were wiped out by epidemics of influenza, measles and smallpox. One hundred Barrow Eskimos perished in a measles epidemic in 1902; two years earlier a visit by a whaling ship at the Point had resulted in the death from measles of some 200 inland natives who had gone there to trade.

For a time trapping seemed to offer the Eskimo a new source of income when whaling and hunting had fallen off. Fox furs, beginning in the 1920s, increased in value. An Eskimo could earn $3,000 to $4,000 and more during a season that lasted from November to April. But at that time of year Eskimos had traditionally devoted themselves to community events—making visits, renewing old ties, storytelling or almost continuous entertainment in the Eskimo dance house, or *karigi*. Trapping isolated the Eskimo not only from the larger community but also from the entire family that had once made the hunt a cooperative endeavor. And when the fox fur market declined sharply in 1929, it forced still another change. The Eskimo went back to hunting seal, walrus, whale and, when he could find them, caribou. He was encouraged to try basket weaving and carving, to take jobs in the villages as postmaster, school janitor, sales clerk in native stores, and—during World War II—to serve in the Army. (Eskimo health was so poor that half of the young men who volunteered for service were rejected as physically unfit.)

In recent years the Eskimo has been given welfare payments and cared for by religious institutions; he has been offered new opportunities for career training by industry and government agencies. But these piecemeal corrective measures served only to compound his bewilderment. In recent years the oil companies, the DEW Line installations and other evidences of an encroaching technology have only stepped up the tempo of his loss of traditional identity. The Eskimo is an individual with a dead past and an uncertain future.

The distribution of Eskimo settlements in the North Slope region, hardly a true representation of their ancient way of life, has come about because of a series of stresses and strains on what was once a balanced ecological picture. Today Eskimos are concentrated here in five major settlements that ring the northern and northwestern coasts: Point Hope, Wainwright, Barrow, Kaktovik and Anaktuvuk. Barrow, with its population of 2,000, is the largest Eskimo village in Alaska. It also claims the title of northernmost town in North America. Soon after I arrived there it occurred to me that Barrow was a microcosm of what had been happening to the Eskimo in recent years—and what would be happening for some time to come.

There are still some Eskimos in Barrow who grew up in the early days when changes in native life were demanding but gradual. They had time to build up an identification with the traditions of the past and yet were able to make an adjustment to the present. Pete Sovalik belongs in this category. He works for the Naval Arctic Research Laboratory at Barrow, where he is highly regarded by his employers who hire about 60 percent of their work force from among the Eskimo population of the area.

Pete, who has been living in Barrow since 1913, keeps watch over the experimental animals at NARL—wolves, Arctic fox, lemmings. He is muscular, craggy-faced, barrel-chested, fiftyish. I asked him what he thought was the biggest difference between the young Eskimo men of today and those of his own youth. "What we wanted," Pete said, "was to become great hunters. Today the young men here at Barrow try to get jobs with a construction company or in oil drilling. It's been a big change. Very big change."

Pete spoke in deliberate, slow tones. "In old days we not spend money for living, for clothes, for sod houses. We wore skin clothing, not fancy but we make ourselves. We have what we need. Nobody was a poor man then. If times bad you got help from your neighbor. Everybody the same. Now nobody seems to have enough. Plenty to buy. But never enough."

He shrugged his shoulders. There was no hint of bitterness in his tone. He had accepted what had happened as part of a process over which he and other Eskimos simply had no control. There was something of the traditional fatalism in the way he viewed the changes.

"In the old days we got sugar and flour maybe once a year from traders, and if we run out of it we don't have it for six months, maybe more. We'd run out of tea, and there was no tea for a long time. Now my kids, when they don't see any sugar in sugar can they say, 'Mama, we don't have sugar.' And Mama goes to store."

Pete seemed to find most disorienting this loss of the constant sense of deprivation, once so much a part of the Eskimo way of life. Scarcity in the old days was perhaps the major thread of his existence. I suspect that to Pete the idea that one could now go to the store and buy something anytime it was needed was slightly immoral. Being proud of oneself for being able to do without the minor luxuries of life was another aspect of Eskimo culture that had vanished. Perhaps it disturbed Pete that Mama and the retail store clerk made life go on, rather than the husband in his role as hunter.

I had seen almost as many television antennas in Barrow village as might be seen atop the roofs of a typical American suburb, and I wondered what Pete thought about the impact of TV programming on Eskimo children. Pete told me that this was the second year of television in Barrow and the entire community had caught the fever. Movie attendance had dropped off, and TV sets were turned on for more than a dozen hours a day, he said.

"I think young children learn more from television which they are not supposed to learn," he said. "They see murders, lots of Westerns, plenty of violence. The little kids maybe they think they can live like that." After one of his thoughtful pauses he added, "I kinda worry about my kids."

What did Pete think about the way the younger generation was developing, I wondered. I began by telling him about the exciting native dances I had seen a few nights earlier. Did Pete think that the new generation would carry on the old dance traditions? "I doubt it," he said. "Maybe twenty years more it will all be gone. Eskimos won't keep it up. Youngster dance American way—jitterbug, twist," he laughed. "Something like that."

Pete agreed with a growing consensus that liquor was a serious problem for the Eskimo. "That's another big change, from the old days to now," he said. "Long ago we not have much liquor around North. They had it in Fairbanks, in the South. Not here. Now we got it here too. When liquor shows up there's lots of trouble."

Pete recalled Barrow before the influx of white people. There were quite a few sod and wood houses then. "People liked to go up to the Point," he said. "It was a good place for whale. People here still catch whale. We already got two of them this year."

I told Pete that I had seen many village natives leave their jobs and go out to watch the whale being brought in the day before. It was still a matter of pride for the community. During the time I spent in Barrow a total of four whales had been caught. Pete told me that nine whales in all had been taken the previous year. The season, he said, lasted from late April to early June, the period when the whales migrate to the northeast around the tip of Alaska. In late summer and early fall they pass by Barrow again heading in the other direction.

Distribution of the whale meat has always been an important ritual among the Alaskan natives. The captain of the crew that catches the whale gets the favored sections; the next most desirable parts are distributed among the crews that have assisted in the catch; the balance of the meat goes to the community. It was always a mark of distinction to be a successful whaling captain. And, according to Pete, much honor is still accorded to the Eskimo whaler. In fact, Pete said, the twenty-eight-year-old whaling captain responsible for the catch the day before was a local celebrity. Typically, he works for the government and takes time off from his job each year at whaling time. Many Eskimos try to maintain just such a part-time commitment to their traditional way of life.

I asked Pete how many children he had. He told me he had nine, now. There were eight boys and one girl. His eldest son, Floyd, died in 1957 while seal hunting. Pete had trained his son well, but one morning after Pete had gone to work young Floyd went out alone. Returning home over the ice he fell through a deep crack and was drowned in the ocean below.

One of Pete's sons, Thomas, has been living in California for seven years. "He has a job," Pete said, a little uncertainly. "It's part work and part school. I don't know what kind of school. One day, long ago, some men came to Barrow and asked if anyone wanted to go to Mexico. Quite a few from Barrow went away. Thomas went too. We get a letter every month or two. He say he like to come back and see Mama sometime. But I don't think he like to stay at home anymore. He tell us in the letter not to worry about him being cold where he is."

Pete's oldest son, who is thirty-five, works with an oil-drilling crew, some 300 miles from Barrow. I asked Pete if he found it lonely to be away from his family. Pete explained that his son worked for twenty-eight days, returned to his family for two weeks, then went back and put in another twenty-eight day hitch.

How did his son make out on his driller's salary, I asked Pete. Was he able to save any money? Pete shook his head emphatically. "There no money to put in bank. My son got seven children. Very hard to get by. Everything pretty expensive here, too. His family want television, clothes. You don't save money. If he get sick he go on relief.

"In old days," Pete went on, "we get help from neighbors if we're sick and can't work or hunt. The neighbors come and bring food. But it's kinda hard now. I gotta big family. You gotta big family. How can we help each other?"

Later I spoke to Pete's boss. He is Dr. Max Brewer, the director of the Naval Arctic Research Laboratory, and a man with a long and extensive interest in the Arctic. His views on the Eskimo's problems, I knew, would be well supported by an abundance of first-hand experience.

There was, according to Max Brewer, a vast difference between the kind of Eskimo represented by Pete Sovalik and the younger group. Pete, he said, is really happy in both worlds. The younger people have not adjusted to either culture—the white or Eskimo. "We can send out a forty-year-old Eskimo with a field party, across tundra—winter and summer—and feel confident that he will return. I couldn't say that of a younger man. The older ones have made the shift. It's the younger ones who are caught up in the radical change. They are hurting right now."

Max Brewer called them city boys with brown eyes. They have become incapable of living the rough life on the tundra, and they are not yet ready to compete with the white man in the job market.

There was little doubt in my own mind as I listened to Dr. Brewer analyze the situation of the Eskimos in his measured, thoughtful way, that he was in favor of relatively complete assimilation—the sooner the better. As he saw it there was little hope for the Eskimo of tomorrow who could not meet the white man on his own terms. This, of course, would mean the eventual abandonment of the Eskimo life style. He would say, I'm sure, that it is going down the drain anyway. What could the Eskimo look forward to if he were to continue in his attempt to recapture his past? His best hope perhaps, Brewer thought, lay in intermarriage. Because of the shortage of white women in the Arctic, assimilation by marriage would come about anyway to a large degree, he said. The Alaska of the future would not be part white and part native, but an amalgamation. The day would come, Brewer speculated, when many an Alaskan would be able to say with pride, "Grandma was an Eskimo."

Education, nearly everyone says, is the answer. But what kind of education? And in the case of the Alaskan native, there is also the sensitive question of *where* the education should take place. Brewer entirely approves of the system of sending Eskimo teenagers to the Bureau of Indian Affairs schools in various parts of the state: Fairbanks, Anchorage, Mt. Edgecumb at Sitka. As a member of the Native Advisory School Board in Barrow, Brewer views with "mixed feelings" the growing demand of some Alaskan natives that they be allowed to keep their children in regional high schools. Admittedly, he says, parents would like to keep their children near home during their formative years. But the native schools, he points out, are "segregated schools." He adds, "And that's something we're trying to get away from." Clearly, Brewer feels that assimilation will be completed more successfully if children are sent to schools where they can get a better taste of white culture. There they will learn how to compete and, most important, they will have a better chance to learn English.

The language problem is another bone of contention. Dr. Brewer is not alone in his belief that the young Alaskan's failure to learn English adequately in the local schools, or at home, keeps him out of the job market—perhaps as much as any other single factor. This belief, fairly common among American educators, welfare workers and government officials in Alaska, was also expressed by Guilford Dudley who teaches eighth and ninth grade English and math at the Bureau of Indian Affairs school in Barrow.

"People look down on the Eskimos because they don't know English," Dudley told me. "I look at it from a dollars and cents viewpoint. If they're going to compete with the white man they are going to have to learn his culture. I know there are many people who say that the Eskimo must learn about his own culture, his heritage. But we just don't have enough time in school to do it all. There is no time for them to learn Eskimo culture and English and arithmetic and everything else.

"In the year I've been here," Dudley went on, "I've noticed that our 'A' group of students had one thing in common that the 'B' group (inferior students) didn't have. The A's came from a home where there were books, where their parents were English-oriented. The others read the words, but they haven't a clear idea what they mean. They really are thinking in Eskimo."

I found an articulate spokesman for the opposing argument in William Byler, director of the Association on American Indian Affairs in New York.

"A language," he explained, "is a response to an environment, and it must be important in relation to that environment or it wouldn't have developed. For example, the fact that there are seven words for snow in the Eskimo vocabulary is vital for survival. There are different implications for the Eskimo depending on the type of snow he is to encounter."

As Byler saw it, the teaching of English at the expense of the Eskimo tongue would worsen the gap between the generations. "By teaching a child English you are giving him a whole new world to live in, and that world is different from his parents' world. If the child's mother-tongue is Eskimo, you impede his general education by forcing him to learn early, basic concepts in a foreign tongue, and you may create a lifelong distaste for learning."

He claimed that boarding schools were "militarized and impersonal—disasters for many Indian and Eskimo children. These boarding schools," Byler continued, "have a custodial mentality. They don't want the kids messing around. You know, everything has to be done according to Hoyle—and not the Eskimo's Hoyle. And the suicide rate is catastrophic among Eskimo and Indian children. Many Eskimo children who come out of schools like Mt. Edgecumb are deprived of their feelings of self-worth."

Byler told me that the government wanted to spend $9 million to expand boarding-school facilities, but the Eskimos protested so strongly that the project was dropped in favor of developing the local native schools.

Byler did not agree with the thesis that unless the Eskimos were educated in American-oriented, white-staffed schools away from home they would be doomed to permanent ne'er-do-well status. Jobs for native high-school graduates were already available or could be made at trading posts, chain stores, in the Public Health Service or the Post Office. There would be opportunities for Eskimos to serve as nurses and health aides and in other social service fields. Crash programs were needed, Byler said, to bring native Alaskans a greater share of the wealth. The Federal government, a huge employer in the Arctic, could make an even greater effort to employ natives.

The Radio Corporation of America trains Eskimos in New Jersey so that they can return to Alaska as technicians and engineers on the DEW Line. Other employers too are discovering that it is to their advantage to train Alaskan natives for jobs in the Arctic instead of employing men from the lower forty-eight who are likely to quit as soon as they have gotten a taste of the harsh climate.

Byler's views were antiassimilationist. Nothing could be further from his thinking (or that of the association he directs) than the view that the Eskimo should be hustled into the mainstream of civilized life at the earliest possible moment. When I told him about the teachers in Barrow who were complaining about getting Eskimo children to come to school on time, and about the problems the native people seemed to have in adapting to the work routine, he told me, "Don't change the Eskimo culture. Change the schools. Why try to change the people? Change the work routine.

"I think we ought to be very careful about changing native cultures," Byler continued. "I don't think that the only way to run a business or school is on a nine to five basis. It might be interesting to sit down with the Natives and ask *them* about the best way to adapt a school system to the needs of children."

And then Byler offered a provocative comment: "We may not be seeing the twilight of native culture so much as the twilight of our own puritanical, work-oriented Western culture. We are becoming nativized, turning from a work-oriented to a leisure-oriented society. Why foist a way of life on the Eskimos that we are learning to abandon ourselves?"

Alaskan nativism was given emphatic support by Senator Ted Kennedy during his visit to the forty-ninth state in April of 1969. Although his attention was focused mainly on the abject poverty of the Eskimo villages, he took dead aim at failure to emphasize native culture in the schools. "I am obviously perplexed by the lack of secondary education opportunities, lack of native teachers, and the lack of the development of a curriculum which is perhaps of more relevance to the experience of the native people," Kennedy told the local press. During an inspection of the library of the school at Kotzebue, Kennedy said that he was "appalled" at the lack of books about the culture and history of Alaskan natives.

While the debate continues as to whether the Alaskan native can best prosper—best survive—with or without strong roots planted deeply in his ancient heritage, Eskimo political sophistication has been growing. At this time and probably for the foreseeable future, native politics revolves around the issue of the land claims—another way of saying that the Eskimo too is concerned about the protection of *his* environment. Linked to this issue is the recognition that the great mineral and oil potential of Alaska is at last nearing the point of realization.

The attitude of many Eskimos to their land is perhaps best summed up in an article in the *Tundra Times*, the native newspaper published in Fairbanks. "Briefly," wrote Helen L. Atkinson, "the natives claim the Russians never owned Alaska, just used it and exploited it, and that the U.S. government had, and has, no right to claim it, lease it, or give it away—it belongs to the native people."

This seems to be strong language, but there is no indication that the 22,000 Alaskan Eskimos, or the 20,000 Athapascan Indians, or the 4,000 to 8,000 Aleuts, or the 8,000 Tlingits intend to secede. Rather they are building an organizational structure and hiring the best legal talent they can find in order to convince the United States Congress that their claims are not only just, but provably legitimate.

The Statehood Act of 1958 gave to the state of Alaska the right to select 103 million acres from the public domain, a total acreage of almost 375 million. The selections were "not to interfere with the Native Rights." The state soon began to pick out lands with the aim of gaining title to them for economic development; they were to be leased to oil, timber and mining companies, or set aside for recreation purposes. However, it appeared that every time the state's Bureau of Land Management would print newspaper advertisements giving the statutory notice of intent to file for title to a given piece of land, a native organization would turn up. Their claims that the land in question was Eskimo or Athapascan or Tlingit property from time immemorial created a deadlock and prepared the way for federal intervention.

If they achieve nothing else, the Alaskan native organizations may help to restore some of the lost pride of the indigenous peoples; they are being welded together with the growing awareness that they need not be swept off the stage of history without a struggle. Even if their policies are seen as wrong-headed (and many otherwise sympathetic Alaskans do view them that way), they are at least serving notice that the Eskimo or Indian will no longer accept passively even the best-intended leadership and guidance of the white man, a passivity that too often in the past has led to the native's self-defeating apathy and despair. There are now about twenty-one regional or community organizations in Alaska, most of them having grown out of the land issue in the last few years, and a statewide organization, the Alaskan Federation of Natives. Summing up the growth of the native organizations, Howard Rock, publisher of the *Tundra Times*, explained. "The reason for the formation of these groups, of course, was that we had begun to realize that we, as native people of Alaska, had many problems. We also found that by speaking as a group, we were heard. As a result, some good things began to come our way. Having tasted the fruits of our labors, we are encouraged to try to perpetuate the existence of these organizations."

Meanwhile, Senator Henry M. Jackson, chairman of the Committee on Interior and Insular Affairs, has promised that Congress will pass a Native Land Bill. The Department of the Interior when under Secretary Walter J. Hickel, former Governor of Alaska, made its recommendations: two townships for each native village, amounting to a total land grant of from ten to twelve million acres; a cash settlement of $25 million a year, with a ceiling of one-half billion dollars; and a statewide native corporation to invest the dividends. Although opinion is somewhat divided, the native organizations are in general agreement that the Interior Department recommendations fall far short of the desired mark.

While these political moves have been taking place, the potential value of Eskimo lands on the North Slope has grown considerably with the discovery of rich oil accumulations at Prudhoe Bay. There is speculation in the oil industry that the exploitation of these newly discovered reserves will by use of an 800-mile trans-Alaskan pipeline, make the United States independent of foreign imports for a long time to come. And occurring at a time when both South American and Middle Eastern oil sources are in jeopardy, the importance of Eskimo lands in the Alaskan Arctic cannot be overstressed. Moreover, new icebreaking techniques may make it possible to ship oil both through the long-dreamed-of Northwest Passage—from the region around Barrow to America's eastern ports—and through the Bering Strait to the West Coast. Thus transportation costs, always a significant factor in the feasibility of developing new oil resources, would be reduced.

What all this means to the Eskimo is not yet entirely clear. But it is within the realm of possibility that the Eskimo may be in for a sizeable share of the new Alaskan wealth. At this time Eskimo living standards are among the lowest in the United States. One is tempted to ask, will the Eskimo be able to survive sudden success? "What will an Eskimo, who doesn't often see ten dollars, do with $10,000?" a business friend in Fairbanks wanted to know. I told him that I thought the Eskimo had a lot more flexibility in him than he was credited with. The more important question may be: Will other Americans permit the Eskimo to exercise his own judgment, to try out his own decision-making capacities? Or must we insist that he be made over in the image of a twentieth-century-model American, which even now may be becoming obsolete?

8 Africa: Tribes into Nations

IN THE PAST DECADE I have gone to equatorial Africa twice, each time after having sworn never to expose myself to the uncertainties of tropical exploration. To be sure, I had, in the '30s, '40s and '50s, documented on film and in print the predictably final scenes of truly primitive life among such African peoples as the Mangbetu, Watusi, Masai, Wagenia, Turkana and the Pygmies of the Ituri Forest. So, why go back in the late 1960s? I returned for a jumble of personal reasons—old friends I wanted to see again, nostalgia perhaps, the explorer's chronic addiction to the land that represents his first love—but mainly because I could not pass up the chance to see for myself what future generations will regard as the pivot of African history.

It was a decade of explosive upheaval. Africa, for centuries a dormant behemoth, had awakened, and within a few shattering years, demanded and for the most part got its independence. Men whose parents lived in mud huts, observing tribal law and ritual, dependent on the spear and the shield, had risen to the demands of running modern nation-states. What had happened here could not have occurred on such a scale on any other continent. Nowhere else were native peoples strong enough in spirit or in numbers to carve out of colonial history their own national destinies.

What happened in the Congo, Kenya, Tanzania, Nigeria and Ghana, for example, could not have occurred among the non-white, non-Western, and preliterate peoples of the Americas—certainly not among the beaten and quasi-assimilated Indians and Eskimos, or among the vanishing aboriginal societies of Australia. But the birth of the new African states was not achieved without costly and devastatingly radical surgery.

Uruhu, independence, meant not only the painful ripping away of vast populations from their former colonial masters; it also meant that ancient tribal and religious loyalties could compete with each other and with the central governments for domination, that people could assert their rights, at whatever cost, to live by their own rules without harassment or coercion. With few exceptions, the new nation-states of Africa were enclosed within boundary lines that reflected the colonial appetites of European powers in the nineteenth century, rather than the tribal territories that predated the conquest. So we find Ibos in ethnically divided Nigeria who fought vainly against a powerful central government for an independent Biafra at the cost of a million lives by the end of the decade. Nigeria was supposed to have been a showcase republic, but it blew apart along tribal lines. In Kenya, the Luo and Kikuyu tribes, once allies in the struggle for independence, have moved from mutual distrust to open hostility and conflict. In the Congo the anti-Western surge reached a peak of ferocity in 1964 when, in one brief but deadly period, tens of thousands of blacks as well as many whites were massacred. The enemy was anyone with a trace of Western education or even affiliation—cultural or political—with the former colonial masters.

The fate of the stately, towering, autocratic Watusi of Central Africa best illustrates the startling changes that have occurred since my first visit there in 1937. At that time they were still masters of all they surveyed, including the shorter Bahutus, their serfs who vastly outnumbered them. They were the proud possessors of the finest cattle in Africa, a magnificent longhorned variety which seemed to fit in perfectly with their imperial style of life. In their twin kingdoms of Rwanda-Burundi, the seven-foot-plus Watusi lived as if the universe pivoted on them; their spectacular dances, now well known and imitated, their dramatic feats of high jumping and their sacred cattle ceremonies gave them an almost Olympian air.

Not too much had changed by 1946 when, for the second time, I met and spoke with the absolute ruler of the Rwanda Watusis, *Mwami* (King) Rudahigwa, whose death in 1959 was widely ascribed to the Belgians. Rudahigwa, I had heard, was exploring the possibilities of converting his kingdom into a constitutional monarchy. He was also an advocate of nationalism and, since World War II, had spoken out against colonial systems. By 1946 the *Mwami* had moved from the traditional Watusi *inzu*, a domed structure of poles and thatch, into a brick and concrete house with flush toilets, picture windows and broadloom carpeting. I had no inkling then of the sudden and revolutionary change that was soon to take place in Rwanda: the Bahutus appeared as docile as ever; the handful of Batwa Pygmies were loyal servants and fiercely devoted to their Watusi overlords. Had I returned to the Watusi during my 1954 African expedition (to film the motion picture *Zanzabuku* for Republic Pictures), I might have detected the first rumbling of Bahutu discontent. Still I would probably have been unable to see any signs of it in the Watusi court or among the dancers or high-jumpers I would have filmed. However, when I again visited the Watusi in 1964 it had already happened—the volcano had erupted and, in fact, was still sending off sparks. In November of 1959, the Bahutu majority in what was to become the independent nation of Rwanda cut down the lordly Watusi in a bloody revolt.

This revolution was as violent and cruel as anything Central Africa had ever seen; it was a harbinger of bloodier days to come. One missionary told me that during the thick of the fight-

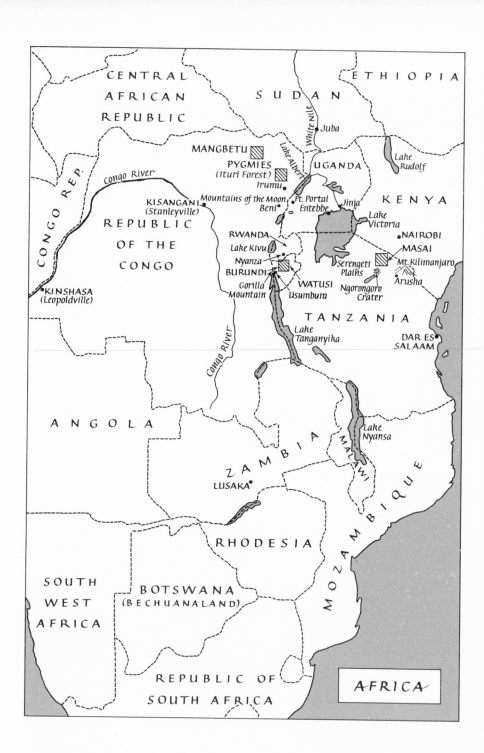

ing he had tried to help a Watusi chief to cross the border. A group of Bahutu stopped his car, ordered the seven-and-a-half foot Watusi out, and hacked off his legs below the knees, a gesture indicating that the Bahutus believed that the time had come for them literally to cut their former masters down to size. There was much wanton cruelty on both sides; Watusis had descended on Bahutu villages in retaliatory raids and, with their warriors, the Batwa Pygmies, they had killed indiscriminately. This violence continued sporadically throughout the sixties, despite the Belgians' settlement of the conflict early in 1960.

In regional elections later in that year, the Bahutus swept into power in Rwanda. The following year the old kingdom was abolished, and Gregoire Kayibanda, a Catholic seminarian, became president and prime minister of the new republic. In 1962 Rwanda and Burundi became independent nations following U.N.-supervised elections. While perhaps 100,000 Watusi eventually remained in Rwanda, many began leaving in the early sixties for neighboring Burundi, which continued in Watusi control. Others accepted exile in Uganda, Tanganyika (later Tanzania) and the Congo.

Those who stayed in Rwanda became virtual hostages against counterattacks launched by other Watusi from refugee camps along the borders. Such raids were heaviest in 1963 and 1964, with high losses on both sides. In retaliation, the Bahutu of Rwanda vented their anger by persecuting their dwindling Watusi population. Outright violence aside, the Bahutus, I was to learn, were downgrading Watusi dignity in Rwanda—for example, by politicizing sexual relations between the two tribes (or perhaps it would be more accurate to say that they were sexualizing political relations). Watusi women, once regarded as beyond the reach of Bahutu men, were serving as mistresses; at the same time, social pressures were mounting against marriages between the members of the opposing tribes. The Watusi were getting the familiar treatment accorded to second-class citizens.

In Burundi, the Watusi position seemed much more secure until later in the sixties when the Bahutu majority there threatened to revolt. Both Bahutu and Watusi elements had voted for a constitutional monarchy with *Mwami* Mwambutsa (later exiled) as king. Despite his reputation as a playboy who preferred to do his governing from various European spas, Mwambutsa was undoubtedly a popular sovereign. More important, however, was the fact that in Burundi the Watusi minority had not lorded it over the Bahutus in years past; instead many of them intermarried, and qualified Bahutus served in government posts. In Burundi the Watusis were something less than divinely appointed rulers of the world—some actually worked in rather ordinary jobs. Nevertheless, a Bahutu uprising was quelled here in 1965, and in 1969 the government—by then under the presidency of Michel Micombero, a former police officer—said that it had uncovered a plan for a Bahutu coup. There were few observers who would venture a guess as to how long the Watusi regime might last.

In 1969 I found Watusi exiles scattered all over Central Africa. Many of them believed that one day they would be able to return to their homes in Rwanda. Others, despairing of such a return, were preparing to spend the rest of their lives in other countries like the Congo where they are tolerated or eyed with suspicion. They reminded me of the Russian emigrés who dispersed throughout Europe and the rest of the world after the Revolution of 1917. Like the Russian aristocrats, the Watusis cherished memories of a dead past when they had everything their way—an abundance of servants and little work to perform. Like the Russians they found the disparity between the realities of the moment and the memories of the past unhappy to contemplate.

I met one such exile in Nairobi in 1969. He was *Mwami* S. M. Kigeli V, who, except for the revolutionary course of African history, would have been the present king of Rwanda. It may be symbolic of the fate of exiled kings that our meeting was arranged by the head of publicity for Pan American World Airways in Nairobi, Joan Weaver, a friend of Kigeli. The pretender arrived at my hotel one morning with no more advance notice than a call from the lobby. At the moment I happened to be shaving, and it was necessary for me to ask the Watusi king to wait until I had finished. He waited downstairs with his retinue. When he arrived we greeted each other through his interpreter, a man whose broken English made impossible any communication beyond the exchange of simple pleasantries. The *Mwami* promised to return in a few days with a more proficient interpreter.

When Kigeli returned he thanked me for having written so sympathetically in the past about Watusi life. He had hopes, he said, that the days of glory would return. It was difficult to put much conviction into my rather perfunctory "Well, I hope so too." I had been cautioned not to refer to him as King or *Mwami* or Your Highness in Kenya. The Nairobi government only recognized the existing Bahutu government of Rwanda. He was, I assumed, a king in only a few eyes in his land of exile.

Over luncheon in the hotel restaurant, Kigeli told me that he was bitter about events in Rwanda. He said that Watusis there had been treated badly, that about 90 percent of them were suffering from malnutrition. He added that the Bahutus would do anything to contribute to the humiliation of their former masters. In Rwanda the Bahutus had done the most menial work; now the Watusis were being made to discover what it is like to be members of a servant class. The Watusi women, he went on, were being used as prostitutes; he confirmed what I had heard about Bahutus frowning on marriages with Watusi women.

Kigeli told me about his brother, Prince Rwicemera, to highlight the present plight of the Watusis. The Prince had remained aloof from the political events in Rwanda; he had not tried to assist the Watusis in their attempt to put down the Bahutu rebellion, nor did he plot to escape. Consequently the Bahutus permitted him to keep part of his large herd of longhorn cattle. However, the Prince found that it was virtually impossible for him to make a living from his cattle—at least not the kind of a living that would have enabled him to live as he would have liked to. With much regret he had sold his herd and with the aid of a small bank loan he bought two second-hand cars which he converted into taxis. Now the former Watusi aristocrat drives one around the capital of Rwanda, while a Watusi friend drives the other.

Before we parted Kigeli gave me his card. In the upper right corner was his royal crest; his Nairobi post office box number was on the lower right. And in the center of the card was his full name and title, the title forbidden in Kenya: S. M. Kigeli V, Ndahindurwa Jean Baptista, *Umwami W' Urwanda*. At the moment, this card, his retinue and a heart full of dubious hopes were all that remained of Kigeli's kingdom.

The questions that occurred to me during my fourth and fifth visits to Africa in the 1960s are not easy to answer. At best I was able to get a better understanding of their significance to the embattled cultures now moving so quickly, if sometimes grudgingly, into the twentieth century.

Above all, I wanted to know what kind of African would emerge from this turmoil. Would he be, in any sense, a tribal man? Or would he surrender his tribal identity as the price of national unity? At the moment, the average sub-Saharan African looks to his kin, his village, his tribe; they are his realities, not the central government, which he is likely to regard as a vague abstraction. But modernization in Africa appears to mean nationalism, as it did in large measure for Europe and America. It took the West centuries to abandon religious rivalries (in favor of nationalistic rivalries, I am tempted to add; and from the shape of things in Northern Ireland, for example, or in Belgium, the road to national unity is a long one). Will it be possible for Africans in our time to begin thinking of themselves as Kenyans, Nigerians, Tanzanians or Congolese, and to draw pride from that identity? Or will they see their traditional cultures disappear before they have had a chance to adapt them to a modern version of their national life?

It would be sadly ludicrous to expect a Camayura or a

Chavante Indian to think of himself as a Brazilian. Brazil has all but crushed them. One could draw up quite an extensive list of peoples who are caught between the death of their own culture and the economic and social barriers that prevent them from identifying with the national culture that has taken over. Many of our own Eskimos and Indians, for instance, find themselves in just such a dilemma. African tribesmen, however, have more power—in some cases, much more—and it is they who are being called upon (sometimes by their own leaders) to abandon traditions before they wipe each other out.

If tribalism must go, and it seems to be the judgment of most African leaders along with the Organization of African Unity that it must, does it mean that "tribes" must go as well? It is pointless to plead for the survival of primitive life on the African continent; roads, airports, hotels, universities, radio and TV stations, machine guns, doctors and missionaries will soon put an end to that. It is my own hope, however, that the Third World of Africa will turn out to be more than a shabby imitation of the West, that the new nations will be able to bring what remains of their primitive vitality and pride into the challenging arena of modern life. And that may be the hardest thing of all, for how can we say, "Give up your spears and your war paint, but retain your courage; give up your witchcraft, but not your wonderful sense of the mystery of nature; give up your crude hunting techniques, but not your encyclopedic knowledge of the forest and its ways"?

I do not have, as I have said, pat answers to questions like these. The answers will come not from white men like myself. We have had our chance in Africa, and now we are out—or soon will be—except as traders, investors, missionaries, technicians and tourists. No, we shall have to look to the African peoples themselves, Europeanized as many of them are, and see what they propose to do with their future. And that is why I returned again in the summer of 1969 and found myself for the fifth time in four decades in a Bambuti Pygmy camp, isolated from the world and even from the continuing African tragedy by the overwhelming foliage of the Ituri Forest.

9 Pygmies of the Ituri: A Place to Hide

THE ITURI FOREST PYGMIES in the northeastern corner of the Congo are something of an anomaly in present-day Africa. They have found a place in which to hide, and there are few people in the world today—primitive or civilized—who can say as much. They may have been the original prehistoric inhabitants of the great African rain forest, and have been able to avoid the depredations of larger and fiercer peoples for thousands of years. Like the Jivaros of Ecuador and Peru, they were protected by natural barriers—in their case, the great "Mother Forest."

To the outsider, the forest is fearsome, a maze of unseen dangers, a place of oppressively leaden humidity. For anyone but a Pygmy it is perhaps the least hospitable place in the world. It is the home of the tse-tse fly and the anopheles mosquito, carriers of sleeping sickness, blackwater fever and malaria, and poisonous vipers and twenty-foot pythons. There are safari ants that travel in solid columns only inches wide that will devour rapidly and systematically anything or anyone in their path unless they are repelled by flaming torches or boiling water. The forest is also a haven for larger and only slightly less dangerous species of wildlife—elephants, leopards, wart hogs, as well as the gentle, vanishing okapi, rowdy baboons, and a tree lemur whose maniacal scream will raise gooseflesh on anyone but a Pygmy.

It is not only the snakes, insects and wild animals that make the forest so fearsome to intruders; even more frightening is the vegetation itself. The forest seems to have a life and a will of its own. Perhaps all forests do, but the Ituri has a way of telling you in very personal terms to get out, that it has decided who its charges will be, and let all others be forewarned.

I doubt that I will ever forget my first trip to the Ituri in 1937. Escorted by a Bantu villager who had offered to take me as far as the nearest Pygmy camp, I was suddenly plunged into a dark and heavy gloom the like of which I had never known. Accustomed to the bright sunlight outside, I was unable to perceive anything at all for a while; then the trees began closing in on me. Until that moment, I never believed that I could be seized by claustrophobia. I knew that the most primitive thing in that forest was, at the moment, my own fear. I was responding to a natural stop sign that had for centuries prevented men from going farther.

Thorns reached out and clawed at my clothes, holding fast until they had ripped through the tough cloth; my face and hands burned with the sting of nettles. Long looping liana vines snagged my footsteps, and giant ferns swished wetly against my face. Farther ahead the tangle of undergrowth became a swampy area where the mud rose and clung to my legs like thick gumbo. A snake, incredibly thin and about nine feet long, probably the deadly black mamba, slithered by into the underbrush while we were splashing across a narrow stream. For a time every vine became a snake.

There are rhythms in the forest that seem designed to throw you off balance—sudden stillnesses when the only thing that can be heard is the "roar" you get when you cup your hands over your ears, or a kind of long and steady asthmatic inhalation; then, just as suddenly, a cacophony of sound and movement: a crashing of feet in the branches, a chorus of screeching birds, the shrieking cries of colubus monkeys, and then the sibilant sound of silence again.

During the night there is likely to be an ear-splitting thunderstorm; you hear it as it gathers force in the distance, and then it descends upon you. For a time it seems as if nothing, certainly not your tent or hut, will remain intact. The rain beats at the canvas with a desperate urgency until once again the message of the forest is clear. This is no place for intruders. "Get out! Get out!" it seems to say. Only the Pygmies or those few who can live like them or with them dare to enter.

There are indeed few men from Africa or elsewhere who have found this forest to their liking. A few anthropologists, such as Pat Putnam or Colin Turnbull, have determinedly adapted themselves to the forest. Turnbull has even discovered in it a spiritual home. Two missionary friends of mine, Bill Deans and Bill Spees, have lived among the Pygmies for nearly forty years. Theirs, I believe, must be the record for endurance.

As a measure of my confidence in the protection afforded to the Pygmies by the Ituri Forest, we remarked in the 1946 film, *Savage Splendor**, that they alone of all peoples might very well survive even an atomic war. Short of such devastation, it is hard to imagine how the Ituri Forest could be endangered. The Belgians, before their departure, had built a road into the forest, and for a time the Pygmies were encouraged to live close to it. A few did so, and were soon victims of lung diseases, sunstroke, a loss of vitality and other ills that generally follow intrusion upon primitive life. Fortunately, the Belgians relented and gave up this attempt to regulate Pygmy life. Even had they kept on, it is doubtful whether some 40,000 inhabitants of the Ituri could have been brought under their control.

The forest is simply too big, it is too much of a tangle for men

* Made with Armand Dennis for RKO.

and machines to mow down, at least not for the price that any government or private organization is willing to pay. And that has been true always of this Pygmy refuge. Today, the Pygmies in an otherwise fast-changing Africa represent the only link with the primitive past that can be depended upon.

My visits to the Ituri Forest in 1964 and again in 1969 convinced me that the Pygmies were going to remain free from external pressures, tribal or political, for a long time to come. And paradoxically the Pygmy is often mistakenly seen as not possessing any genuine culture of his own. His condition is that of a servant to the Bantu natives who live in villages on the edges of the forest. The Bantus own plantations, grow bananas, rice and peanuts; they have a well-developed ritual life, and they employ metal implements. The Pygmies, on the other hand, grow nothing, have no initiation, marriage or funeral rites of their own, and so far as implements are concerned are still living in the Stone Age. So the Pygmies, whom the Bantus regard as their slaves, are dependent upon their supposed masters for cultivated products, ritual and religion, and metal implements. In return for these, the Pygmies supply their Bantu overlords with forest products: game, ivory tusks, honey, broad leaves used for roofing, rattan, and occasionally with a sturdy and hard-working wife.

On the face of it, the Pygmies seem to be guilty of a form of cultural parasitism. This view was probably reinforced by the fact that it is virtually impossible to make contact with the Pygmies until one has first spoken with their Bantu "owners." This was not only my own experience, it was even necessary for missionaries Deans and Spees to make their first contact with the Bambuti Pygmies through their village masters. Pat Putnam, a legend among Ituri hands and for many years the only white settler there, found it necessary to approach the villagers before he could meet "their" Pygmies.

One might suppose that the Pygmies were an inferior, cultureless breed by listening to the self-serving Bantu legends about their "slaves." According to one myth the Pygmies were originally Bantu-owned dogs who were badly treated and who disappeared into the forest until their masters agreed to feed them in return for their services in hunting.

The Pygmy and the Bantu are actually interdependent; in true symbiotic fashion they satisfy the needs of one another. The Pygmy prefers not to cultivate land, while the Bantu has little desire to hunt; like everyone else, he is in awe of the forest. If either of the two peoples has, in fact, a greater capacity for independence, it is the Pygmy; he has proven many times that he can survive, without advice or assistance, deep in his forest home.

The Bambuti may be regarded as "owned" by the Bantu villagers, who indeed measure their social status by the number of Pygmies they have. Yet visitors who have observed the four-foot-tall Bambuti in the forest would agree that there never were "slaves" more fiercely independent of their masters. And since very few outsiders have had such a unique opportunity, the true life style of the Pygmies has seldom been reported.

If the Pygmies were easily manipulated by the Bantu or other peoples outside the great Ituri Forest, they would not have survived the winds of political change and tribal conflict sweeping over Africa. In the mid-sixties many Pygmies were, in fact, engaged by the Congolese rebels to fight on their side, and they were soon caught in the deadly cross fire between government regulars, rebels and mercenaries. Most of them quickly recognized their mistake and returned to their forest sanctuary.

The Pygmies know that they can get just about all of their necessities from the forest that, for the most part, their "masters" dread and despise. The villagers are all too aware of their own dependence on the Pygmies, although they are not likely to admit it. They know that when the hunting is good in the forest they cannot get "their" Pygmies to come out. The Bambuti might be lacking some of the goods they trade, wheedle or borrow from the villagers—beer, palm oil, bananas—but they can get along without them, and they very often do. During my last visit to the Ituri, one of the villagers grumbled that he had been waiting for such a long time—weeks—that he was beginning to suspect that perhaps "his" Pygmies had abandoned him. He complained that they had been getting less reliable all the time. A rough translation of what the Bantu was saying is, "They are getting so damned independent these days."

But the evidence suggests that the Pygmies always were, and will continue to remain independent at heart, even when they seem to be subservient to their "masters." When the wayward Pygmies eventually did make an appearance, incidentally, I noticed a look of pleasure on the face of the villager who had been complaining only a short time before. And though he went through the motions of expressing chagrin over having been kept waiting, he was careful not to hurt the feelings of "his" Pygmies. There is a delicate balance of power in this interdependence, and each side seems to know just how far it can go without alienating the other. For this reason the relationship between the Negro Bantus and the Bambutis has been longstanding and uniquely workable.

The bonds of loyalty between the Bantu and Pygmy are strong because they are united on a family-to-family basis. If, for any reason, the Pygmies go to another part of the forest and serve another Bantu family, there can be much bad feeling. It is, as Pat Putnam has observed, very much like a divorce.

Pygmy families may remain in the service of Bantu families for generations. On the Pygmy side, father teaches son to maintain loyalty to a village family and to deliver game, ivory tusks and forests products so long as the villager is generous with his bananas, axe blades and spearheads. In times past, intervillage warfare erupted as a consequence of Bantu communities luring Pygmies away from one another.

So the concern of the Bantu villager who was waiting for his more than usually tardy Pygmies was understandable. During my 1969 visit to the Ituri I found no letup in Bantu reliance upon their Pygmy allies—a word that seems to me to be more appropriate than "slaves." The villagers continued to look down upon the forest-dwellers for their apathetic cooperation, their seeming restlessness, their easy-come, easy-go attitude toward possessions, their joyful lack of concern over the dangers of the forest and their exuberantly daredevil hunting methods. However, the villagers have not been doing so well in recent years; they need their Pygmies more than the Pygmies need them.

Since the coming of independence the Bantu villagers have suffered a series of economic setbacks. I learned this from Bill Spees at his mission in Lolwa. The Bantus, unlike the Pygmies, have no cushion against the vagaries of economic fortune imposed by the outside world. In good times they were able to buy manufactured items, and it must have been highly satisfying to them to learn to use the tools of civilization while the Pygmies could not or would not do so. But prices of imported goods have skyrocketed since independence and, to make matters worse, markets for Bantu farm products have diminished drastically. Belgian authorities arranged for buyers of Bantu rice, plantains and peanuts to drive their trucks into the villages in the past; these days few trucks are to be seen. Moreover, the Belgians obliged the villagers to work hard and productively on their gardens. The present government merely asks that the villagers cultivate their gardens. As a consequence of this policy, some do and some do not. Because the central government has had its hands full with other matters, the villagers have been left to their own devices. Caught in an economic squeeze between rising prices and dwindling markets, the Bantu villagers have lost many of their former incentives.

But the Pygmies seem to go on at the same steady pace. In 1969 they were no better or worse off than they were when I first visited them in 1937. During this thirty-year interval the rest of Equatorial Africa underwent tremendous changes. Only on the Uganda fringe of the Ituri have Pygmies lost some of their primitive innocence; tourists visiting the game preserves have been coming into contact with them. It was here, a few years ago, that Jack Paar filmed a TV documentary and concluded that Pygmy life was edging toward modernity. No wonder. For a fee, you can get the Bantus here to bring their Pygmies out of the forest and have them put on one of their tribal dances for the benefit of the tourists and their cameras. The Pygmies spend the money they get for their choreographic displays at the village *duka*, a small store usually well stocked with the manufactured products of civilization: clothes (Western style), bicycles, sewing machines, umbrellas. Pygmies will usually buy tobacco, salt, shorts, perhaps some cloth to replace the bark "cloth" worn by both sexes.

I saw no Pygmy contact with modern life to speak of, however, on the vast and inaccessible Congo side of the Ituri Forest. There have been no tourists here as yet, nor are there the dusty roads, the Western diseases or the social upheaval that generally accompany a sudden and heavy influx of outsiders. I doubt that such an incursion will take place in the foreseeable future. For one thing, it requires something approaching divine intervention to obtain a visa for the Congo these days. Furthermore, roads leading from major cities into the Itrui region are few and in poor condition. A small plane with a seasoned bush pilot is the safest way to get there. Finally, few tourists care to take a chance with the vagaries of Congo politics. Many recall the bloody rebellion of 1964, the massacres and the regrettable death of Dr. Carlson, the American medical missionary.

If I do not seem to be touting tourism in the Itrui region, this is intentional. Personally, I like the Pygmies as they are—self-reliant hunters who are as free of care as one can expect any imperfect human being to be. And despite a grumbling contempt on the part of the Bantu villagers, the members of the Walese tribe, who inhabit much of the Congo side of the forest, want them to remain that way too. In the coming years, should there be an invasion by tourists or soldiers or engineers among the Walese Bantus, the Pygmies will simply abandon their beehive-shaped huts and—with much commotion and singing—move deeper into the Ituri Forest. And this is not wishful thinking on my part. The Bambuti seem to have an instinctual feeling about outsiders—white or black—whom they regard as a clear indication that it is time for them to move on.

Should this take place, the Bantu villagers would, of course, be the losers. Especially now that the Bantu two- or three-crop economy is suffering, the Pygmies are needed for the forest products they bring into the villages. The Bantus are sometimes guilty of shamelessly marking up the value of the skins and ivory for which the Pygmies receive palm oil, plantains and arrowheads. But the Pygmies somehow make their own pragmatic calculations based on their own peculiar needs; in one way or another they receive what they regard as a proper return on their labors. They may beg, borrow or steal to make up any inequity and, if all else fails, they will threaten to leave. That usually gets results. Peculiarly, the Bantus are often the victims of a similar system—as much as they may seem to take advantage of the Pygmies, they themselves realize only a small percentage of what the next one in the trading chain gets.

This is the owner of the *duka* and he is likely to be a Greek. Although a number of *duka* owners were killed in rebellion, I found several still operating their shops along the roads near the Bantu villages; they trade with members of the Walese tribe, not the Pygmies on the Congo side of the Ituri. If a Pygmy wants something in a *duka*, his master must make the purchase. And it is the villager who brings to the *duka* the forest products brought in by his Pygmies.

The *duka* is not only the focus of economic activity in village life, it is also one of the few reliable sources of social change in the Ituri region. Because it funnels into both Bantu and Pygmy hands almost all of the manufactured articles they will ever get, the *duka* epitomizes the materialistic values of the civilized world. On my last trip to the Ituri, while making my way toward a Bambuti camp, I met a Pygmy woman carrying in from the forest an enormous bundle of phrynium leaves, used for roofing Bantu huts. Around her middle was the typical primitive loin cloth made of bark, but above that she sported what could only have been a very small brassiere and which performed no visible function. Through Filippo, the Bantu who was guiding me to the nearby camp, I learned that the Pygmy woman had gotten the brassiere idea from a Walese girl in the village. She had had her heart set on getting one and had finally managed to acquire one on her last trip out of the forest.

The brassiere was not worn out of modesty or for any other purpose but the dictates of fashion; it had come from the local *duka* where a Bantu villager had bought it and then traded it to the Pygmy woman for a load of nuts she had gathered in the forest.

At the Pygmy camp I discovered that a number of other Pygmy women had taken to wearing brassieres, most of which were off target. I decided that if this was an example of acculturation, it was a very unimportant one, since the Bambuti were hardly aware of the true function of the brassiere other than the casually decorative use to which they put them.

Filippo, a Christianized Bantu who did evangelical work at the Lolwa Mission, told me that intermarriage between the Pygmies and the Bantu villagers was increasing. I knew that he could only be referring to marriage between Pygmy women and Walese men, for no village woman would think of subjecting herself to the forest life. On the other hand, Bantu men had good reason to marry Pygmy girls, even though they regarded the forest hunters as subhuman.

For one thing, Filippo explained, there was the poor economic situation. The bridal price of Walese women was as high as ever, even though the village men were earning less money from their crops than in years past. Pygmy women were much less expensive, so a polygamous (non-Christianized) Bantu could, if he so desired, acquire two Pygmy girls for the price of one village wife.

Another reason for the increase in Bantu-Pygmy marriages, Filippo told me, was the high incidence of sterility because of venereal disease among Bantu women—one of the earliest fruits of civilization. Lately the health of Bantu women has improved in areas where medical missionaries are available, but farther afield the problem persists. Pygmy girls, protected from contagion by their forest isolation and their customary distrust of strangers, have remained fertile and healthy, and by Bantu male standards they are a hardy, energetic and relatively uncomplaining group. Here I must agree; I have never seen harder working women anywhere. But for pure, selfless devotion under the rigorous demands imposed on hunters' wives, Jivaro and Eskimo women, in my view, get the nod.

Although Bantu-Pygmy marriages are still very much the exception, the physical evidences of these unions are apparent among the village people. The children of the mixed marriages remain in the villages (a disgruntled Pygmy wife may occasionally pack up and return to her forest family), and they are likely to represent in stature, pigmentation and facial features a compromise between the two groups. Because these children will probably not marry back into Pygmy families, the next generation will more closely resemble the Bantu norm, though crossbreeding has produced a wide variety of physical types among the villagers. By contrast, because of the Pygmies' genetic isolation—Pygmy genes flow out of the forest, but no Bantu genes flow in—they have remained little changed in thousands of years.

There are other Pygmies, so-called. The Batwa, in the Watusi country, are really pygmoids, a hybrid of the true (Bambuti) Pygmy and the Bantu or Sudanic Negro. There are also the diminutive Bushmen of the Kalahari Desert in southern Africa who share with the Bambuti the distinction of being the only peoples on the continent who do no cultivating, but who live as their Paleolithic ancestors did—by hunting and by gathering wild vegetation. The Kalahari Bushman culture is fast disappearing, as I learned on my last trip to Africa; they have nothing like the Pygmy's impenetrable forest to protect them. Although a recent count listed some 55,000 Bushmen still living in the vast arid wilderness and scattered farmlands of southern Africa, many of these now work as laborers on European ranches or in Bantu villages.

While Pygmy women may represent sound value to a Bantu villager, to her family she is an essential worker as well as a potential producer of more Pygmies. And when Pygmy marries Pygmy, the father of the bride not only asks for what he considers fair compensation for the loss of a daughter—arrows, spears, bark cloth, a piece of iron—he also demands a replacement from the family of the groom, a practice known as head-for-head, called *kichwa-kichwa* in Kingwana (a Swahili dialect used throughout Central Africa). A Pygmy suitor of, say, sixteen or seventeen, who wins a girl of perhaps thirteen or fourteen from a neighboring group, must then become a matchmaker and convince one of his sisters to marry into the family of the bride-to-be. If he has no sisters, he may have to look around the camp for another candidate. All else failing, the Pygmy suitor hopes that his future father-in-law will accept a more attractive bride price in lieu of head-for-head. Since the Bantu villager who "owns" this Pygmy has a vital interest in the prospective marriage, because of the numerous offspring it will produce, he will more than likely provide the bride price when his Pygmy is unable to do so himself.

The Pygmy will then take his wife home—without benefit of any marriage ceremony. The husband makes an additional payment when his wife bears a child; if there should be no child there is still another payment at the end of six months or a year when the marriage partners are reasonably sure that they will get along together. If the girl should prove to be sterile or if the couple decides that their marriage will not work out, the husband can return his bride and receive his payment back. Since the husband may have already traded his sister in the head-for-head arrangement, he, or his father, will probably demand her return, and this could be rather complicated because she and her husband may wish to continue their marriage.

So it is unlikely that a marriage will break up for frivolous causes. Still, a girl's strongest ties are to her original family, and she knows that she will be always welcomed back by her parents. Her husband knows this, too, and although a wife is a Pygmy's private property and has been given to him as both a worker and a child-bearer, there are limits to the amount of abuse he can heap upon her. A slap on the head now and then is permissible, but if he hits her too hard and too often, philanders excessively, denies her the necessities of life or is cruel to their children, he knows that she will leave him, whatever the consequences.

The head-for-head system was still operating in 1969 when I last visited a Pygmy camp. *Kichwa-kichwa*, despite the complex squabbles it sometimes engenders, seems to knit families closely together—brothers from one family marry sisters from another—and that is a peculiarly good arrangement in the Ituri where hunting and forest survival demand close cooperation.

According to Bill Spees, whom I visited again at his missionary station at Lolwa, the *kichwa-kichwa* system is partly responsible for maintaining polygamy among the Bambuti. As a Christian missionary Bill would not be unhappy if polygamy disappeared, but it is not his custom to rush social changes; he has been in the Ituri for more than four decades, and he is grateful for even minor concessions to our sexual attitudes. When a Pygmy male is lucky enough (from his point of view) to be born into a family with more sisters than brothers, he will go to his father and ask him to arrange a head-for-head deal with another family or two so that he can have a second or even a third wife. As Bill sees it, the extra sisters represent a potential extra wife, worker and child-bearer, and are too much a temptation for any Pygmy to resist.

For missionaries like Bill Spees and Bill Deans the objective is not to remake the Pygmy into the image of civilized man. Any attempt in that direction would be as futile as it would be wrong and harmful to the Pygmy. They do believe, however, that it is possible to distinguish between the good and bad qualities of Pygmy life and, by persistent evangelism, to correct the bad while reinforcing the good.

Bill Spees told me in 1969 that four Pygmies had learned to read and write the local Swahili at the Lolwa Mission bible school, and that they were going to travel the Ituri as Christian evangelists. What would they teach those Pygmies who would listen to them, I wondered. Bill's answer came down to this: they would tell their potential converts not to fear the evil spirits of the forest, believed by Pygmies to be centered in a devil figure called *Keti*. Instead they would be taught to believe that Christ, an all-seeing, all-knowing benign force, is forever watching over them.

Although the Pygmies are as free from care as the Camayuras in South America they do have some deep-rooted fears. They love their forest, but they believe that evil forces are present always, and Bill and Ella Spees would like to see this fear allayed. I cannot help thinking that they have taken on a nearly impossible task. It is difficult to imagine living in the Ituri Forest without being attuned to a sense of danger, whether it is expressed in superstitious or rational terms. Many of these fears, of course, have survival value.

There are numerous sounds in the forest which will set an outsider's teeth on edge, but will not disturb a Pygmy. For example, while visiting a Pygmy camp with Bill and Ella Spees, I heard the sudden call of the tree lemur, an almost-human, blood-curdling cry repeated some thirty or forty times. This sound was upsetting to both Bill and myself, resembling as it did the signal for the entrance of a legion of furious demons. The Pygmies were only interested in locating the tree it was in; the next morning they hunted it down and ate it. But the hooting of an owl—also a forest-dweller—is regarded among Pygmies as foretelling some terrible doom, and is enough to start a panic in the camp. The Pygmies are also frightened by the sound of the forest grasshopper, which they call *Ama Songu*, "the one who brings trouble." This insect is three or four inches long, makes a noise like a roaring motor, and is likely to mean to the Pygmies that a leopard is on its way to the camp.

The leopard is particularly feared, especially when it gets too old to hunt its usual prey, because it will enter a Pygmy camp or a Bantu village, attack a dog, a goat, or even a child or an adult. In the camp we were visiting we heard about a marauding leopard that had entered one of the leaf huts some months before and attacked a sleeping child. When the Pygmy father awoke and tried to pull his child away, he was killed by the leopard. At another camp this same leopard killed a woman. For three weeks after these incidents, a number of Pygmies with children in that area lived and slept in the village of their Bantu masters.

One night we were awakened by an uproar in the camp. What we witnessed was difficult to understand. A group of Pygmies was hurling burning sticks and embers over one of the huts and making as much commotion as they could. I could observe nothing but the agitation of the Pygmies and their curious fireworks display. It was Filippo who explained; the Pygmies had seen evil spirits that the rest of us could not see. Later, in discussing the incident, Bill and Ella Spees admitted that they believed that such forces might indeed be "visible" to the Pygmies' eyes. They were hoping, of course, that they could make their own benign God equally visible, or at least knowable. For my part, I could not help wishing that the destructive forces still hovering over primitive man in Africa could be as easily frightened away as those which troubled the Pygmies that night; I would be the first to pick up a burning ember and hurl it.

Perhaps what the Pygmies have to fear most is the turbulence surrounding them in Africa and, although they are unaware of it, the fate of other primitive peoples in distant places. They have, however, a forest sanctuary with ample game—buffalo, elephant, antelope, monkeys and the rare okapi and bongo—and an environnent that is sternly hostile to the hopes and instruments of civilization.

If any primitive people are exceptions in this time of rapid acculturation and social change, it is the Pygmies. My own belief —and faith—is that they will hold out for many years to come. They may, in fact, still be hunting elephant as they have for so many centuries when our society is gasping for its last polluted breath.

10 Masai: Cowboys and Lions

THE MASAI, proud practitioners of the pastoral life in Kenya and Tanzania, are no strangers to many of the conditions that have spelled disaster for other primitive peoples. They cannot thank nature for having fenced them off from civilization; unlike the Jivaros or the Bambuti Pygmies, they are not surrounded by dense forests. On the contrary, they live on a plain as open and wide as the lands east of the Rockies, where American Indians were driven off by soldier and settler a century ago. Their climate is a beckoning paradise compared to the soggy weather of the Congo or the Amazon basin or New Guinea's Sepik River valley. They have known disease, famine and wars. They have been exposed to rapid political change: a powerful colonial government, then independence in a new African state beset by intertribal tensions. And they have seen more than their share of tourists. Still—when all is said, if not yet done—the Masai, who call themselves *Il Maasai* (accent the first syllable), remain today a healthy, growing, independent and very self-reliant people. They have also proven themselves to be a flexible people, and that quality may be their salvation.

The Masai have not somehow sidestepped the processes of cultural absorption and change. Rather, the pace of change has not been for them quite so devastating as for the Bororos, say, or the Chavantes or the Watusi. The twentieth century has not yet overwhelmed them because of their own personality and culture, combined with some uncommonly good luck, and the fact that they had to deal with the modern, enlightened British colonialist who—with all his faults and mistakes—is a far cry from the European imperialist of former centuries. In short, in this twilight of their traditional culture the Masai are maintaining their tribal identity.

To meet the Masai today all you have to do is step off a bus an hour or so after leaving Nairobi. (Those you meet in Nairobi are likely to be successfully camouflaged in Western dress.) The Masai will happily pose for you and will feel justified in asking for a fee of perhaps a hundred shillings, since as a rich tourist you can certainly afford it. For the camera the Masai—tall, slender and fine-boned—will wear his traditional attire: the simple, long, flowing robe of dark cloth, the head glowing reddish-orange from ochre mud. You will note the pierced earlobes distended in long loops from which dangle heavy ornaments of copper and iron. And you will probably feel the same admiration I experienced when I first saw a Masai warrior—called *Il Moran* —in 1937. But it is not quite so easy to learn about the inner life of the Masai, the sources of their pride and strength. To get to know them it is necessary to detach them both from their role as tourist-camera subjects and from some of the myths that surround them.

The Masai are a Nilo-Hamitic people who swept down through East Africa perhaps from Ethiopia some two centuries ago. They poured into the funnel of the great Rift valley, evicting the Bantu inhabitants, and became the sole possessors of the dry grassy plains. This land was and still is well suited for cattle herding—their principal way of life and the basis of the Masai culture. There are other Masai—notably the Arusha—living in Tanzania who practice agriculture, but only the pastoral Masai have the peculiar qualities which make them such a remarkable society, whether in traditional or modern Africa. They subsist almost entirely on the milk, meat and blood of their cattle. They, like the legendary cowboy of the American West or the South American gaucho, look disdainfully on any other way of life. For them the farmer's monotonous routine is demeaning. Nothing can compare with the nomadic life of the open plains, and this spacious life—both in the elbow room and the abundance of livestock—has made the Masai the envy and the despair of neighboring tribes.

The Masai believe that their god, *Enkai*, saw to it long ago that they alone should be the herders of cattle on this earth. The ownership of cows or steers by other tribes is taken as *prima facie* evidence by the traditional Masai that they have been stolen, and he will fight to the death for their return. Naturally enough, other tribes have often tried to appropriate Masai cattle, and the Masai themselves have been known to raid one another. So the entire warrior life of the Masai is geared to the protection of their cattle and their grazing land or, when necessary, to the recovery of real or supposed loot from past losses.

The old-style cattle raids and range wars between the Masai and the Kikuyu or Wakamba tribes are fast becoming as outdated as their American prairie equivalents, but the Masai herder still retains his self-reliant personality. The pride and independence are still there, even in those Masai who are well educated and hold important positions in Nairobi. I have spoken to men in modern Nairobi office buildings who have accompanied me to their *manyattas*—warrior villages—or to their kraal camps, where they are quite capable of taking up a spear to confront a marauding lion or leopard. Unlike many of the younger Eskimos I met in Alaska, the Masai, even in the presence of wrenching change, still regard their traditional identity with great pride. In their early training they are taught to respect certain values which fortunately can be incorporated into the new, Westernized life of an independent Kenya.

I had always known, for example, that Masai were regarded as the bravest lion fighters in Africa. Their technique is to encircle their prey, shields and spears poised, and wait for the lion to attack one of them. As soon as this occurs the other warriors quickly run in with their spears, making the lion resemble an old-fashioned pin cushion. In the meantime, the Masai who bore the brunt of the lion's charge may have been badly mauled and is often lucky to survive. Still, I was rather surprised when a well-dressed young Masai, whom I met in Nairobi in 1969, took me to his *manyatta* and showed me where only a few months before he had singlehandedly attacked a lion. He and his friends assured me that this was not uncommon. He had heard the sounds of disturbed cattle in the enclosure, the *boma*, and had gone outside to investigate. There he found a male lion about to feed on a prize steer. The eight years of Western education were of little help to him; taking up a spear, the young Masai went for the lion. The spear found its mark in the lion's shoulder, but the wounded animal was still able to charge at the Masai, biting him in the head, shoulder and leg. The lion was eventually driven off by other Masai, to be tracked down and finished off the next day. The young man was temporarily patched up at home (the Masai regard themselves with some justification as good surgeons) until he could be moved to a hospital about twelve miles away.

Alan H. Jacobs, an American anthropologist working in Nairobi and an expert on Masai society, told me that lions usually give these cattlemen a wide berth; they seem to know, as does almost everyone else, that they are not to be trifled with. The older, male lions, abandoned by their mates (who do the hunting for the family), too slow or too weak to stalk the usual wild game, usually become desperate enough to attack Masai cattle. Such lions hover around the *boma* at night (they wouldn't dare to make an appearance during the day) so that the cattle catch the lion scent. Then they wait until the frenzied livestock break out of the cattle gate and knock one down with a paw, dragging it off into the bush.

The Masai are not really lion *hunters*. They go after lions as they would any predator—human or animal—that threatens their livestock. A Masai might also attack a lion as part of his initiation process—possibly even to impress his women. But the unnecessary killing of wildlife was forbidden by the colonial administration, and slowly, painfully, this practice has died out. Today the government prefers to be consulted when a predatory animal has been attacking the livestock, and in such cases, poison is supplied (usually a slaughtered goat is used as bait). Of course, when a predator attacks, a Masai is not likely to wait for government intervention. Nevertheless, the Masai does not see himself intrinsically as a hunter.

As a matter of fact, the Masai look down upon hunters as they do upon farmers. The word for "poor man" in their language is the same as the word for "hunter." The Masai have traditional prohibitions against the eating, growing or hunting of most foodstuffs other than the meat, blood and milk of their cattle. They disdain fish and fowl; in their view they are somehow connected with reptiles. And they have strong taboos against taking anything out of the earth or putting anything into it. Only evil comes from below. All that is good, like the rain which makes their pasturage grow, comes from above. They hire members of other tribes to dig their wells; a shovel or a spade is unwelcome and a superfluous tool for the Masai. Traditionally, they do not bury their dead because they believe that the corpse will poison the earth and bring misfortune to their cattle. So the dead are washed, given a good coating of sheep fat, and left out on the plains to be devoured by vultures, hyenas, lions or other predators. (Incidentally, their technique of disposing of the dead helps to attract predators to the area—one of several disadvantages of the Masai attitude toward the earth.)

The true basis of Masai courage and self-reliance is their commitment to pastoralism in a hostile tribal setting. Living on wide plains, with large numbers of cattle to protect and with a low population density, the Masai have had little choice over the centuries but to adopt virtues like steadfastness and bravery. They have been surrounded by too many populous tribes, too many hungry eyes—animal and human—to have survived very long without learning to be wholly confident of their ability to repel an attack, no matter the size or power of the enemy. It is not at all uncommon for only two Masai to be charged with the protection of an entire herd of cattle against as many as twenty-five members of another tribe. No Masai would dare return home and say that his cattle had been taken from him—even with the odds at twenty-five to two. He would be beaten and scorned. Any two Masai must be prepared to drive off an attack. Their enemies know this and do not undertake a raid lightly. Neither do lions. The Masai have been known to drive their herds right through a pride of lions without incident. It is no wonder that thus far the Masai have successfully braved the winds of change.

Civilization can be infinitely more disastrous to primitive ways of life than any company of lions or, for that matter, a full-scale charge by spear-wielding Wakamba. The Chavante Indians in their heyday were every bit as feared as the Masai, but once the Mato Grosso was penetrated by the Roncador-Xingu expedition, they quickly succumbed to the virus of civilization. Whatever special qualities the Masai have cannot be packaged and exported, and although their old ways of life are slowly eroding their fundamental pride remains untouched.

In 1969 I avoided venturing too deeply into one of the Masai mud-and-dung huts. The first time I did so, back in the thirties, I learned that living in these hive-like structures so patiently smeared over a framework of sticks by the Masai women was not for anyone who did not love the smell of cattle. Yes, the huts were still there, but opportunities were increasing for the Masai to move into Western-style homes. Would they, when they could afford it, be able to part with their traditional way of living without losing their Masai-ness? Somehow I believed that they could, and my feelings were confirmed by Professor Jacobs, with whom I spoke at the University College in Nairobi, where he is a research director in the cultural division of the Institute for Development Studies. "The Masai," Jacobs said, "are not—contrary to the romantic view—tied by sentiment to the mud-and-dung huts. They wouldn't mind in the least living in a handsome cottage with a white picket fence around it. Just so long as they could do one thing: look out of that cottage and see cattle."

It had occurred to me that the Masai were in many ways a pragmatic and flexible people. And these were qualities that I found lacking among other primitive peoples more often than not. The Masai were willing enough to change—if the change could be of some benefit. Moreover, they were able to change without the usual social chaos and personal dislocation. The "why" of all this is a complex matter, but the Masai self-confidence is a large part of the answer. The Masai had been taught two extremely important things early in life: to rely on himself and to take pride in his people.

A Masai tribesman may take an active role in the government of Kenya or he may for a time turn his back on the heady national political life, but in any case he is always a Masai first, a Kenyan second—or even third. This may pose a problem from the standpoint of national unity, but tribalism and nationalism need not *always* be incompatible, especially when the individual tribesman is convinced that government stability will really be in his interest and if he is able to bring into national life some of the qualities of personal courage and tenacity born of his group pride. America itself is less than the melting pot it is often supposed to be. "Irishmen," "Texans," "Blacks," "Swedes," "Bostonians," "Jews" and "Italians" are in a sense names of tribes that have brought strength into our national life insofar as individual members have been able to draw upon their group identity with pride. It is quite possible that long after the Masai have left their mud-and-dung huts they will still carry with them the conviction that their name is synonymous with the best qualities a man can speak of: a blend of self-reliant individualism and steadfast cooperativeness, courage and friendliness.

I recognize that these are rather far-reaching generalizations and that the Masai produce their share of misfits—individuals who fail as herdsmen or warriors and become derelicts in the towns. But in this twilight period of primitive man the few remaining peoples who will not be defeated stand out rather clearly. The collective ego of the Eskimos, for example, suffered a punishing setback when they learned that they occupied only a minute portion of the world's consciousness. But the Masai will certainly be able to cope with the larger world that they are about to enter, unless I am very wrong, because it is another challenge for which they have been prepared. Given the likelihood of an expanding population (there are at present about 300,000 pastoral Masai), they may be heard from one day.

The Jivaro headhunters, like the Masai, are taught self-reliance and group pride from the earliest age, but their traditional toughness—as attractive as I have always found it—was based upon a fairly rigid commitment to the blood feud and an equally fixed concept of the soul. The pragmatic and flexible Masai, although they have their traditional enemies, are not the prisoners of a fragile past; they can take their feuds or leave them because their character has developed out of their productive pastoral life rather than ritual revenge. Moreover, the Masai attitude toward religion is as relaxed as one is likely to find outside the Unitarians or the Society for Ethical Culture. They do not find it necessary to vindicate the souls of their ancestors because ancestors, in their view, do not survive in the spirit world. A curse is something else, and for that reason a Masai will never antagonize an aged person for fear that the old one will speak a malediction that will remain in effect long after he has departed this life. As for what happens after death, the Masai practice a version of old-fashioned agnosticism; they admit that they frankly do not know. There is no preparation for an afterlife, no heaven or hell. Neither do they believe that they will be punished by some supernatural power for their "sins." Their somewhat sophisticated view is that sin is made by man and should be adjusted by the actions of men. The wrong-doer must make amends, and there are councils of elders who make the moral judgments.

The Masai god is neither a Moloch nor a Jehova nor a Zeus; he requires no sacrifices, no blood offerings; he hands down no commandments and fires off no thunderbolts. Ever practical, the Masai have one god with two names, red and black. When things are going badly they speak of the red deity; good times are the work of the black deity—different aspects of the same god, *Enkai*. The Masai word for rain is also *Enkai*, and so when the Masai pray for rain they are also praying to god for more god.

Asked about their belief in god, a Masai will probably tell the questioner that he really isn't sure. He isn't an atheist, but neither is he a confirmed believer. He is as open to evidence as any man, primitive or civilized, yet willing to try to define and describe the limits of his religion. It is uncommon to find men in Masailand praying to their god. Prayers are only heard in formal ceremonies where they are repeated by the elders as part of the ritual. Women may sometimes be heard praying to *Enkai* for something. There are superstitions, but not the kind that tend to enslave people. These are treated as casually as any in modern societies. A Masai may spit on his hands before offering to grasp yours, dispelling some evil in the process.

If the Masai have an obsession, it is their belief that anything to do with the earth is bad. Consequently, they use gourds to catch and carry milk in, rather than earthenware utensils. To use anything from the ground would surely bring bad luck—their cows might dry up or it might not rain when it should. On the other hand, their most prized objects come from trees that grow quite tall and from the vines that climb these trees. Their deity resides in the sky, and whatever rises upward has particular merit for the Masai.

The Masai are, on the whole, unfanatical. They do not count the heads they have taken, but rather the cattle they have kept safe from raiding parties. Neither do they require an intoxicating beverage or drug in order to prepare themselves for an encounter with a lion or a traditional enemy or—in former days—a gang of slavers. Their favorite alcoholic drink is a wine made from honey and mixed with water and the roots of several shrubs, and fermented for about four days. Two or three glasses of it are remarkably refreshing; it tastes vaguely like a Rum Collins. Of all the European beverages, they were most fond of South African sherry as being the closest thing to their honey wine.

I am unaware of drunkenness as a behavior problem among the Masai, and it is not likely that one will see much solitary drinking. If a Masai has been away from his kraal camp, he will probably look forward to sitting under a tree with the local elders with whom he will go over, event by event, all that has happened while he was away, all the while sipping honey wine from a common gourd. It is a common practice, in fact, for a traveling Masai to stop off on his way home and send a message ahead so that the wine will be ready for him when he returns. The idea is that the wine is an energy restorer, and having tasted some, I am not inclined to dispute that belief.

This is not to say that the Masai are a placid people. They do vent their feelings in various ways. Mahutu, the young Masai with the scars from lion's teeth on his shoulder and legs, insisted that his tribe was "hot tempered" and "high spirited" and they find various reasons to fight among themselves: cattle stealing between Masai groups, he told me, is a leading cause, along with disputes over waterholes. The fear is that water sources will become polluted through indiscriminate use; diseased cows may infect others by drinking at the same waterhole. There is some intratribal fighting over women, but if any real violence is done, the chief inevitably hears about it and the guilty party is turned over to the government police. If, however, an accidental death results, the matter is taken up by the local elders and if in their opinion there was no malice intended the government will never get the case. Intertribal fighting is unlikely to occur over women, but the Masai fight fiercely to protect their cattle.

Masai are sometimes given to an epileptic-like seizure, which to an outsider can indeed be frightening to behold. As Alan Jacobs views these attacks, they are an entirely acceptable way in Masai society for individuals to give vent to their frustrations. He explained that when a Masai is unable to express his feelings on a certain matter, he will simply throw a fit. And while a European (in East Africa all outsiders are designated as Europeans) may be conditioned to regard such loss of control as an affliction, to the Masai it is a most natural process.

One of my first experiences with a Masai seizure was during the filming of *Zanzabuku* at Monduli, about fifty miles from Arusha. The headmen of three Masai *manyattas* brought a number of their *moran* together with shields and spears, since in this remote area the Masai were permitted to carry weapons. The subject was a good old-fashioned war dance during which a number of the *moran* broke into convulsive seizures. At the time I surmised that recollections of old wars had excited these out-of-work warriors, and it occurred to me that I might be able to film a realistic Masai charge for my documentary while spirits were high.

Through my interpreter I was assured that I would be able to record a truly authentic running attack with menacing spears held high, just as in the old days. So, with cameras grinding away, ten beautifully built warriors gathered behind a slope and began their charge. I heard the wild, chilling war whoops before I saw the *moran* closing in for the attack. When the charging warriors were less than twenty feet away, I became aware that for one or two warriors—the pacesetters—this was no game. Their mouths were frothing, and the wild look in their eyes was that of men who had lost contact with reality. I was much too frightened to budge, and anyway there wasn't enough time. When they were not much more than a spear's length away, several of the Masai onlookers threw themselves between the attackers and me, creating a sudden pile-up of writhing, kicking warriors all frothing at the mouth. They recovered after a few minutes and seemed bewildered by all the fuss. A few months later, while describing this incident, I learned that the men filming *King Solomon's Mines* had been forced to scramble away from their cameras during a similar mock charge of Masai warriors.

Many peoples have drawn group pride from their memories of military victory, our own included. But an important source of Masai personality strength lies in the manner in which self-reliance is taught to the young as a means of maintaining the traditions of pastoral life, which they are convinced is a superior way of life.

When he reaches the age of eighteen, the Masai is deemed ready to undergo circumcision. He wears a long, robe-like garment for five months, during which time he may neither fight nor carry weapons. After this period his clothes are removed, he is shaved, and he begins life as a *moran*. He now enters a rank appropriate to his age—that of junior warrior; later he will become a senior warrior, and one day he will move up to the rank of elder (first junior and then senior). Only the elders can sit in the council. In this way the Masai is taught to respect those in the age-set above him. At the same time he learns to trust and depend upon members of his own age-set. Each age-set selects its own leader on the basis of courage, intelligence and the ability to command respect. This age-set system, known throughout the world, is also found in Melanesia, among certain South American tribes and among the Plains Indians of the United States.

A Masai junior warrior will give particular respect to a junior elder, a senior warrior to a senior elder. The members of the next alternate age-set in the Masai system are called the firestick elders. The firestick is the wooden tool the Masai use to start a fire by running it through a wooden base. They take a rather consciously Freudian view of this process, interpreting the stick as the male element and the receiving disc as the female counterpart. (In Masai language "to blow a fire" is expressed in the same terms as "to have an orgasm.") A firestick elder's threat to break his stick, as a means of punishing a member of the alternate age-set beneath him, is really the most serious curse, the strongest sanction among the Masai. It is equivalent to denying the offender's manhood, the ultimate humiliation, and is quite enough to maintain a deep-rooted loyalty to the principles of Masai life.

Deference to the Masai firestick elder and loyalty to Masai traditions continue despite modernization. The Masai do want new things, consumer goods—European clothes, automobiles, new houses—and they would like to travel. Many of the younger *moran* want the benefits of education, but they will bring with them a respect for what they have left behind. They are not likely to look down upon their parents or their firestick elders, who are their second parents. The point is that the Masai can change clothes, but they do not lose their identities.

One of the new breed of Masai I spoke with in 1969 is John Ole Mpaayei (*Ole* means "son of"). John is a Cambridge graduate with an advanced degree, and he heads the East African Bible Society. He has seen much of the world, but when he returns to his family, it is as a Masai.

Like other Masai, John's father, a recruiting officer, had more than one wife, and when he converted to Christianity it became necessary for him to put away one of his wives in order that he might be baptized. He refused since he had had children by both wives. He was never baptized but considers himself a good Christian as well as a loyal Masai.

John told me that many of the older people were opposed to sending their children to school. There is undoubtedly a certain amount of fear that education may deplete the manpower required for cattle raising. But according to John (as well as others I have spoken with), education without Christianization does not adequately prepare the young Masai for progress in the national life and he will inevitably return to his pastoral life. The East African native seems to assimilate along with Christianity the particular virtues needed to become a fully modern man, at least in the kind of transitional society represented by Kenya where enterprise, hard work, sobriety and industry (what is usually termed the Protestant Ethic) still go hand in glove with economic and social progress. Only with this double education, John made clear, will the young Masai make a place for himself in the new society.

Ironically, the British colonial administration was largely responsible for keeping the Masai in their traditional mold. They treated the Masai like pets, discouraging their warlike tendencies, while at the same time encouraging them to stay put, undisturbed by the changing world around them. The colonial administration may have feared the possibilities of Masai expansion. Certainly they had no objection to showing off these pastoral people, so often photographed and written about. On the credit side of the ledger, the British desire that the Masai retain their less aggressive traditions gave these cattle herders time to prepare themselves for the dramatic changes in the sixties. On the debit side, colonial policy made it difficult for many Masai to demonstrate their very apparent and considerable talents or to receive educations.

John complained about the British attitude, and was pleased that the new, self-determined Kenyan government was encouraging changes among the Masai. Since independence, he said, there has been a willingness to try new things: schools, churches, medical outposts have all increased in number. I told John that in many other parts of the world a sudden growth of new institutions would have brought on a period of serious confusion. "We are ready for it here," he said with assurance.

John was especially resentful of the way the colonial administration had handled the problem of game in East Africa. The British feared that the Masai, should they turn to agriculture, would take away grazing land available for wild game that was becoming a major tourist attraction. So they wanted the Masai to maintain their nomadic, pastoral existence—in spite of, or because of, the fact that British farmers had already killed much of the game in the Rift valley. According to John, the British often showed more concern for the wildlife than for the needs of the Masai or other tribes.

But now that Masai are represented in the Kenya government, as John put it, "The government will have to come to terms with the need to establish a balance between animal and human needs."

I asked how. John said the answer was more game parks, with the Masai sharing in the economic benefits of tourism. "Perhaps for once the game will be an asset to us. We will be able to share in it," John went on to explain. "I don't think it is the game

To prove the depth of their grief over the deaths of relatives or close friends, a once-prevalent practice of New Guinea natives was to cut off part of a finger.

Native of Kankanamun wears a basketry woven ancestral mask with grass fringe at boys' initiation ceremony.

A study in contrasts. Danga, a shapely New
Guinea girl from the Minj tribe, was reared
in a Stone Age culture but has been trained
as a laboratory technician in a malaria control
laboratory. At home in her native village she
wears traditional attire, but dons western
garments for her job, which includes the
identification of mosquito larvae using a
modern binocular microscope.

No two alike. The Bororo Indians of Brazil's vast Mato Grosso display amazing creativeness and ingenuity in devising highly individualized costumes for their ceremonial dances.

This House Tambaran in the village of Kankanamun is the most famous and finest example of all the villages along the Sepik River. Such structures contain carved figures representing the ancestors of the villages, and here village leaders meet to plan their wars, their economy, and their food production. Females are forbidden to enter a House Tambaran on pain of death.

Dani tribesman from the Grand Valley of the Baliem in the central highlands of western New Guinea. These Stone Age warrior-farmers still practice ritual warfare (conflicts which occur regularly and which are considered necessary and sacred to their culture). Their greatest triumph is to eat a slain enemy in full view of his clansmen. The penis gourd is their chief and sometimes only article of clothing, and they would not think of being seen without it by anyone outside the family.

wo chiefs from the Minj
rea of the Wahgi Valley
n New Guinea attend an
mportant festival, adorned
with bird of paradise
lumes, cockatoo feathers,
earl shells, face paint, and
woven wigs strangely re-
embling those worn by Brit-
h barristers.

Tanyaga, the wise and much-revered elder of the
village of Kankanamun on the Sepik River in New
Guinea. In his left hand he proudly displays the
sacred pole, or *bengal*, carved from the heartwood
of the *sacsac* tree. Each stick inserted in its 15-
foot length represents a village man killed in battle.
The hardwood spear with serrated edges that he
holds in his other hand has been employed in
numerous bitter engagements with enemy tribes
jealous of the village's very desirable location.

Lewis Cotlow and Pygmy friends.
About 40,000 Pygmies inhabit the
dense Congo Ituri Forest. Their
average height is 4 feet and weight,
70 pounds.

In recent years, intertribal wrestling has become a feature of the
guarup—the annual ceremony of
the dead—taking the place of yesterday's bloody warfare. In the
upper Xingu River region of
Brazil's Mato Grosso, magnificently
muscled members of four different
tribes intently watch a spirited
match. Always conducted to the
accompaniment of loud grunts by
the contestants, it ends when a
wrestler manages to catch hold of
his adversary behind the thigh;
throwing an opponent on his back
is particularly humiliating.

Unseasonably warm weather caused the melting of the 5-foot-thick ice covering Jones Sound, but it did not impede the progress of this Eskimo 10-dog team and sled. Scenes like this have virtually disappeared now that planes and snowmobiles have replaced the traditional methods of transportation. Modern vehicles not only travel more quickly than dogs, but they don't require feeding when not in use.

Woman's work (indoors). On the right, Quisa repairs a caribou skin parka for her husband inside their igloo in a hunting camp near Jones Sound. She must do a perfect job; should it split while he is out hunting at 60° below, he might not return. Quisa's mother-in-law has just finished chewing the boot she holds in order to soften it for her son; a stiff boot in contact with the ice quickly cracks. (*right*) Woman's work (outdoors). The omnipresent Eskimo knives and scrapers are evident in this photograph of Quisa, shown skinning a seal on the ice of Jones Sound.

trappers and the tourist hotelkeepers who alone should make the decisions."

The Masai are quite often mauled and killed by the wild game in their area. Rhinos, elephants, lions and wild dogs take a high toll among them. These carnivores come into the kraal camps, attracted by the cattle, and in the course of their depredations a certain number of children who are watching over the cattle are badly hurt or killed.

But as John pointed out, the wildlife of Kenya is beginning to pay off for the Masai. Tourism is presently the number one contributor of foreign exchange to the Kenyan economy.

"In 1961," Alan Jacobs explained, "people here argued whether tourism brought in £750,000 or £1,000,000. Now they argue whether this figure is £17,000,000 or £19,000,000." Coffee and sisal have declined in importance; the disappearance of the sisal market is a result of the increased use of synthetics as well as America's high protective tariff in favor of domestic cotton. The Kenya government must continue to encourage tourism, but not, it is hoped, without giving the Masai their fair share—especially since many tourists come to Kenya to see them as well as the wildlife.

In 1961 the Masai began to receive a share of the Amboselli Reserve gate receipts: 35 percent, which brings in from £52,000 to £54,000 annually. None of this money reaches the hands of individual Masai; most of it is consumed in the construction and maintenance of schools. But it all adds to the feeling among Masai that they really have an important stake in the national life, something few other primitive peoples have been able to feel.

Another change in Masai life since colonial days centers on the new position of the local chiefs. During the high water mark of British colonial administration, local chiefs were given power that had little, if any, traditional justification. They were not selected by the age groups and were responsible mainly to the colonial administration. Since the coming of independence these chiefs have lost their power. The Masai, under the aegis of the central government, are reestablishing much of their autonomy. They are not being forced to change, but they are being encouraged to change by being given a greater stake in the larger Kenyan society. In Tanzania, incidentally, government policy restricts the dress of the Masai who, because they can be too easily seen by tourists there, are made to wear trousers. A certain high Kenyan official, I am told, promises to position himself on the border between the two countries with his backside bare, pointing directly at the trousered Tanzanians as his way of protesting the policy of the neighboring state.

The few Masai who have been given the opportunity to participate in modern life have gone far. There are between sixteen and twenty Masai studying at American universities in fields as diverse and as difficult as range management, political science, economics and nuclear physics. It will be easy enough for them to find jobs when—and if—they return. But the vast majority of the Masai are changing very slowly. It is perhaps hardest for those with only a little education because there are not enough jobs yet. But the situation will never be hopeless, for as long as they regard themselves as Masai there will always be a place for them.

11 Australia's Aborigines: How Do You Save a Culture?

THE AUSTRALIAN ABORIGINES had a special meaning for me even before I learned that their fate was in many ways similar to that of other disappearing cultures. I had seen the others wither and rot away under the impact of civilization; "ethnocide" is the word that is coming into use. My main consolation was in the knowledge that I had seen the face of pride and innocence before it turned to bitterness, bewilderment and despair. For the indigenous Australian peoples, as for the Alaskan Eskimo, it was already too late when I made my plans to see them in 1967.

At least I was told as much when early that year I wrote to Harry C. Giese, a very knowledgeable official in Darwin, to get his cooperation for a documentary film on the Pintubi and Wailbri. These people, I had learned from correspondence with another Australian official, were likely to be the only extant primitive tribes there. But Giese wrote back that there were, in fact, no Wailbri living in the manner of their ancestors, and the Pintubi were now living in government settlements. Moreover, Giese explained, I could not expect to find many pure-blooded Aborigines living in the traditional way in other parts of Australia because the remote desert areas had been well combed by government patrols. The Aborigines were now gathered in or around missions, government settlements, cattle and sheep stations.

It seemed that the gloomy predictions of anthropologists in the last decade were correct. Aboriginals there would be, but they would inhabit a dying culture. Giese should know, I thought, not only because of his official title—director of social welfare for the Northern Territories Administration—but because he has dedicated his life to building bridges between the Aboriginal traditions and modern Australian life. In some ways he reminded me of Orlando Villas Boas who, though building no bridges into his Brazilian Xingu National Park, was as devoted to the primitive people in this twilight period.

Despite these disquieting presentiments, I stopped off at Sydney during a world tour in 1967 and made the rounds of government, missionary and academic authorities there. Nothing I heard then led me to believe that enough authentic Aboriginal life remained in Australia to warrant the time and expense of making a film. I put in a call to Giese, who was then in Darwin, near the northernmost tip of Australia. He told me that the best he could offer was a five-day gathering of Aborigines there, to display some of the relics of their traditional culture, dance and sing, exhibit their quite remarkable art, and show their prowess in modern, Western-style sports activities. It sounded like a sincere attempt to maintain old tribal identities, without actually holding back the process of assimilation. But it wasn't at all what I wanted—it sounded altogether too contrived, too well supervised, too much like material for a travelogue. They would be wearing modern dress, and that was the last straw. I abandoned the idea and left Australia.

Some two years later, my wife, Charlotte, and I were winging our way from Johannesburg in South Africa to Perth in western Australia, this time with a book about dying primitive cultures on my mind. Since my last visit to Australia I had gone back to the Indians of Brazil, Peru and Ecuador, had seen the Eskimos of Alaska, and had returned to the primitive peoples whom I had filmed and written about in Africa. I had seen a pattern emerging on a global scale. To the degree that technologically advanced societies were able to penetrate the once-isolated sanctuaries of primitive life, disruptive changes had shaken the native cultures. How well these cultures would fare depended upon a number of considerations. Among the more obvious were the presence of natural bulwarks, or certain internal strengths such as strong warrior traditions. (A tradition of cooperativeness and hospitality to strangers might well be fatal in dealing with civilized societies.)

An extraordinary sense of group identity might be another saving factor, along with time enough to learn how to adapt to new ways before a feeling of worthlessness overcame the members of the group. I wondered if the pattern would hold true for the Australian Aboriginal. From what I had already heard I suspected that it would. After all, the same civilization, with all its virtues and defects, its good and bad intentions, had had its way in Australia as it had in the Americas and, for so long, in Africa.

This time I decided to go to Darwin and see the Aborigines there for myself. But first there would be a few days in Perth, and I decided to make the most of my time. I saw Griff Richards, managing editor of the *Western Australian*, and learned that the issues surrounding the Aborigines in present-day Australia were lively and often fairly hot. The questions that had been raised were reminiscent of those concerning the Eskimos and the American Indians. How much separatism? Were government reservations adequate to the needs of the Aborigines? How successfully were these reservations serving as buffers between the native populations and the expanding frontiers of the pioneering Australians? Were the Aborigines being

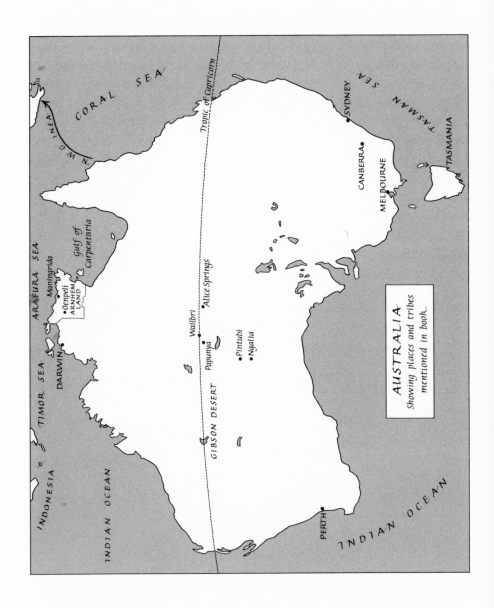

AUSTRALIA
Showing places and tribes
mentioned in book

treated fairly as workers in the towns, on the farms and at the sheep and cattle stations? What kind of schooling should they—or could they—be exposed to? The questions, seemingly endless, and at the same time very familiar, were in the clippings given to me by the newspaper's librarian, C. L. Aris, a former commander in the Royal Navy.

Before taking off for Darwin I had the opportunity of speaking with Ronald M. Berndt, professor emeritus of anthropology at the University of Western Australia and for many years the pre-eminent scholar in the field. Like so many anthropologists, Dr. Berndt despairs of the word "primitive." To him it is an inadequate characterization of the rich cultural life of peoples like the Australian Aborigines. I asked him what he thought would be the fate of that culture. He was hopeful that it would not die out, that while it might not survive as an independent and self-sustaining tradition, it would find its way into the mainstream of Australian life.

I could not help wondering about that Australian future. How much influence remains in American society of its own Aborigines, the Indians? Many motion pictures still portray the Indians as bloodthirsty savages. Would the Australians draw from the Aboriginal traditions a more accurate and enriching spirit? A society takes from the past what it can use, or adapt to its needs, and what it believes in; thus, earlier cultures survive in one form or another. But how much of the Aboriginal way of life will survive? To answer questions like these it is necessary to abandon, for the moment, the possibilities of the future and to deal with the rather murky present, itself in part a result of the historic clash between white and Aboriginal interests.

Scientists are certain that the Aborigines were originally immigrants who came from southeast Asia through Indonesia to Australia's northern coasts possibly 20,000 years ago. But the exact origins of the Aborigines are still open to speculation and controversy; attempts to classify these first Australians as one "racial" unit still generate heated academic debate. Dr. Berndt and his wife, Catherine, have pointed out in their book *The World of the First Australians* that there is no single physical or even cultural "Aboriginal type," just as there is no "European type," although there are obvious similarities among all groups of Europeans. In physical terms, one can find Aborigines in the south who are extremely hairy—men with chest and body hair nine inches long, women with very apparent facial hair—while others in the Great Victorian Desert have copper-colored skin, prominent brow ridges and sloping foreheads. Some Aborigines in the north are taller, heavier and bigger-boned than the thin and wiry people who inhabit the borders of the Northern Territory and western Australia. Except for their dark-brown eyes and chocolate color, they are almost European in appearance. In central Australia there are people who conform to the stereotype of the Aborigine with their distinct brow-ridges, broad nostrils and deep-set eyes. But in western Arnhem Land, in the north, you can find people less than five feet tall, some small-boned and delicately shaped, others thickset and squat. In the Alice Springs area, there are children who are blond. Despite this diversity, many people throughout the world still wrongly consider native Australians as a species apart, the nearest living relatives of the Neanderthal Man.

Culturally, the Australian Aborigines have traditions which bind them together and set them apart from all other peoples I have seen. But here again the diversity of styles and attitudes, implements and art forms, defies generalization. There was no common language to unite the Aborigines before the Europeans arrived. The word "tribe" is in fact a European designation for a group of people who speak a single language (perhaps with different dialects) and who occupy a certain territory where they hunt and gather food, and which they call their home. It has been estimated that anyone who wished to speak to all the Aborigines in Australia (before English began to serve as a *lingua franca*) would have needed to acquire fluency in about 150 separate languages, comprising more than 600 dialects.

Elaborate rules governing marriage, sexual activity and family relationships vary significantly among—and within—these tribes, which once numbered as many as 500. Religious beliefs, rituals and mythology differ not only from tribe to tribe, but also among the important subdivisions of clan and horde, extensions of the nuclear family. The clan—not the tribe—functions as a political and economic entity, hunting and gathering food as a unit, sometimes feuding or warring together. Unified by a belief in its own totemic ancestors, the clan traces a common descent through father or mother, and preserves from one generation to another its own legends and songs.

The Aborigines' adjustments to the varied Australian environment are reflected in differing economic styles and ways of hunting and gathering food, and various attitudes toward the particular natural surroundings. The boomerang, widely regarded as the symbol of Aboriginal life, is an example of these environmental adaptations and differences. In some areas it is used for hunting; elsewhere the boomerang serves as a clapper to provide rhythmic accompaniment to songs; in still other places it is used for purely ceremonial purposes. There are even communities where boomerangs are totally unknown.

There has never been a single name for all the indigenous peoples of Australia. By common usage "Aborigines" refers to the people as a whole, and "Aboriginal" to an individual, perhaps because "Aborigine" is felt to have derogatory associations.

Because the Aborigines had neither a sense of common nationality nor the traditions of banding together when faced with an external threat, the first Europeans to arrive in Australia were able to prevail easily. The rather crude technology of the Aborigines was no match for European weapons; nor were they culturally adapted for the kind of persistent bellicosity that might have discouraged some of the newcomers. From the time the British established their first Australian settlement in 1788, a penal colony at Port Jackson (now Sydney), the Aborigines were systematically pushed back from their traditional lands and forced into regions which held little interest, at least temporarily, for the newcomers. From time to time the Aborigines made efforts to resist the invaders, but these attempts to retain possession of sacred Aboriginal territories were usually put down by merciless punitive raids.

While official British policy regarded the Aborigines as subjects of the Crown, with all the benefits of citizenship, British justice and law, Western culture and Christianity, neither the colonists nor the Aborigines themselves (for quite different reasons) saw much point in fulfilling the spirit of this enlightened, if somewhat ethnocentric, policy. The Aborigines, of course, were perfectly satisfied with their own culture. But the colonists, many of whom had only recently quit unpleasant circumstances, were of a mind to carve rich farming lands from territories to which no savage, noble or otherwise, could be expected to lay claim. (As I have already pointed out, nomadic or seminomadic peoples have a remarkable indifference to land deeds.) No colonial official back in England could tell the self-reliant settler that his Aboriginal neighbors were anything but irresponsible heathens, unfit to receive the rights, privileges and immunities that went along with British citizenship. Colin Simpson, in his *Adam in Ochre*, quotes a nineteenth-century author, a Mrs. Thomas Mortimer, as typical of the British view of Aboriginal culture:

I have already told you that the natives have no God; yet they have a devil, whom they call Yakoo or debbil-debbil. Of him they are always afraid, for they fancy he goes about devouring children. When anyone dies, they say, "Yakoo took him." How different from those happy Christians who can say of their dead, "God took him."

People who know not God, but only the devil, must be very wicked. . . . These ignorant savages have their amusements. Dancing is the chief. At every full moon there is a grand dance, called a Corrobory. It is the men who dance, while the women sit by and beat time. Nothing can be more horrible to see . . . and they play all manner of strange antics, and utter all kinds of strange yells; so that you might think it was a dance in Hell, rather than on earth.

In general, the colonists took matters into their own hands. There were no official treaties, and orderly administrative and legal procedures were left behind in the dust of frontier expansion. Aborigines were tolerated if they behaved themselves, if they "kept their place." If not they were "bad niggers" and were dealt with brutally as less-than-human creatures, partly out of simple racism and partly out of convenience. For example, it was difficult indeed for the colonists, many of whom were criminal outcasts eager for a new start and intent on accumulating wealth, to understand the Aboriginal's indifference toward property. That alone would have marked them as worthy of contempt. And the fact that Aborigines did not fence off a particular piece of land and post "no trespassing" signs both fed the settlers' contempt and served as the rationale for their unchecked expansion into native territories.

The Europeans could not or would not understand that every jutting rock, tree or stream might have a sacred meaning for the Aboriginal, or that it was essential to his traditional life that he have freedom of movement, or "walkabout," in his tribal lands. Aborigines were not simply aimless wanderers; there were always practical and religious reasons for breaking camp and moving on to a new location. When water ran short, when firewood supplies were too distant to be carried easily, when the birds migrated or when fruits and yams were ripening somewhere else, it was time to move. Moreover, when a death occurred it was customary for the Aboriginal family to leave their camp and not return, a practice that has complicated recent attempts to locate Aborigines on permanent government settlements.

Another feature of Aboriginal life which both served the colonists' needs and confirmed their European prejudices was the apparent laxity of the Aborigines in sexual behavior. Actually, they had as detailed a code governing sex and marriage as any other tradition-oriented people. There are, even now, in the various tribes and clans, highly complex rules specifying who may be intimate with whom, to what degree and when. There are strong taboos, for example, against a man and his mother-in-law speaking or even approaching each other, except on ceremonial occasions when many restrictions are temporarily abandoned. In some tribes a man is permitted more than one wife; in others marriages are arranged during infancy; and in still others young girls are wedded to older men. The rules are enforced mainly by social pressures in the tightly knit family and clan units, where there is probably less opportunity to lead a double life than in a small New England village.

Yet Aboriginal society has never been tyrannical. It has always permitted individual freedom within well-understood limits. There are husbands who prefer one woman although they are entitled to more, and there are those of both sexes who look for satisfaction beyond the scope of a disappointing marriage. The range of human behavior is certainly as wide as that among the Ituri Pygmies or, for that matter, in a typical American suburb. There are wives who are shrewish and tax the patience of their husbands, possibly because they know that women are highly valued as child-bearers and workers, or simply because that is the way they are.

And there are others who suffer quietly the indifference, the hostility and the infidelities of their husbands. A philanderer knows that his people will wink at his indiscretions, but a habitual wife-stealer will be severely punished, perhaps by exile or a fatal beating. Wives, too, can exhibit a certain degree of independence because they know that in small nomadic groups both their economic value and their sexual desirability are important. The colonists' taking Aboriginal women as concubines probably did little immediate damage to the native way of life, especially in view of the broader dislocation caused by the outsiders. But in the long run such liaisons contributed to the general undermining of the host culture.

One reason why the Aboriginals so readily accepted the use of their women was their failure to relate childbirth to the sexual act. While anthropologists still disagree about the extent of the Aborigines' connecting sexual intercourse with procreation, the Aboriginal clearly placed much emphasis on myths about a "child spirit" that entered a woman's body—a mystical event made possible but not actually caused by coition, as though the sexual act "made a path" for the child spirit. Another view is that the sexual act merely produced the physical being that is the child, but that it was animated only by the presence of spirit.

Nevertheless, the Aborigines do not seem to have regarded paternity in quite the same way as the white settlers. Nor did they complicate paternity with the same economic rivalry common among property-minded whites. To us the son is the eventual recipient of some portion of his father's estate, and so it is important that there be no doubt as to whose son he really is. The Aboriginal son and father traditionally shared the same "estate" along with all the other members of their tribal community.

Moreover, the Aboriginal sense of relatedness extended far beyond the boundaries of the nuclear family, which in our society is a basic unit of property ownership (think of the misery caused by the distribution of community property when a family breaks up; think of a family, if you can, that is totally property-less or that does not aspire to owning possessions). So the Aboriginal is accustomed to living in a world where there are many "mothers" and "fathers," "sisters" and "brothers," all expressing appropriate family feelings toward each other, regardless of the immediacy of biological connection, and all participating in a common cultural "estate," viewing every square yard of their communal lands as invested with spiritual meaning.

For reasons such as these, it was not really "sinful" for an Aboriginal woman to give herself to a white settler, although he may have regarded her accommodating attitude as just that. Sometimes, according to the Berndts, these relationships were treated as normal and natural, but frequently there was what they refer to in their book *The World of the First Australians* as a "triangular situation in which a young woman lived almost simultaneously with her Aboriginal husband and with a white man. In practice the latter had more rights over her than her husband because of the tremendous difference in status between the two men."

These relationships eroded the position of the male in Aboriginal society and upset the social balance. Often the woman in the family would serve as a go-between since she was in a more favorable position for asking favors from the male white settlers.

She might, for instance, ask for consideration for a husband who had stepped out of line. Alternately, she might return with the message for her family that failure to work for the colonists without complaint would be punished by cutting off the hand-outs to which they had grown accustomed, or—even worse—by banishment from settled areas. This would force the Aboriginal group to take up in unfamiliar areas the rigorous subsistence life with which they had undoubtedly lost touch. Under such circumstances, the Aboriginal male who did not suffer a loss of confidence in himself must have been rare indeed. Similar situations are recorded among the Eskimos of Alaska and Canada, where a scarcity of white women resulted in an appropriation of native girls, with an attendant loss of pride among Eskimo men.

These sexual arrangements affected Australian life beyond their impact upon the Aboriginal social structure. One result was an increasing number of mixed bloods, subjected for many years to discriminatory practices and attitudes by the white Australian community, who were not able to call upon the supportive identity and tribal or clan membership of the full-blooded Aborigine. They were the in-betweeners who generally appear at the confluence of two cultures and who suffer the ambiguities of an ill-defined status. As it happens, the mixed bloods now outnumber the full-blooded Aborigines by a ratio of nearly two to one. When the British first settled the land, there were (according to the best estimates) about 300,000 Aborigines in Australia. Today census figures indicate that the total is 130,000—about 83,900 part-Aborigines and 46,100 full-blooded Aborigines, most of whom are, to a significant degree, acculturated. But census takers do not ask citizens whether they consider themselves Aborigines or "Europeans," the blanket term for the ethnic stock of Australia's white majority.

There are part-Aborigines, regarded by census takers as Europeans, who may call themselves Aboriginal. Others, 50 percent Aboriginal or more, prefer to think of themselves as European. Until quite recently the individual Australian states in charge of

Aboriginal affairs, attempted to define who was and who was not Aboriginal—with only a great deal of confusion to show for their efforts. In some states an "Aboriginal" or "native" was anyone with an "admixture of Aboriginal blood." Other states decided that an Aboriginal had to be at least a "quarter-caste" and in others "more than a half-caste." In the last few years, statutes of this sort have been recognized as discriminatory, even when they are used to determine who shall receive welfare benefits, and although many of them have been stricken from the books, some remain in force.

In general, the laws, policies and official attitudes determining the Aboriginal's fate in Australia reflect changes in the mood and conscience of the white-majority society. They have never accurately reflected what was best for the Aborigines, nor could they, for that would have called for the whites never settling in Australia. Furthermore, the rules of the game have always been laid down by the Europeans, who may or may not have had good intentions. It is another example of the irony we find everywhere in the clash of cultures: by the time a conquered primitive people is able to join in the councils that control their destinies, they have already been deprived of their ancestral life style.

The myth that Aborigines could be regarded as ordinary British subjects was abandoned in a *de jure* as well as a *de facto* sense by about 1860, and until 1910 new laws were passed by each colony or state to keep settlers and Aboriginals apart as much as possible. During this period, known in Australia as the protection era, there was also an attempt to compensate the Aborigines for their hardship by setting up administrations to dispense flour, blankets and medicine. (It should be remembered that during much of this same period, the United States was virtually in a state of war with its own aboriginal tribes.)

While much of the "protective" legislation remained in effect until World War II, a new attitude toward the Aboriginal began to develop in the twenties and thirties when it became clear that disease, hunger, poverty and social disorganization were threatening to wipe out the native community. A series of official conferences, begun in 1937 and continuing after the war, helped to crystallize the growing feeling among concerned Australians that something must be done to bring the Aborigines into the national life on an eventually equal footing with the white majority. At first, part-Aborigines and then full-bloods were included in the official welfare programs. In 1967, the Constitution was amended so that the Commonwealth government could share responsibility for Aboriginal affairs with the states, which had been placed in charge of the Aborigines when the Commonwealth was established and its Constitution adopted in 1901. Recently, the tendency has been to extend government assistance in the fields of child welfare, old-age benefits, health care, minimum wages, industrial relations, housing and other social services in a more-or-less even-handed approach to Aboriginal and white. Various discriminatory laws have gradually been abolished, and it has even become possible for the Aborigines to vote (a right not yet enjoyed by our own Aborigines). Laws forbidding Aborigines to drink have been struck down in favor of right-to-drink legislation. Aborigines are now required to pay income taxes along with other Australians. In theory, if not always in practice, the Aboriginal is permitted equal access to public facilities, transportation and places of entertainment. He is supposed to receive equal pay for equal work.

Many problems have arisen in this period of adjustment: a typical situation is that of the Aboriginal stockman who works at an outback cattle station. In the old days he accepted virtual serfdom as a way of life. He received a little money, perhaps the equivalent of fifty cents or a dollar a week, and he and his family were fed and housed. He was permitted a certain amount of "walkabout" but he nevertheless belonged to his master who, in turn, regarded "his" Aborigines paternalistically. With the coming of the new liberalism and specifically the minimum wage, the owner began to demand an efficient and regularized work day. At the same time, the older fringe benefits previously granted by the owner tended to be withdrawn.

The result of such situations was much bitterness and tension between the Aboriginal stockman and his employer, whose position was tantamount to a declaration that "I'm not your father anymore." In reality, the Aborigines have gone through a series of culture shocks, beginning with the initial invasion and continuing right up to the present when they are being made to give up some of their early adjustments to a white-dominated world.

On the other hand, the extension to Aborigines of health and social welfare services has helped to reverse the population decline. In fact, their rate of increase in some areas is now greater than that of the Australian population as a whole. Recent census figures show that 55 percent of the population described as "Aboriginal" is under twenty-one years of age, while only 40 percent of the white majority is under twenty-one. It is expected that by the end of the century the number of Aborigines and part-Aborigines will double. Whether there will be any point in calling them "Aboriginal" by that time will be open to question.

The present policy of assimilation says, in effect: let us make up for the thoughtlessness of the past, give the Aborigines the careful attention required to prepare them to live side by democratic side with other Australians, as brothers and equals. Under this policy, championed by Sir Paul Hasluck, a former minister of territories, more recently governor general, and a longtime student of Aboriginal culture, special consideration is to be given the Aboriginal only during the period of adjustment. According to a policy statement agreed to by the Commonwealth and state government ministers at a conference on native welfare in Canberra in 1961:

... any special measures taken for Aborigines and part-Aborigines are regarded as temporary measures not based on colour but intended to meet their need for special care and assistance to protect them from any ill-effects of sudden change and to assist them to make the transition from one stage to another in such a way as will be favourable to their future social, economic and political advancement.

The "special measures," intended to advance the assimilation policy, included government settlement work aimed at encouraging the nomadic and seminomadic peoples to adopt "a more settled way of life"; health services and health education; special schools and preschools to educate and train Aborigines who were not yet ready for regular schooling; encouraging participation in sports and other community activities; special vocational preparation; transitional housing intended to prepare the once-propertyless Aborigines for the management of a European-style home; and the availability of welfare workers who would instruct the native peoples in Western-style community living. There would also be a program for educating the Australian community in general to the importance of accepting "advanced" Aborigines and part-Aborigines into the community without prejudice.

It appears, however, that the white majority is going to need its own period of adjustment. On the whole, they seem as unprepared to accept the Aboriginal into their community as their counterparts in America have been to accept Negroes, Indians, Mexicans and Puerto Ricans as neighbors. There are proportionately fewer Aborigines, of course, and there is a possibility that the native peoples of Australia can be assimilated into the life of the majority before the inevitable rise in population poses special problems.

The most serious question, it seems to me, turns on Professor Berndt's hopes that the Aboriginal way of life will not completely vanish under the policy of assimilation. In the policy statement of 1961, are the following words: "The policy of assimilation means . . . that all Aborigines and part-Aborigines are expected eventually to attain the same manner of living as other Australians . . . observing the same customs and influenced by the same beliefs, hopes, and loyalties. . . ." This sounds like a recipe for a well-mixed, homogenized society with no cultural or subcultural lumps, a rather difficult feat for an expanding, dynamic and democratic nation. The statement deserved, and got, a considerable amount of attention, and in 1965 another conference of Commonwealth and state ministers responsible for Aboriginal welfare changed the wording to read, in part: "The policy of assimilation seeks that all persons of Aboriginal descent *will choose* to attain a similar manner and standard of living to that of other Australians and live as members of a single Australian community. . . ." [italics mine] The element of free choice had been added, but given the far-reaching policy of assimilation, would it be a real choice? Later, the Commonwealth minister for territories added his personal reassurance: "This change was made to avoid misunderstandings that had arisen that the assimilation policy sought the destruction of the Aboriginal culture. It does not."

12 Aborigines:
The Ethics of Assimilation

THE PROGRAM DESCRIBED at the conclusion of the previous chapter was the very program that Harry Giese was administering in the Northern Territory. I wanted to ask him about the care taken to maintain freedom of choice among the Aborigines. Giese is a tall, raw-boned man of about fifty-seven, quite amiable and, like many Australians I've met, plain spoken. He is a disciple of Sir Paul Hasluck, the father of assimilation policy, and frowns upon the "academic circles" which tend to disparage the program. I called him soon after I arrived in Darwin; he immediately remembered my long telephone conversation with him from Sydney of two years before. After picking me up at my hotel, he gave me a comprehensive tour of Kormilda College (a secondary school), where I saw young people studying English, handicrafts and art. Aborigines were being schooled in map reading, in health care, in how to use the telephone "properly and politely," as the instructor put it. Boys were studying carpentry and masonry, and girls were learning sewing, cooking and the making of marionettes.

As we moved from group to group, Giese would greet the young Aborigines by first name, always in a casual manner, speaking as if he were one of their peers, not at all like a Big Brother. He reminded a few of the girls that on the following day they were to appear in an important softball game. "Mary," he would say, with all the enthusiasm of a high school cheerleader, "I expect great things from you at the plate. We've just got to win tomorrow." And, turning to another girl whose painting he had interrupted, he said, "Sadie, you are going to pitch a great game tomorrow, I just know it." He asked me if I'd care to join him in the grandstand. I told him that I wouldn't miss it. I couldn't ask for a better example of assimilation in action, as it were.

Giese gave me some basic statistics before we got down to the question that was uppermost in my thoughts. There were at present in the Northern Territory 20,500 full-blooded Aborigines scattered over 525,000 square miles. Most of them, he told me, are still living in their traditional areas, but not their traditional ways of life. There were also 70 different tribal groups speaking 70 different languages; some of these groups numbered as few as 100 members, or about 12 families. Larger groups in central Australia, like the Pintubi and the Wailbri, numbered from 2,000 to 2,500. Until the last decade there were comparatively few Europeans in the Northern Territory and contacts between the two cultures were rare. According to Giese, the missions there served as a buffer between many of the Aboriginal groups and the newcomers, especially the pioneers who might care little for preserving the nomadic inhabitants and their traditional hunting grounds. Recently, discoveries of bauxite and other ores have brought a steady flow of Europeans into the Northern Territory. Now the government, in the belief that an isolated Aboriginal culture is no longer possible or even desirable in a growing Australia, has pushed the assimilation program forward. Overall, the Commonwealth is spending more than $20 million a year on assistance to the native peoples, and this is only a start.

When Geise and I met on the following day, before the big softball game, he told me that those fears prevalent in "academic circles" about Aborigines losing their traditional culture—at least in the totality of its aspects—were unjustified.

"We do not intend," Giese said, "that the Aboriginal should lose those elements of dance, song, and art that would enrich the dominant society. The assimilation policy is difficult to explain to people who see it as an attempt to make the Aboriginal the same as the European, a kind of white black fellow. That isn't the idea at all."

"Then what is the Aboriginal becoming?" I asked.

"Part of the constituency of Australian society, and that means he must accept some of the mores and customs of that society. How much and how far he accepts these norms will be up to him. He does have a choice."

I had heard about the principle of free choice which had been incorporated into the government policy statement back in 1965. I was not, however, quite sure what it really meant. In what sense can you have a culture comprised of individuals who are in the position of having to choose how much of it to accept or how much to reject? I turned to Giese for the answer.

"Many of the older people," he explained, "will probably not want to make the move that will set them on the road to assimilation. They will go on living in the old way insofar as they can. But the younger generation, partly because they are being educated, and because they desire some of the things that other Australians have—they will want to come into the dominant society."

I reminded Giese that I had seen some of those younger people the day before. They had looked very happy to me.

"There are others," he went on, "who, after being trained, will want to go back and work within their own society. They'll teach their people to develop aspirations and goals beyond those of their local community."

The point was that technology and the European way of working and living would win them over one way or another, the question of free choice notwithstanding.

"For assimilation to succeed we must develop educational facilities from preschool to adult education. The problem is how to reach the many groups scattered over wide areas in the Northern Territory. The government has established a number of settlements in remote areas."

Did the Aborigines walk into these settlements on their own? Was it really their choice?

"There has been no compulsion for the Aborigines to become members of these communities," Giese assured me. "But the kinds of facilities that have been provided in them have attracted the Aborigines, and when they have been attracted the government has then had the opportunity of providing health services, educational and training programs."

It all amounted to something of a lure, but a lure in the direction that the Aboriginal was heading anyway. Giese, as a government administrator, had to deal with a host of practical considerations. That I understood. And it was necessary to have a fairly clear-headed notion of what the goals were in order to make decisions affecting the lives of many people, sometimes on a day-to-day basis. So one had to have some kind of model which could characterize the future, and for Giese that model was an Aboriginal who would maintain a pride in his heritage, a familiarity with the artistic culture of his people and possibly their language, but be quite capable of holding a job and living in the dominant society, intimate with its technology, its laws and its traditions. There were other models of the Aboriginal's future, too, and they would be heard from. Conflict is the one really inevitable result during a period of cultural change, especially when the changes are charted for the future by men with individual attitudes, personalities and philosophies.

This kind of conflict is something that we of the West need to understand, for it will go on as long as we believe that men can sit around a conference table and decide which way a culture is to go—what to add and what to delete. Possibly because we are no longer convinced that ways of life were divinely decreed since the beginning of the world, we have taken it upon ourselves to change what at any moment in history seems necessary to change. And that willingness to change things, especially values, morals and life styles, seems to me to be the major difference between those people so loosely described as "civilized" or "modern" and those described as "primitive."

The practical considerations facing the administration in Darwin included the preference of many Aborigines for living in small groups of four or five families at great distances from each other. Because this situation involved the role of education in the process of assimilation, a number of mobile units were set up, comprising a classroom, a residence for the teacher, a small wash unit and kitchen facilities. Whenever possible, students are brought to settlements where a working balance can be achieved between the influence of European-based education and that of the Aboriginal community. In other words, the administrators do not want to cause too great a gap, too soon, between growing children and their parents.

Because the children come from widely scattered tribal groups, there is a many-sided language barrier hindering communication between student and teacher, teacher and parent, and among the students themselves. This is not an uncommon problem in frontier education, by which the expanding society seeks to absorb and indoctrinate indigenous peoples. We have seen the problem in the education of the native peoples of Alaska and Canada, the Indians of South America, and in Africa. In teaching a people a new language, more is involved than the simple addition of knowledge. All that we describe as "education" supports fundamental beliefs and assumptions which hold a culture together. One administrator at the government settlement at Maningrida in North Arnhemland told me that he did not expect Aboriginal religion to survive among people who were studying the concepts brought in by Western education.

Loss of native language is especially disruptive because it is the means by which the practical knowledge, the wisdom and the folklore of a people are transmitted from generation to generation. Each Aboriginal tribe, for example, is rich in language expressing personal and kin relationships that do not exist in Western society, and in names for the countless topographical features of their traditional lands. (Imagine, if you can, two doctors trying to discuss a patient's illness without resorting to the complicated anatomical vocabulary that is only vaguely familiar to laymen.) What we call a "language barrier" is usually just as significant a protective shell for a culture as a natural barrier.

In the Northern Territory, Aborigines who have mastered English are used as assistant teachers to bridge the gap between the Aboriginal child and his teacher. When the children have been taught English, their *lingua franca*, they are encouraged toward greater proficiency by their desire to participate in urban life and in the school community composed of children from many different tribes and language groups. What they are learning, it appears, is how to become an Aboriginal with a capital A, rather than a member of a particular tribe, in an Australia where, theoretically, all Aborigines will be accepted as a single group—as if they were Roman Catholic Italians or Protestant Swedes, with a tradition of their own that can enrich the larger society without disrupting it.

But the Welfare Administration is not hurriedly yanking Aboriginal children out of the clan or family communities. When the children have completed the special readiness programs, either in the mobile units or in a settlement, they leave their families and go to a major city or town such as Darwin. After about a year of additional schooling, they are ready to compete with white Australian children in the high schools. (At Darwin High School there were, in 1969, 50 full-blooded Aboriginal students, and 200 are expected by 1975.) At the end of the term, however, they return to their families, who also have been able to visit the students during the school year.

Students are encouraged to study their own language. They receive additional training in linguistic principles which enables them to return to their people and transcribe languages that have never been written down. (This is similar to the work that the Summer Institute of Linguistics is doing in South America and other parts of the world, with the difference that the missionary *linguistadas* are engaged in Bible translation.) At present, fifteen of the seventy Aboriginal languages in the Northern Territory are being studied, but only four of them have been put into written form. The Aboriginal of the future may be not only literate but bilingual. So, whether or not the culture survives outside museums and textbooks, no one will be able to call it "primitive"—and certainly not "preliterate."

Aside from the language barrier, there are a few additional sources of concern for administrators of the assimilation policy, particularly in the centrally important area of education. Among certain tribes, for example the Pitjandjara, boys are initiated during early adolescence, from ages eleven up to fourteen or fifteen. The young Aboriginal undergoes a series of spectacularly elaborate rituals—with circumcision usually the focal point—intended to prepare him for manhood as his culture defines it. He dies, symbolically, and is reborn; he has mastered the ultimate fear. Among certain tribes the boy is swallowed by an Ancestral Spirit, who vomits him back to life as a new being. In other tribes the boy is returning to the womb of the Fertility Mother—the cutting of his foreskin symbolizes the severing of the umbilical cord—and he is born again. He learns some of the mysteries of life that will enable him eventually to marry, to have children of his own, to participate in the sacred rituals of his people.

As important to the culture as initiation may be, administrators know that if a boy is taken out of school during this crucial period of his education his chances for further progress will be limited; assimilation, in his case, will be set back. I learned that government administrators were speaking with the elders in Aboriginal communities in the hope of reconciling the cultural demands on the young Aboriginal with the educational program. Although "teaching respect for Aboriginal traditions" is an established part of the curriculum, there is little doubt that initiation rites would lose out in any contest with schooling.

Another conflict between Aboriginal tradition and the educational programs arises from the frequent marriages of young girls and older men. These marriages, often remarked upon in studies of Aboriginal culture, take place when the girls are about nine or ten—a time when they could be preparing to enter primary or secondary education. Traditionally, however, they are given to men of about fifty or sixty to whom they have been promised since birth. Their wifely duties do not begin until they reach puberty. Many of the girls who have already begun the educational program are reluctant to break contact with the settlement life and the opportunities that lie ahead for them.

When individual girls do resist such marriages, legal steps can be taken to free them from any "obligation," but only after there has been a full discussion with her community of the implications of her decision. There also has been an attempt to do away with plural marriages, especially among older men who are provided for under pension plans. With money to disburse, the government is able to be more persuasive in encouraging Aborigines to adopt moral attitudes which conform to those of the dominant society.

I asked Giese if he thought that such conflicts between the two cultures could be resolved. He was optimistic, but it would need some give and take on both sides. As he put it: "There has to be a full understanding of Aboriginal culture and background. On the other hand the Aboriginal people themselves must come to some understanding of the sorts of changes that must occur in their own society if they are to give their children the opportunity to make viable choices."

"What concerns me and many others," Giese added, pinpointing the problem, I believe, from the administrative viewpoint, "is how we can make sure that those elements in traditional Aboriginal life that are not inimical to the acceptance of Aborigines in the wider community can be retained."

That was a very straightforward comment on the pattern I had seen emerging in many parts of the world. The Aborigines would have to do their part in modernizing themselves in ways acceptable to "the wider community." Yet if a culture is seen as a living organism, how can you cut out a piece here, a piece there, without affecting the whole?

Part of the answer under Australia's assimilation policy is to encourage the older Aborigines to come into the schools and teach those traditional elements of their community which do not conflict too painfully with the conventions and attitudes of that "wider community." Dancing, singing, music and folk legends are elements that the administrators hope can survive. Each year Aborigines from all parts of the Northern Territory come to Darwin and compete in contests of artistic expression. There are Aboriginal theater groups playing to large audiences in Sydney. Plans are being made for an Aboriginal school of the dance in Darwin that may attract students of this art from all over the world. There are plans under way to establish an Aboriginal Theater Foundation, with the blessing of the government, and to launch it on a world tour by 1975. As a preliminary to this, fifteen Aborigines from the Northern Territory attended Expo '70 in Japan as part of the Australia Day program and were well received by a large and enthusiastic audience.

Aborigines are widely known for their ability to mime, as are many primitive peoples whose theatrical abilities have served my camera well over the years. The Aboriginal theater will reflect this talent for imitating the ways of birds, land animals, and the mythical creatures created by a once-unfettered imagination.

Aborigines have also demonstrated a high degree of athletic ability. They have shown that they can develop proficiencies in Western-style sports: basketball, football (Australian version), and as I was to see for myself, women's softball. In 1968 Lionel Rose, an Aboriginal boxer, received a hero's welcome when he returned home to Melbourne after winning the world bantamweight championship in Tokyo. A full-blooded Tiwi, David Kantilla, has starred with a leading South Australian football team. He is now retired and working as a coach. In 1971, a shy nineteen-year-old tennis prodigy, Evonne Goolagong, whose father is a hinterland sheep-shearer, stunned the world when she won the French Womens Singles Open Tournament and then went on to become queen by winning the prestigious Wimbledon.

The wider Australian society is prepared not only to view such expressions of Aboriginal artistic and athletic ability as culturally acceptable—they are becoming justifiably proud of them. In fact, Australia is gaining a sense of national identity by preserving, even at this late date, some of its Aboriginal past. The native peoples are becoming "Our Aborigines" and eventually will stand for *the* Australian national culture in foreign theaters, sports stadiums and at the international expositions of the future. The Aboriginal will be welcomed as a dancer, mime, singer or athlete—yet it is not likely that these can be expressions of a living culture in any real sense. Rather, they will represent memories—happy ones, perhaps—but memories just the same. The Aboriginal will have company in his culture of memory, not only among other primitive peoples, but among all those ethnic groups and displaced nationalities who re-create their traditional life with national costumes and colorful pageants on holidays and special occasions.

Of course, I did go with Giese to the big softball game that afternoon, and his encouraging words of the day before had not been wasted on the girls. They played well against a rival school in Darwin—and it was difficult for me to imagine them settling down as one of the wives of some superannuated Aboriginal. I could be wrong; marriage customs die slowly. Yet it seemed to me that any husband of Sadie, the pitcher, or Mary, the long-ball hitter, would have to fit the image of younger heroes. Giese stood up and cheered every well-executed play, and he gave every base runner booming encouragement that could be heard throughout the park. Didn't I think that Sadie had a superb delivery, he asked. I agreed that she was great. His enthusiasm was infectious and soon I found myself urging "our team" on to victory.

That evening Giese and I and our wives celebrated the eventual triumph with huge buffalo steaks, served al fresco at the Darwin Hotel. Nearby Europeans were taking a last dip in the swimming pool. It seemed, on an evening like this, that the world had been created for gentlemen in neatly pressed slacks and sports jackets, and for their ladies in gay summer dresses.

We had just finished our brandies when a light breeze whipped against our faces, carrying the fragrance of a sea that had lured so many adventurous spirits away from hearth and home. But not far away to the North, there were black, brown and yellow men whose immense numbers were known and usually spoken of in guarded tones. The West had come to the East confident of its superior wisdom, power and virtue. It had fought to stay here, and was still fighting, and would continue to fight to assert that wisdom, power and virtue. There are 12,500,000 white Australians, but a few hours away by jet one could reach the bulk of the world's population—and it is not white. It was impossible—or at least unforgivably shortsighted—to forget this fact when considering Australia's attempt to assimilate its 130,000 full- and mixed-blood Aborigines. And Australia's future role as a frontier of Western civilization in the East might depend on its ability to deal wisely with its own dark-skinned people.

I chartered a Twin-Beech and flew to the government settlement at Maningrida on the Arafura Sea, about 225 miles east of Darwin—a flight of about 90 minutes. My pilot incidentally asked me if I remembered the disappearance of Michael Rockefeller in 1962 in the Arafuru Sea off the coast of New Guinea. I said that I had spent a day with the Governor's son in New York before he left on his ill-fated trip to New Guinea. The pilot told me that when he was recently in Biok in western New Guinea he learned that Michael had been killed by cannibals. Two chieftains had boasted about it to him, and there was convincing evidence to support their stories. I had heard as much from an American missionary a few years earlier as well as from a Dutch patrol officer now living in the Midwest.

At Maningrida I was met by Jack Wilders, the assistant superintendent there. He is a lanky forty-two-year-old with much of the same zeal and dedication I found in Giese. Accompanied by Wilders I toured the native settlement. What I found did little to raise my hopes about the fate of Aborigines in this period of transition. I saw men and women wearing rather shabby Western-style clothes that looked as much like hand-me-downs as the second-hand culture into which they were moving—not quite Australian and not their own. The small, metal-sheeted huts they occupied did not seem to be an improvement over anything they had known in the past—with the possible exception that they kept out the rain.

With Wilders' help I spoke to a number of Aborigines who, like their parents, were born in this part of Arnhem Land, along the Liverpool River. Near the mouth of the river, in view of the sea, I met John, a typical coastal Aboriginal in build—husky, five-foot-six, once a man of considerable strength. His English was adequate for a conversation, and we joined him on the riverbank. He said that he and his brother lived in one of the huts, along with their wives. The brothers were both over sixty-five and were each getting a government pension that amounted to about $28 every two weeks.

Curly-haired and grizzled, John had been at the station for many years, but, until recently, had maintained the seminomadic life of his ancestors. Now, he rarely left the station. He loved to fish, and he was just as fond of telling fish stories. He spoke of the days when he was able to hunt in the hinterland as well as in a bark canoe along the shore. On land he had hunted Kangaroos with a spear which he made from a flexible shaft with a sharpened stone point affixed by means of a piece of bark rope. A similar spear is used for offshore fishing. John recalled filling his canoe with turtles, salmon, barramundi and rock fish. I asked about sharks which abound in the waters here, and John told me that he would never eat them. Wilders explained that the Aborigines were opposed to eating sharks for religious reasons— although this was not true of the very young. I learned, by the way, that the local sharks were apparently quite satisfied with their regular diet and posed no threat to the native peoples who swam in the waters off Arnhem Land. Nor did I observe any fear of sharks among Darwin residents.

John was happy to have me photograph him. He posed along the shore holding his spear. It was a beautifully clear day, and you could feel the salty sea spray in the air. Some Aboriginal children were gathering nearby. I could hear them giggling during the picture-taking; they seemed to be entertained by the sight of two grown men facing one another, one with a spear, the other with a little metallic box. I wondered how many times in recent history this tableau had been reenacted: spear-holder and photographer, standing on opposite sides of a chasm that no amount of time or instruction in each other's ways could hope to bridge. When—and if—we came to understand the differences that separated us and accepted them, then we could really begin to be friends.

I learned that John was a respected elder in his community, that some still relied upon men like him for advice and insight. I asked if John could take us fishing. It was possible; the sea appeared to be in the right mood, and I understood that the fish were always cooperative. It wasn't a bark canoe this time, just an ordinary dugout with a makeshift sail. John pointed to a shimmering shadow and raised his spear. Somehow he was able to compensate for the aberration of the image caused by the water. He took aim—not at the fish but somewhat to its side and a little ahead. Then a quick thrust, and out came the wriggling prey to join the others in the bottom of the boat.

The Maningrida settlement is one of the more recently developed government projects for Aborigines. It came into being out of simple necessity. Aborigines living in the central Arnhem Land coastal plain had begun to get a taste of the Western style of life during and after World War II (a period of increased traffic throughout the entire southwestern Pacific). At least 100 Aborigines wandered into Darwin hoping to find what seemed then a better life: tools, weapons, clothes, amusements, as well as the intangibles that civilization had exhibited to them over the past decade.

Social Welfare administrators in Darwin attempted to turn back the Aborigines, but without success. They kept coming back like lemmings to an urban fate they were totally unprepared for. And so the government decided to set up the Maningrida settlement as a half-way station that would enable Aborigines to adjust to civilized life in an artificial urban situation. Life in Maningrida is infinitely better than among a band of city derelicts, and it places less strain on the welfare resources of the government. But for many Aborigines—and there are some 800 in Maningrida at present—it may be too late in their lives to make the changes that would enable them to live among and be accepted by the white Australian community. Many find themselves with neither a wholesome tribal life nor anything more than a shabby imitation of urbanized society.

On our return flight to Darwin we made a detour to Oenpelli Mission, about 175 miles to the southeast. Before the Church Missionary Society took over this property in 1925 in a weedy, rundown condition, it had served as the setting for a noble but unsuccessful experimental plan to make this area an important center for dairy farming, cotton and vegetable crops. All went well until insects that had for ages contented themselves on plants like the river fig discovered the cotton; weeds, nut grass and termites did the rest. Moreover, there were incidents in which union workers refused to handle Oenpelli butter (before it spoiled) because they objected to the use of "black labor." The worst of the Oenpelli failure was its effect on the Aborigines. Having grown used to working for the white man, they wandered westward dejectedly and settled along the railway line in small towns—a detribalized people.

Aborigines who have suffered setbacks like these have relatively little to lose by entering the missions. At Oenpelli I saw Europeans and Aborigines who worked nine hours a day in abattoirs through which we were guided by a young missionary. Here they butcher twelve buffaloes daily and pack them for shipment. But Oenpelli has continued to have more than its share of bad luck. The buffaloes here are wild, like those on Brazil's Island of Marajo, and they are not indigenous. A few years ago a severe drought struck the area and thousands of them converged on the dried-up lake on the mission grounds, where they died in large numbers. The depleted herd departed just before the rains came.

Back in Darwin I had the opportunity of talking with a few patrol officers at a hotel bar. We got around to speaking about the differences between Australian law and Aboriginal tribal codes. It was a subject, I pointed out, that had always interested me: men accustomed to Western concepts of justice imposing their laws on people who have worked out over many centuries a perfectly adequate system of their own. For example, among the Aborigines incest, as they define it, is frequently punished by death. The same punishment applies to Aborigines who disclose ritual secrets to inappropriate members of their group, like young boys or women. Would anyone responsible for carrying out a death sentence be charged with murder under Australian law? On the other hand, stealing is not thought of as a crime among the Aborigines because they simply do not recognize property as private. One officer explained that Australian law had been modified in recent years so that judges were legally required to take into consideration all tribal aspects of acts of violence. He gave me several examples of this attempt to respect tribal law, one of which, I think is worth repeating.

In 1955 in central Australia, an Aboriginal named Selly had undergone a highly secret ritual which involved smearing blood on his body. According to tribal law the blood could not be exhibited to a woman, at least not until it had worn off somewhat in the normal process of everyday activities.

Like many other young men in other times and places, Selly was interested in a young girl, and for her he broke the taboo: he showed her the ceremonial blood, and what took place between them is not known. However, the tribal elders learned of the incident, and they decided that death was the appropriate punishment. They also determined that the young men in Selly's age-set should do the killing.

The appointed executioners found themselves in a quandary because they had attended school and knew what the consequences of such a killing might be. The elders, told of their reluctance, used the full power of their ceremonial and age-set influence. Eventually, the young men who had been commissioned to satisfy Aboriginal justice gave in. Although they were still fearful and possibly may even have felt a Western sense of guilt, they agreed to carry out the traditional act.

Somehow Selly learned that his transgression had been discovered and that he was to be punished. Dreading punishment, he lived very cautiously and spent most of his time in the nearby government settlement in the company of Europeans. But a few members of his age-set reassured him and won his confidence, at least to the extent that he permitted himself to attend a relatively unimportant tribal ceremony on a Sunday afternoon. It was a Corroboree (a word used by whites to describe a wide range of Aboriginal ceremonies—anything from a campfire *singsing* to an important religious ceremony with song-cycles and dances), and having lost his apprehension he joined in the dancing, singing and eating. At a prearranged signal one member of his age-set came up from behind, grabbed him by his right hand and under his chin, twisting his head and breaking his neck. Selly was dead; the patrol officers were told that the victim had fallen from a cliff. The story was believed in the settlement, at least for a time.

Selly's relatives in south Australia learned the true circumstances of his death and came north seeking vengeance. They complained to the superintendent of the settlement who, in turn, began an investigation. Eventually, the young man who did the actual killing—and only that young man—was brought to trial. Found guilty, he was sentenced to one year in prison at hard labor.

This sentence may seem like a reasonable compromise between Western standards of justice and criminal law on the one hand and Aboriginal justice on the other. It certainly does not represent an eye for an eye, and I doubt that Selly's relatives were entirely happy with the sentence. However, for an Aboriginal even one year in prison is a terrible fate. Selly's executioner tolerated prison life for only about six months. A resourceful and hardy young man, he escaped and traveled at the rate of thirty-five miles a day, racing over sand hills on his way to his home southwest of Alice Springs, pursued all the way by a party of police trackers mounted on camels. (These had been introduced into Australia many years ago, just as they were once unsuccessfully introduced into the American Southwest.)

His trail led them to a place where he had killed a couple of rabbits and tied their skins to his feet so as to conceal his tracks. The pursuit ended there, but about six months later he turned up at a mission in southwestern Australia, and there he was apprehended and brought back to trial again in Alice Springs. The judge did not hand down an additional sentence; the offender was told that he had only to serve out the remaining six months of his original sentence. This he was able to do as a result of having had a taste of freedom.

On this 1969 trip I also spoke to the author and journalist, Douglas Lockwood. Lockwood has accompanied a number of patrols into Pintubi country, a barren wasteland extending about 500 miles west of Alice Springs, which is the geographical center of the continent of Australia. In 1963 he headed a patrol and covered much of this area in a four-wheel-drive Land Rover on an assignment for Harry Giese's Northern Territory Administration Welfare Branch. The Pintubi were widely scattered, many living nomadic lives in the Gibson Desert where only the hardiest plants—spinfex, mulga, ti-trees and desert oaks—can survive, and where the available food is limited to lizards, rodents, grubs, dingoes and wildcats. Water is, of course, the scarcest commodity there, and only small family groups of five to ten men, women and children can hope to be supported by the environment. In these circumstances, many Aborigines remained beyond the reach of Europeans for the better part of two centuries. They were protected by the harshness of the desert, a region the outsiders have regarded as unnecessary to conquer. Here they survive by owning little, wearing nothing, and carrying only a few implements that might be regarded as essential.

To the Western mind the more you can possess, the more secure you will be; the greater your capital, the more you can accomplish. The Aboriginal viewpoint is quite the reverse. In his desert home, the Aboriginal does more on less—possessions are pointlessly encumbering. A few spears, a spear thrower and a firestick are all he needs. His wife will carry a digging stick and on her head a large wooden bowl in which she will put winnow grass seed, an important food resource. Anything else would cut down their mobility, their comfort and their sense of well-being.

Modern man cannot understand an attitude which rejects property and possessions. For the civilized person things are an extension of his ego, his sense of self-worth. At the same time modern man has very little connection with the land; the earth for him is something to pass through or over as quickly as possible, something to pollute or to cover with houses and factories, capital to use up. For the Aboriginal, it is an extension of himself; he belongs to it and it belongs to him. He is everywhere at home, and no single place is his house.

This was, at least, the pattern of Aboriginal nomadic life in the past. When Lockwood visited the Gibson Desert in 1963, important changes were already taking place. A few years earlier in 1959, the government set up one of its major settlements at Papunya, about 132 miles west of Alice Springs. Here, as part of official Australian policy, Aborigines would theoretically learn to adjust to the ways of the white, civilized world, so that eventually they could take a position of equality along with Australians of European origin. Lockwood told me that at Papunya he saw the Aborigines who might be called seminomadic. He found children at the settlement school who were still eating dingoes, lizards and desert rodents. But they were being introduced to bread, beef and fruit—foodstuffs they had never seen in their nomadic days. Before coming to the settlement, the Aborigines had never seen water coming from a tap, or a tin of food, a building, a cow or a horse. Aircraft had flown over their lands, but they were regarded as some inexplicable, supernatural phenomenon like flying devils. When they appeared the Aborigines would hide themselves in the shrubs or bury themselves in the sand.

How well was the assimilation process going now? I decided that a visit to Papunya was an essential part of my itinerary.

On the way to the airport I had a last good look at Darwin. It still is very much a frontier town, but because of its strategic location it is growing in every way. Our taxi driver was a chatty Aussie who told me that the owner of the cab was part Aborigine, a really nice fellow, he said, who usually takes over the night shift. He added that in his thirty years in Darwin he had seen many Aborigines become first-rate electricians, carpenters and craftsmen of all kinds. He was proud of the fact that they were some of the best athletes in Australia. I asked him if he thought that there was much prejudice in Darwin. He offered to bet me that I would find less bigotry there than in any other place in Australia. "It's a town of many nationalities," he said. "We have learned to accept one another." As I was paying the fare, he leaned closer and said proudly, "You wait until they get a bit more education. They'll do great things!" I told him I was sure they would and started to look for my plane. At the airport I saw American troops from Vietnam on their way to Sydney for holiday leave. The newspaper I bought to read on the plane was full of tributes to the late mayor of Darwin, a very popular figure who had received a spectacular funeral. He was Chinese.

It was a five-hour flight from Darwin to Alice Springs in an old Friendship plane—a distance of about 900 miles with many stops. The town is situated on both sides of the Todd River, which is about 100 yards wide and only a dry sandy bed for the greater part of the year. On this dry bed I saw many Aborigines living in lean-tos; they move onto the banks during the wet season. There are no other places for them to stay while they are in town. Alice Springs functions as an administrative center for the southern part of the Northern Territory and as a supply center and railhead for the outlying cattle stations. The town is a base for the flying physician who tends patients by radio, except when they require hospitalization—and then he picks them up in a specially fitted plane. Here there is also a "school of the air" for children in the Outback, as the undeveloped lands are called. The town is a marketplace for Aboriginal art and artifacts, and tourists (mostly from the larger Australian cities) use it as a base for their trips into the surrounding country.

I decided to spend a day or so in breath-catching before flying on to Papunya. The Alice Springs hotel was not really first- or even second-rate. The owner was a burly, unkempt and rather loud-talking bloke. He told me that he had converted the adjoining lot into a beer garden with the hope of attracting Europeans. However, it was now patronized exclusively by Aborigines— when the Europeans saw a few of the native people there, they abandoned it as a drinking spot. The Europeans congregate on the second floor of the hotel where in the evening a crowd of young Aussie swingers dance to rock music. A few half-bloods venture up to the second floor occasionally, but they seem self-conscious there.

From our first floor terrace I was able to watch the Aboriginal beer garden directly beneath. As early as nine o'clock in the morning men and women could be seen building a fire in the center in a gasoline drum. They bought their beer at a kiosk bar run by a slender Aussie barmaid. Many of the Aborigines had come in from outback cattle stations and were costumed like cowboys in movie westerns.

Despite the fact that a visit to the beer garden was frowned upon by Europeans, on the following day I noticed an Aussie there wearing crisp khaki shorts and decided to go down and join him. He was a taboo-breaker of sorts himself, an engineer who had lived in Aboriginal country for fifteen years. We went over to the kiosk for a couple of beers, and there I had the opportunity to meet the barmaid—a matriarchal personality who ruled her Aboriginal customers with the proverbial iron hand in a velvet glove. She treated them gently but firmly, telling them when they had had enough to drink. She kept them in line and, as far as I could tell, no one attempted to contest her rulings.

Around me were small knots of men and women, uninhibited in their talk, singing and playing on various stringed instruments. As the morning progressed, I saw that some would stagger around from group to group. At one point we were in the center of a cluster of people, and one Aboriginal weaved in among us and walked off with my beer. I ordered another from the barmaid who shrugged slightly and gave me a smile as if to acknowledge this gentle theft. She seemed to be saying that there were worse things in this world than sharing your beer with an Aboriginal.

The barmaid turned from me and spoke to a young woman with very large black eyes, wavy hair, sensuous lips.

"Aren't you supposed to be at work, Minnie?" the barmaid asked.

"I walked out. Not for me that job," the young woman answered.

"How are you going to pay for your beers now?"

The young woman did not respond. She tilted her head back and smiled at the clouds. I wondered why she had left the job and asked the barmaid.

Minnie did, in fact, tell me what I wanted to know, getting right to the point as though she were accustomed to being questioned about her personal life by strangers. I offered to buy her a beer which she accepted with a pert nod.

"The Boss," she explained, "likes to play around every time Missus go away. Missus away, Boss play." She laughed at the unintentional rhyme and continued. "I don't care. Lots of black girls in town have the same thing happen. Bigfeller Boss always say 'Now you come here Minnie. This time you make it good.' And he go into bedroom. I better follow."

Minnie told me that she had had her share of romances with stockmen, bagmen, prospectors and white hunters in the bush; she was no prude. It was somehow different with them.

The barmaid cut in at this point to explain that Minnie had worked in the household of a well-to-do and socially respected businessman in Alice Springs. But why, I asked, did Minnie object to the sexual advances of her employer and not those of the men she had met in the outback? Were they more subtle in their approach? It was only partly that, Minnie explained. Some of the white bosses she knew were as crude in communicating their sexual needs as the stereotypes of the Aborigines who knocked their women on the head with a club and dragged them off. They treated black girls like chattel and expected them to follow whenever they headed for the bedroom.

"And there *is* something worse than that?" I asked.

"It's the worst thing of all," Minnie said. "The Boss always hate himself when everything is finished. He say or look like he has done something very bad. Then he hates me. First he love me, then he hates me. That is bad. That is the worst thing of all. He say he can't help it that he want 'Black Velvet.' But he make himself feel dirty.

"I like it better out there in the bush," Minnie concluded. "Those stockmen want me, and they never say they feel bad. And they know what I like, too. They give me things. I got a dilly bag full of dresses. Out there I don't even wear them all the time. I can be naked if I want. Not here."

"Yes, the good ladies of Alice wouldn't like that at all," the barmaid interjected.

I ordered another beer for Minnie, thanked her, and left. It was time to make plans for getting to Papunya.

Papunya seemed to epitomize all the problems left to be solved in the assimilation program. It is situated approximately 150 miles west of Alice Springs; there are about a thousand Aborigines there, comprising four tribal groups: Pintubi, Ngalia, Wailbri and Aranda. There are also some members of the Loritja tribe. The buildings were designed to enable the more primitive or unsophisticated Aboriginals to move in with a minimum of stress: aluminum frame windows, galvanized iron roofing, a fireplace, a surrounding veranda. There are also washing and toilet facilities; attempts to explain their importance in maintaining public health have met with indifferent success. And no matter what the roofing is, the Aborigines do not like the feeling of being boxed in. They prefer to encamp at the fringes of the settlement among their own people and apart from the members of other tribes. Here they live in miserable shelters and lean-tos covered with branches and dirty pieces of tattered canvas. I saw them sitting about, bewildered and lackluster, wearing filthy European clothes, believing for some reason that this was the place for them to be, yet resisting the settlement itself—as if they had abandoned both the past and the future. On the whole, they were the saddest looking group of people—primitive or otherwise—that I had ever seen.

Of course, there were explanations; there were reasons for this failure to induce Aborigines to live in "settlements." And if there were causes there might also be cures. But at what cost?

The Aborigines do not take to living in houses in the Papunya settlement because it has always been their custom to live out-of-doors, to sleep on the earth and to move with natural changes in their environment. They are natural conservationists and prefer to do more with less. The Pintubi lived where there was little water, and they simply are not accustomed to lavishing water on themselves. When a death occurs, they abandon that dwelling place, as do the other Aboriginal groups at Papunya. A centrally organized village seems pointless to them.

It will take time, but sooner or later I suspect that the Pintubi will be willing to live in common villages with the Wailbri and the Ngalia. They will surrender their attitudes toward death and remain where they are when a member of the family dies. They will give up living under the sky and accept the galvanized-iron roofing and the encircling veranda, along with what the Australian administrators refer to as the "ablution facilties." They will keep their children in settlement schools. This much is quite predictable. What type of person will eventually come out of the settlements is not.

Richard Gould, an anthropologist with the American Museum of Natural History, in his excellent book *Yiwarra* quotes from a report issued by the deputy commissioner of Public Health in Australia. It sums up fairly my impression of the Papunya mission: "There is some irresistible attraction towards centers of white man's culture that leads more and ever more natives from being aristocrats in the seclusion of their own hunting ground to graduate to a form of rudimentary education and a system of missions to become unemployables in the squalor of native camps."

The administrators point out that they are hampered by lack of funds; if they had more money, they say, they could make the settlements and reservations fit the Aboriginal needs more closely. And they are partly right. But money doesn't solve all the problems. The anthropologists say that assimilation of traditional peoples, especially rapid assimilation, will bring an inevitable disorientation. And they are right, too.

As for the Aborigines themselves, they have only begun to make their feelings on assimilation known. There are few nationally recognized leaders among them, not enough to make very much noise. They are accustomed to the leadership of groups or councils within clans and tribes and have little concept of nationhood other than that of the non-Aboriginal Australia which has been imposed upon them. When they do produce individual spokesmen, the whites, who are better attuned to national political voices, will listen more attentively than the Aborigines. There is often an open channel of communication between the educated Aboriginal and the media-oriented white Australia rather than between the same Aboriginal and his alienated people. Moreover, as the Aborigines are deprived of their land-based social identity, they lose the only kind of home it makes sense for them to defend, as Aborigines.

Despite the problems of leadership and national identity, Aborigines are voicing increased opposition to the official policy of assimilation. Some Aboriginal spokesmen are practicing a form of militancy comparable in method and rhetoric to that of the Indians and blacks in the United States. The National Tribal Council in Melbourne, which offers to speak on behalf of all the Aborigines, has called for a "Reacculturation" program to restore native traditions through seminars and courses similar to the black studies approach in the United States. In 1970 there was an Aboriginal sit-in on some British-owned cattle land northwest of Alice Springs, and in 1971 a vigorous movement to protect Aboriginal land rights on the Gove Peninsula of Arnhemland, near Yirkalla, was gaining force until blocked by a court ruling in favor of an international bauxite combine.

In the Yirkalla land rights case the judge ruled that the colonial philosophy of opening "the whole earth . . . to the industry and enterprise of the human race" took precedence over the Aboriginal's "spiritual" attachment to the land. "The more advanced peoples," Justice Richard Blackburn said, "are justified in dispossessing, if necessary, the less advanced." Decisions of this sort can only stiffen the Aboriginal's resistance to assimilation. Some months before this case came to a head, Bruce McGuiness, a leader of the National Tribal Council and a man who likes to use Black Panther terminology, had already served notice to white Australia. "We want our land and the wealth that honky dug out of it," he said.

To resist assimilation through some kind of militant front, Black Panther style or not, might only prove to be a short-cut toward the loss of tribal identity. It would be a sad irony if, in order to be heard, the Aborigines had to create a national style that was remote from their own most precious traditions. It would be another instance of the primitive being stymied whether he fought back or not.

One Aboriginal leader, Robert Maza, had spoken out for a union of black Australians shortly before my arrival in 1969. And what he said as president of the Aborigines' Advancement League of Victoria may represent an emerging point of view. Whether it prevails or not, it is worth hearing, I think, because in a sense he may be speaking for traditional cultures in the process of assimilation in all parts of the world.

"We see the fruits of the white man's coming," Maza wrote in the League journal, *Smoke Signals*, "where he has beaten the black man into submission. He has taken away his culture and land, made him wear clothes, turned him into a beggar, forced him into becoming a black parasite, continually living on handouts."

Maza went on to call for a national "welding together" of black men with a new sense of pride in their heritage while offering pity to "black integrateds who are playing the part of white men."

He adds: ". . . Let us not be too hasty in rushing into a society that is at present floundering, where purse strings govern the outcome . . . where the leaders of the country smear each other's names for their own selfish gains, and require armed guards to protect their own people.

"Can't we take what is good of this society and improve on it by adding the knowledge of our forefathers—so-called primitives—whose society had evolved a perfect harmony of coexistence?

"... We could teach the whites how to live simply by adopting the ethics and principles of our people which are almost completely lost."

13 New Guinea:
Time Was No Enemy

NEW GUINEA, with the Mato Grosso, represents the last important bastion of primitive man to feel the impact of civilization; it is changing more rapidly than the other transitional societies I have seen in recent years. Here, ten thousand years of cultural history have been experienced in only a few decades. To Western minds accustomed to almost daily challenges to traditional beliefs and to new discoveries and ways of life, this kind of leap out of the past may be difficult to conceive. The wonder is that about 3,000,000 New Guineans have not only been putting aside ancient methods of governing, dressing, fighting and moving about, but that they have so far remained on the whole a vital people who believe that they have a distinguished future.

When I returned to New Guinea in 1969 (my two earlier visits had been in 1958 and 1959), I learned that modernization was bringing problems faster than even the wisest and best men were producing solutions. However, the New Guineans are not about to die off or disappear into government settlements and reservations, leaving behind only a few bad consciences. Unlike the Aborigines of neighboring Australia and hard-hit primitive communities on other continents, they had been spared much of the callousness of earlier colonialism by virtue of some of the world's most rugged terrain. Mountains, gorges, dense forests and torrential rivers are packed more closely here than anywhere on earth. New Guinea is big; it is, in fact, the second largest island in the world.

The New Guinea highlands have been especially free from the incursions of outsiders. As recently as 1933, only twenty-five years before my first expedition there, the gold-prospecting Taylor-Leahy expedition brought back word that more than half a million primitives lived there with no knowledge of metal, the wheel, pottery or the sea. Of this region, the Wahgi Valley, Mick Leahy was to report after a second reconnaissance that it was "an island of population so effectively hemmed in by mountains that the rest of the world had not even suspected its existence." Several hundred thousand more primitives were discovered in 1938 in what was then called Dutch New Guinea and is now Indonesian West Irian. It was still possible during my 1969 visit to New Guinea to search out and talk to Mick Leahy and to Keith McCarthy, a former patrol officer and legendary explorer, so recent has been the opening up of the island's interior. Not until World War II did outsiders get a really good look at the large green stone axes, the elaborate cassowary and bird of paradise headpieces, the nose shells and grass skirts, all of which are exhibited in annual festivals that attract thousands of tourists to yesterday's *terra incognita*.

More like the warlike Jivaros of South America than the unfortunate Aborigines of Australia, the primitive people of New Guinea were never a passive people, nor much given to trusting intruders. The earliest German explorers, traveling up the Sepik River in the 1880s, were forced by the hostile natives to remain in the middle of the stream throughout most of their 380-mile trip. Mick Leahy was severely clobbered by club-wielding Kukukukus while prospecting for gold in the 1930s. The only thing Europeans have found amusing about that people is their name. The Kukukukus, known for their ritual cannibalism as well as their unpredictable tempers, eat the leg and arm muscles of their victims in order to acquire their strength, and have been the subject of numerous grisly stories even within the past decade. Headhunting, too, is far from unknown in New Guinea. It is a curious commentary on civilized man's relations with primitive peoples that a really "bad press" is sometimes the most effective means by which the "natives" are permitted, at least for a time, to live as they always have. However, atrocity stories have often served as a pretext for genocidal raids, as the history of the American Indians instructs us. But here again, the people of New Guinea have been fortunate. With only a few exceptions, the Australian-administered eastern portion of the island, comprising Papua and northeastern New Guinea, has been the beneficiary of one of the more enlightened and tactful patrol services anywhere. This cannot be said for the Indonesian portion of the island, where government troops have had to be sent in to quell uprisings of tribesmen.

In short, this chapter is not an obituary of the people of New Guinea; they have not been overwhelmed. They may have been divested of many of their ancient beliefs and in many cases old ways are giving out before new ways can be apprehended and adopted. The primitive splendor is fading, but viable communities have survived and leaders have emerged with keen minds and Western-style professional skills. There is even much talk in Australian-administered Papua-New Guinea about the eventuality of self-government. In April, 1971, a special committee of the territorial legislature called for self-government between 1972 and 1975, with full independence to follow at an unspecified date. Although there is not much agreement about the pace at which complete autonomy can be realized, the very existence of this controversy is proof that New Guineans, with a Stone Age past fresh in their memories, do take their future in the space age very seriously.

There is a certain historical irony in the fact that most primi-

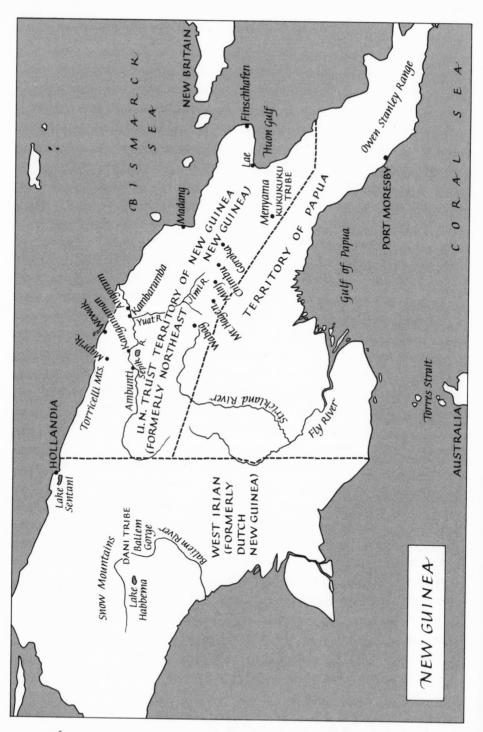

NEW GUINEA

196

tive societies were overwhelmed by invading colonizers, wealth seekers and military forces at times when Western life was still fairly simple—at least by today's standards. Had the original settlers of the Americas, for example, looked at the "Indians" as at least potential equals, both newcomer and host culture might have grown together in an increasingly complex world. Primitive societies presently emerging under relatively enlightened guidance, on the other hand, have much farther to go. They are, in fact, being asked to take on the style of the industrial West just when the Westerner appears to be throwing up his hands in despair over the complexities of a machine-heavy, atmosphere-polluted and ideologically fragmented civilization.

The people of New Guinea have come out of their cultural cocoon and are getting civilization in big doses. One day it is stone axes and digging sticks, blood feuds and sorcery, elaborate pig-roasting feasts and sweet-potato patches, wife-bashing and ancestor worship. The next day it is transistor radios, jet planes and helicopters, classrooms, law courts, democratic elections, unions and protest meetings. The typical emerging New Guinean may have seen some of the most advanced electronic equipment before he has seen a newspaper; a Land Rover, truck, or Jeep before he has seen a paved road; he may even have flown in a plane before he has seen a bicycle.

At the moment, many New Guineans understandably see technology as a magic that has literally been thrust upon them. The "miracles of modern science" have appealed to primitive imaginations and bizarre cults have formed, mysteriously fusing traditional superstitions with the artificially created product-hunger of today's consumer. But there are many New Guineans who are learning modern agriculture, who are receiving advanced training in engineering, law and medicine—many of them in their own country at the new and rapidly growing University of Papua-New Guinea.

In the 1950s the Australian administration assessed the intelligence levels of selected groups of these Stone Age people, using supposedly "culture-free" IQ tests, and discovered that the intelligence of peoples in Papua and New Guinea was "most likely" equal to that of Europeans. All New Guineans may not be moving into the twentieth century at quite the same pace, but that should not be attributed to native dullness, but rather to problems that might well affect any people in a period of rapid change. "They are moving," Margaret Mead has said, "more quickly than any people have ever moved at first contact."

Beyond all this, it is not easy to sum up New Guinea as it prepares to take its place in the modern world. The island itself hovers over Australia like some huge prehistoric bird, with a spine more than 1,000 miles long. In Papua and northeastern New Guinea alone (referred to as Papua-New Guinea and administered jointly by Australia), there are over 700 linguistic groups with an average of a few thousand members per group. There are still many mutually hostile tribes. No one is quite certain where the New Guineans originally came from, except that there were probably a number of migratory waves from Melanesia and Polynesia and probably from the mainland of Asia.

Europeans began arriving after the Portuguese Jorge de Meneses discovered western New Guinea in 1527 and named it *Os Papuas* (*Papuas* meaning "frizzle-haired"). Since that time the Dutch, French, Germans, British (later the Australians), Japanese (1942–1945) and Indonesians have barely left their impress upon the island. It has a frustrating way of swallowing its invaders. Now that the indigenous people are themselves taking a hand in shaping their future—especially in the eastern half—a new culture amalgamating both the old and the new is beginning to emerge.

What the future will bring may be as difficult to forecast as it would have been to predict the future history of the British Isle after 1066. It is possible, however, to speak of the individuals who are in the process of making the future: the white Australian minority (sometimes referred to as "expatriates") as well as the indigenous people who will understandably be shouldering increasing responsibilities and burdens in the years ahead.

Port Moresby, the territorial capital, is not typical of Papua-New Guinea as a whole, but that is where much of the business of the country takes place, and it is where a visitor is most likely to arrive. There are nearly 33,000 indigenes there, many of them from other parts of the territory. There is also a high percentage of Europeans—about 10,000—and almost 1,000 Chinese and people of mixed races. We were met at our hotel by Lady Rachel Cleland, wife of Sir Donald Cleland, the retired administrator of Papua-New Guinea and our host during our stay in Port Moresby. We all agreed that the new university would be a good place at which to begin our tour of the city. The future of New Guineans certainly depends on the quality and quantity of education they will be getting, and here the potential leaders of the decades to come will be trained, and here future difficulties are most visible.

My first impression of Port Moresby was that everything had gotten up to date, like Kansas City in the song of the same name from *Oklahoma*. I soon grew tired of hearing myself exclaim, "But that wasn't here in 1959!" or "Where did all this come from?" As we drove toward the university grounds on the outskirts of town, we went down streets that hadn't been paved or hadn't even existed ten years earlier. There were new air-conditioned hotels, motels, theaters and shopping centers, and there were many more crisply dressed indigenes than I remembered. There were others, too, more shabbily dressed, who seemed to have just come in from their villages that day.

The university was still being constructed then and the temporary buildings were replaced by permanent structures in 1970. The campus sprawls over a beautiful 1,000-acre site with the foothills of the Owen Stanley Range in the distance. It was first envisioned during a walk over this property by Cleland and Dr. John Gunther (now the university's vice chancellor). In 1966 its first students, representing the class of 1970, began arriving. Before its founding, native New Guineans who wanted advanced education had to go to Australia, where they had no alternative but to accept roles as minorities and outsiders. Now they are able to attend a school which is dedicated to the future of its own people. Eventually there will be room for 10,000 students, but as of 1971 there were about 800 attending full time, most—but not all—native New Guineans.

A university is an expensive necessity in any society. The first major building complex at Port Moresby cost $1.5 million and contains an impressive library, science block, classrooms, laboratories and a lecture theater. But the cost of producing education is not the only problem, as Americans have been learning in the last few years. Traditionally, the idea of a university, as the word itself suggests, implies a single and unified sphere of values and belief supported by the originating culture. The question in America might well be whether the universities, having grown physically immense, can any longer represent themselves as reflecting either a unified culture or a national society that is or will remain in one piece. In New Guinea the problem is not entirely dissimilar, but it has obviously different sources.

The lack of national unity in New Guinea is not the result of the kind of fragmentation that occurs in an advanced industrial society with global commitments and with rapidly changing values at home. For centuries New Guineans have lived in tribal societies, at war with their neighbors, influenced by mutual fears and the practice of sorcery, kept apart by forbidding terrain. As a consequence they have grown apart culturally and linguistically, and these differences have further reinforced their separateness. For many of them the village and the clan are their universe, and the idea of national institutions is one of the most perplexing of foreign imports.

Although I have not heard it expressed in so many words, the new university is intended to weld some kind of national consciousness. Its major problem is that such a consciousness does not yet exist—for these are a people without a history of national leaders or national politics and, perhaps most important, without a national language. In short, without nationhood. For many of the students English is a second or third language. They must deal with the same irony that has confronted emerging preliterate peoples in all parts of the world: having to learn an unfamiliar language in their own land if they wish to have a significant role in running their country.

Some forward-looking missionary groups, notably the Summer Institute of Linguistics, are using the latest linguistic techniques in making the scriptures available to the indigenous people of New Guinea (as they have done in South America and elsewhere) in their own dialects. There are also bastard tongues like Pidgin and Motu that have eased communication between the administration and the indigenes. However, English is inevitably the language of technical manuals, advanced texts in all fields, and it is the language that the English-speaking instructors are best able to use. Although English is being taught in Australian-administered New Guinea beginning with the primary grades, there has been no adequate home or social environment for this language to reinforce the students' grasp of it. As a result teachers in the university complained about the "language gap" as the principal cause of the slow progress of many students.

This reminded me of what I had heard in northern Alaska, where teachers on the primary and secondary levels told me that because English was not used in the students' homes, both they and the young Eskimos were having difficulty discussing the same subject in the same terms. On the other hand, those Eskimos who had broken away from their own language and their own culture were experiencing a separation from their families and the traditional authority of the village elders. And this, too, seems to be a disturbing pattern in New Guinea—although I do not believe that the rupture is as serious there as it seems to be in both Alaska and among the Aborigines of Australia.

In New Guinea there is still a surprising amount of family togetherness evidenced in the way an entire set of relatives will often descend upon one of their number who has gotten a good job in town. Shanty villages have sprung up around the perimeters of many cities. These are filled with family members who are dependent upon a few job-holders in the group and who, in turn, accept the burden with a stoicism that usually exasperates the work-ethic-oriented Australian expatriates. Many of the university people believe that the progress of education in New Guinea is being slowed by genuine fears that learning, Western style, will result in a gradual but irreversible alienation between the learner and his family with their traditions.

These are not, of course, unreasonable fears. There may be no way in which higher education in New Guinea can serve as a matrix for the new Western-influenced culture while at the same time serving as support for the indigenous cultures that are about to disappear. Students can indeed be taught about the history of their people, and they are certainly better off if they can take pride in it rather than feel a sense of shame. But studying one's history is not quite the same thing as living it or believing that ancient ways can serve for tomorrow.

Margaret Mead, in a film made during a recent visit to New Guinea, admonished a group of young people to remain true to their heritage, to remember always that their past should be a source of pride, for however far from home they might travel— socially, educationally or geographically—their futures would otherwise be built on sand.

This piece of advice impressed me because what I have seen in the course of my own travels points to its truth. Yet it will be difficult advice to follow for those who have already gone to school without participating, for example, in the lengthy and painful initiation rites that have been practiced for perhaps over a thousand years, or for those children who will grow up without being taught to distrust women and to shed some blood which is the woman's part of them. The past will be less meaningful to those children who will never see an authentic pig feast or attend a ceremonial *sing-sing*. For future generations it may be more like remembering that grandmother was a Chimbu.

The best hope for cultural continuity in transitional New Guinea may rest with educated middle-aged New Guineans and a few younger men who still preserve memories of their Stone Age childhood at the same time that they are learning how to live in a Westernized future. It may be up to them to develop a sense of cultural identity with roots in the past, one that can be transmitted to coming generations. They will not be able to carry over the feuds and the initiation rites, the terror of the sorcerer and the joy of the feast, but they may be able to produce by their own example an idea of what it means to be an emerging New Guinean with a Stone Age heritage in the twentieth century.

One such example might be Albert Maori Kiki, a former patrol officer and medical student who has gone on to help found and lead the Pangu Party of Papua-New Guinea. In many ways he typifies the New Guinean who has been brought up under ancient traditions and has made himself heard—although not to everyone's liking—in the New Guinea of today. For this reason and because his life mirrors the changes that have taken place there I should like to describe him and to record his views. I did not get to meet him until near the end of my trip in 1969, when Sir Donald Cleland arranged it, explaining that Kiki's background and views were a portent of the changes to come in New Guinea.

14 New Guinea: Politican with a Stone Age Memory

KIKI AND HIS FAMILY live in Hohola, one of the suburban villages in the Port Moresby area that have mushroomed in recent years. Another local village, Hanuabada, is a prime example of an exploding coastal community which, since the war, has turned into a cluster of shanty-towns built from metal scrap, abandoned military equipment, packing cases and other available junk. Although impromptu settlements like Hanuabada supply much of the urban labor force, the number of squatters far exceeds the employed. At their worst such slums seem no better than the slums around Alice Springs in Australia or in other parts of the formerly colonial world where native peoples have been uprooted from their traditional lands and have streamed like lemmings toward the bright lights and the expected handouts.

Hohola, by contrast, represents an attempt by the administration to establish healthful and attractive living conditions at least for those New Guineans who can afford them—men like Kiki who hold respectable government jobs or organizational posts in the capital—and who form the new indigenous elite. Naturally, the accommodations for Australian expatriates are infinitely superior; they must be "attracted" to work in New Guinea and the bait is air-conditioned hotel and apartment accommodations. These differences in living standards as well as the obvious disparity in jobs and pay rates have done little to advance interracial understanding—a point that Kiki has been making for more than ten years.

The living conditions. in the indigenous villages around Port Moresby are not without political overtones. Everything that happens in the capital area is, so to speak, in the national spotlight and moreover is likely to attract even global attention. Besides, colonial administrators have become aware that slums and ghettos are potential trouble spots; they breed not only crime but the anger and resentment that fuel radical discontent. That is where the "bad apples" are grown.

In Hohola there are neat rows of houses, many of them of concrete and brick; they are designed for families already accustomed to Western standards of living rather than for people who have only recently left their grass huts. There are no training settlements here like those near Alice Springs with their "external ablution facilities" to serve as transitional housing.

Kiki's house, although modest by Australian standards, is one of the larger cottages in Hohola. It is surrounded by a wooden fence, and there is a neat garden with flower beds. He pays $10.25 (Australian) each fortnight under the terms of a thirty-year mortgage. Kiki injected himself into the housing issue in 1963 when the government began to allocate even smaller one-room bachelors' quarters to large families. As chairman of the Hohola Progress Association, Kiki passed along to the administration what he calls "a strong resolution" protesting the fact that kitchen, bath and sleeping accommodations for all were in the same room; there wasn't enough room for beds; women had to dress in the presence of others; there were holes in the brick walls for ventilation, but no adequate protection against the rain; the houses, he insisted, were substandard. This is one battle that Kiki must still fight; scores of families still live in these houses despite the headlines his protest stirred up ("New Houses Not Worth a Penny").

There is no doubt in New Guinea that Kiki is a scrapper. He takes his personal motto from his uncle's name, Haure, given to the old man in his warrior days. It means "I don't like" and suggests, says Kiki, "one who fought to the finish, one who does not accept compromise." This same maternal uncle, many years earlier, tied the shell band to Kiki's forehead during the sacred initiation ceremonies of the *Kovave* festival. (The *Kovave* is the first mask a young man is made to wear, and it is only the maternal uncle who can make the gesture which symbolizes the transfer of power from one generation to another.) Only recently, Kiki had visited his uncle, and old Haure had placed his hand on his nephew's forehead, using the ritual gesture, and told Kiki to keep on fighting for what he believed no matter how difficult or lonely the way might be and without being swayed by what people might say about him. Kiki had been moved, of course; he obviously loved the old man and everything he stood for: determination, bold confidence, pride and strength. Kiki is certain that he can feel Haure's strength flowing in his blood.

This advice is reminiscent of Margaret Mead's admonition to the young New Guineans, but Kiki is all the more fortunate for not having to hear it from an outsider—even a distinguished American anthropologist. I do not believe that all the anthropologists on earth are capable of instilling pride in a people once they have allowed themselves to be convinced that they are only the refuse of history.

Kiki will not participate in any more *Kovave* festivals. His children will receive a standard Western education. If he is to pass along to new generations of New Guineans a sense of their own strength it will have to be accomplished through imported political institutions and modern communications techniques. And this he has learned—or is learning. He knows how to campaign—although he had recently lost a hard-fought election—and he can speak to his own people in their own language while at the same time crashing into print a thousand miles away; he generally gets himself heard. His party, *Pangu Pati*, wields wide influence when it votes as a bloc in the House of Assembly, where occasionally (but hardly often enough for Kiki's followers) important decisions affecting New Guinea's future are made. Kiki's forbears had a village, a clan, an extended family; he has a constituency.

Kiki is not a person you would have difficulty picking out in a crowd. He is self-assured and carries himself with the air of a man who has worked out his moves in advance. Yet he is spontaneous and entirely unguarded. He is articulate both in revealing his convictions and his passions. He is an easy man to talk to. His eyes are deep set and expressive; he is muscular, stocky, serene—the overall effect is one of solidity. During our talk he was visited by some of his political associates, and he asked them to wait in another room until we were finished. There was no attempt to rush our conversation along. He seemed very much a born leader. His middle name, in fact—Maori—was given to him by his father. It is an Orokolo word for the hornbill that leads its mates in flight.

Kiki is the inheritor of two cultures. He was born in 1931, the son of an Orokolo father and a Parevavo mother. The semi-nomadic Parevavo tribe live in the Papuan highlands along the banks of the Purari River; their customs and language resemble those of the Kukukukus who live in the east. The Orokolo are coastal people who live about 150 miles to the west of Port Moresby on Otokol Bay between the mouths of the Purari and Vailala Rivers. The latter were more knowledgeable of the ways of the white man, having had many more contacts than the Parevavo tribe. The elder Kiki was a village constable, a widower undergoing a two-year period of mourning when he met his future wife. Eau, Kiki's mother, had been married twice, had borne two children, and was herself in a state of mourning when the constable appeared in her village, accompanying a white patrol officer.

According to Kiki, the administration favored marriages between the native police and women from the outlying tribes as an effective means of introducing "civilized" concepts into the lives of "savage" peoples. The marriage suited Kiki's mother because she had already borne the number of children considered acceptable by her tribe and was therefore regarded as something of a matrimonial deadweight by her fellow villagers. Kiki's father was happy to marry again after a long period of mourning and, besides, here was an opportunity to avoid the usual lengthy negotiations and bride price arrangements. (Kiki explained that the men of the Parevavo tribe, unlike the Orokolo, did not bother with long and rigorous periods of mourning; they were too often fighting and could not afford to be shorthanded in their warrior strength.)

Soon after Kiki was born his mother took him back to her own people, where he spent his early years; she was uncomfortable with the coastal Orokolo, probably from the moment she had appeared among them—a strange sight, caked with mud and with a few leaves front and back to signify that she was a mourner. The Orokolo people must have recalled that many of their men had been killed by the Parevavo tribe when they accidentally strayed into their territory while hunting pigs. Eau tried to make herself useful in Orokolo; she was an expert midwife, and Kiki in later years accompanied her on many of her rounds, unaware that one day he would study medicine as it was practiced in the white man's world. Kiki remembers how his mother would rub the belly of the woman with her left hand, while her right hand supported the exposed head of the infant, and there would always be an incantation admonishing the child not to cling to the womb like a parasite, but to "let go, let go . . ." The future pathologist was proud that his mother had been successful in every case except one; the woman had died from loss of blood, and Eau had adopted the child. (It died a few years later.)

Eau was happy to be back with her own people; she had never learned to speak Elema, the language of her husband's people, nor could she accustom herself to fishing in salt water. It did not, then, much advance the cause of intertribal marriage. Kiki did not see his father until he was about five years old—there were no visits in either direction. So his early life was filled with the memory of living among a hunting and fighting people. There were no intrusions by Western institutions: no schools, no churches, and only an occasional visit from a *kiap*, the white patrol officer. It was, Kiki remembers, a pleasant, happy life with nothing about it to suggest that there was an outside world of any importance. The Parevavo tribe was constantly moving about. When they would deplete the game in one region, they would move on some fifty or sixty miles to the next hunting area. There were no gardens. There was, on the other hand, plenty of intertribal warfare. Attacks were constant: "If someone came to attack our village," Kiki told me, "next week it would be our turn to go and invade their village."

As the son of a village constable, even one more than fifty miles away, Kiki was taken to the coast where he was sent to the mission school. Tribal education, however, was still an important facet of Orokolo life, and when Kiki reached the age of ten, mission school or no mission school, he was put through the traditional initiation rites that would prepare him for manhood. The missionaries were accustomed to the disappearance of their pupils when they reached the age of ten or twelve. Anyway, there wasn't much they could do about it, and they usually offered their tacit consent. Kiki was taken to a sacred place in the bush, where he was subjected to a series of harsh beatings, following which he and the other initiants were given head masks to wear. Once he had demonstrated that he could stand pain, he and the other boys were brought back to the village and taken into the *eravo*, a ceremonial long house and keystone of New Guinea village culture—usually called a house-tamberan. There they remained for six or seven months—women were absolutely forbidden to enter—during which time they learned the customs and secrets of the society. Unlike the other boys, however, Kiki participated in the rituals of both his mother's and his father's peoples.

Massive jewelry proclaims that this Masai woman is married, but her husband will hardly ever get to see her without her unusual earrings. Masai women shave their heads while the men do not.

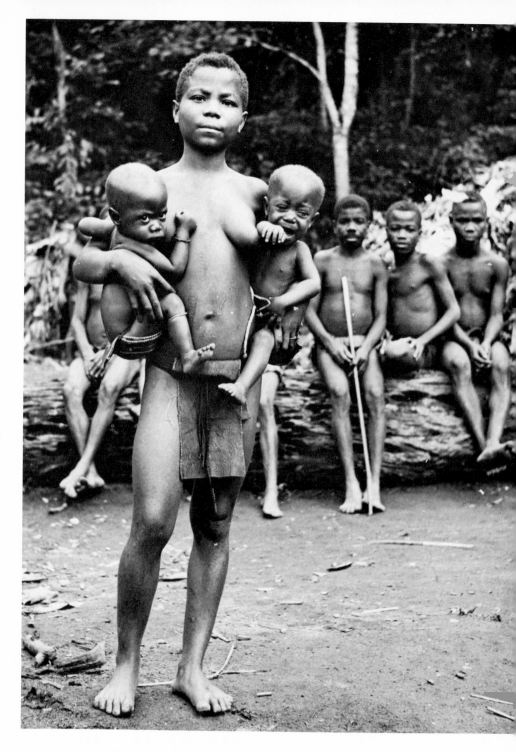

A rare first. Traditionally, among the Pygmies, twins were regarded as an ill omen and one was always put to death. As a result of the influence of missionary Bill Spees, this young Pygmy woman defied superstition and kept both babies. Curiously, the custom probably had its origins in the inability of a foodgathering mother (who must carry her child with her everywhere) to manage the burden of twins.

Hunter-gatherers *vs.* farmer-entrepreneurs. Pygmies from the Congo's Ituri Forest trade ivory and elephant meat with Bantus for iron spearheads and plantains. The agricultural Bantus will eat the meat and trade the ivory to the local *dukka* owners.

Pygmies living in the inaccessible Ituri Forest are among the few primitive cultures unaffected by the civilized world. The woman with the suckling baby is cooking plantains, while another pounds roots gathered in the forest. The hut is constructed from saplings lashed together in the form of a dome and covered with various broad leaves. In the background, a male Pygmy checks the straightness of an arrow.

Watusi women. There is a striking contrast between the regal-looking Watusi women shown seated here in this photograph (made before the bloody uprising of 1962) and the Bahutu female servant seen standing in the background.

Watusi are famed for their flamboyant dances, which recreate the heroic battles of their past glory. Their recent tragic history provides them with little to celebrate. *United Press International, Inc.*

In exile. The author chats with deposed Watusi king, Kigeli V, in Nairobi, Kenya, where he now lives in reduced circumstances with his entourage and his memories of the past. Like all refugee Watusi outside their homeland, Kigeli hopes one day to see the Watusi monarchy restored.

This towering 7-foot 2-inch Watusi, Rudahigwa, once ruled the kingdom of Ruanda. On his death, 2,000 Watusi chiefs chose as his successor Kigeli V, but in 1962 the shorter but numerically predominant Bahutu tribesmen revolted and slaughtered thousands of their Watusi overlords.

A Babira woman from the northeast Congo wears a wooden disk in her upper lip, stretched during childhood by the insertion of progressively larger plaques. The old woman is the last survivor of the curious practice that originated in tribal initiation rites.

The dramatic hairdos of the Mangbetu women are intended to accentuate the elongated skull that results from the binding of their babies heads. Although physicians have said that the practice causes no harm, it is dying out as the Mangbetu increase their contacts with civilization.

Matu, a great hunter, personifies the best qualities of the Pygmies of the Congo Ituri Forest—independent, cheerful, courageous. When the author queried him on the number of elephants he had speared in his lifetime, he modestly replied, "Without number."

Masai in a spirited war dance. These once-powerful raiders of southern Kenya and northern Tanzania are cattleherders who do not eat the flesh but only drink the milk and the blood of their animals. Although the days when they were fierce warriors are past, if lions attack their precious cattle, they hunt them down using slender 6-foot-long metal spears, protected only by shields of buffalo hide.

One of the exemplars of the emergence of a Stone Age man into the 20th century is Kondon Aguando, a respected chief of the Chimbu tribe. He successfully ran for election to the New Guinea Legislative Assembly in Port Moresby, where he was a forceful fighter for legislation that would assist New Guinea's native population. Nevertheless, Kondon maintained his roots in the primitive culture at home in the Wahgi Valley, where he lived happily with his eight wives and many children and grandchildren.

Chief Wamp, Mt. Hagen Local Government Council President wears traditional sing-sing makeup (in the photograph on the left) and (on the right) the same Mr. Wamp presides over a council meeting. *J. L. Anderson.*

Two warriors of the Kukukuku tribe, who inhabit a harsh and forbidding region in eastern New Guinea. An extremely short people, these truculent fighters have the dubious distinction of having killed and wounded more patrol officers, native assistants, explorers, and gold prospectors than any other tribe on the world's second largest island.

Warmth in a cold climate. Language and a totally different way of life were no barrier to deep understanding and affection between the author and the Eskimos of Ellesmere Island, who inhabit the northernmost permanent settlement in the world.

The technique of snow-house building can be clearly seen in this view of a temporary hunting village on Ellesmere Island showing the igloos in various stages of completion. Without such shelters, Eskimos could not have survived their never-ending battle with a harsh environment.

In order to survive under the ice, seals must keep small breathing holes open throughout many months of the year. Here, Markosie and his nephew tug at a seal they have just harpooned off Ellesmere Island. (The breathing hole has been considerably enlarged in order to haul the dead seal out on the ice.)

Eskimo with harpoon awaiting the appearance of another seal. *United Press International, Inc.*

Having roots in two cultures not only subjected Kiki to a kind of double jeopardy in connection with the initiation rites, it also gave him a number of cross-cultural insights and a degree of objectivity which perhaps made it easier for him to confront the outside world. In any event, his dual cultural background has not done his political career any harm. It has enabled him to visit one community after another and to appreciate the differences in attitudes resulting from contrasting and frequently antagonistic traditions. It has helped to produce in him the kind of total New Guinean consciousness that will be needed if the multiplicity of tribal interests are to be one day welded into those of an autonomous and unified people.

Objectivity, however, need not rule out a commitment to one's own traditions, and Kiki has not departed from his early feelings of love and respect for the customs and ritual life of either the Orokolo or Parevavo cultures. Not long ago he took time out from an election campaign to search for certain sacred objects in Orokolo. The *hohao* is an oval-shaped wooden board carved with the image of a face; in times past each clan kept its *hohao* in the *eravo*, and these objects were always consulted whenever there was danger or before important hunting expeditions. Each has a name, a personality and sacredness. Many had been destroyed along with the *eravos* during the war, and those that remained were often feared because of the magical power they had accumulated. Consequently, they had been buried, cast aside or allowed to crumble. Some had even been sold to Europeans. One which Kiki remembered as a child had found its way into the Port Moresby museum. Angered, Kiki attempted to retrieve as many as he could—not as a collector of rare primitive art treasures, but as a member of the society that had produced them and to some extent still believed in their magical properties. He had seen the entire process of making a *hohao*: the cutting of the wood, the carving, the grinding of the colors, the incantations. How could anyone be so insensitive as to sell a *hohao*? In all Orokolo and Arehava villages combined, Kiki said, there were only about ten left. The *eravos* have all but disappeared, too.

Kiki's initiation ceremonies in Orokolo were among the last before World War II finished off traditional culture there.

I asked Kiki if the *eravos* had been destroyed by bombing. They had not. The young New Guinean men had gone off to war. While they were away, the *eravos* were left to rot or burn. After the war the break with the past was too severe and nothing was rebuilt. The old leaders, chosen because they were better at doing most tasks and more able to get others to join them, were supplanted by new local councils. In the old days the *Karikara Kiva Haela*, as the leader was called, inspired people to work harder. Now the councils *command* people to do the work of the government and, as yet, the government is for most of these people an abstraction. Work, always related to meaningful incentives, goals and purposes, has lost its significance. The people along the coast have lost their connection with the past, and they are uninspired by the authority of the present.

Sir Donald Cleland had explained that these local government councils, begun under his administration in 1952, were now spreading throughout the territory. From his vantage point as the former administrator, it meant that the people had moved a giant step forward in learning democratic procedures by electing their own representatives to these councils. Within the limited jurisdiction of the councils, admittedly guided in most instances by Australian administration staff members, New Guineans have begun to control their own affairs, even if "in a minor way," to use Cleland's phrase.

Just as the Australian-administered authority has not replaced the traditional authority of the village leader, so, too, according to Kiki, the coming of Christianity has not made up for the loss of traditional beliefs. Kiki acknowledged that many of his people attend church services, "but they put their Bibles aside during the week, and when they hunt, fish or farm the land, they are likely to remember the old magical incantations." Kiki's wife, Elizabeth, and their children are Roman Catholics, but Kiki still follows the religion of his mother.

I asked him what his beliefs implied.

"After death I will return to the lake where my clan origi-nated, Lake Eihovu. We came from this lake and we will return to it."

"What will you find when you get to the lake?" I asked.

"When you die," Kiki replied, "your spirit goes to the lake and lives among the fishes . . . That's how we originated in my clan—as fish."

"Then you will find serenity?"

"We believe that this lake belongs to us, and you stay there among the owners. It will be a happy time."

I asked Kiki why his people prayed so hard when someone died.

"It is because we are mourning for him," Kiki explained. "His body is gone from the earth and so you put mud all over yourself to clean him off. Later you go and wash, which means that you are taking all the death off. But he will always be nearby. If you are attacked by a pig, you call the name of someone near to you who has died. I do, even today," Kiki went on. "If I'm attacked by a pig or fall, I call my mother's name. We were traveling from the market on the truck; I slipped and immediately called her name. I knew that she would be near me. Subconsciously, I knew it."

Kiki told me that he called his mother instead of his father because he had less affection for the elder Kiki. Nevertheless, he assured me that they were quite close. I wanted to know if he thought most New Guineans felt as he did about their traditional religion, whether coast dweller or highlander. He answered emphatically.

"Yes. This feeling for our traditional religion is quite common throughout New Guinea. Quite recently," he added, "a relative on my father's side went to a large college to train as a priest. He preaches on Sunday morning, and on Sunday afternoon believes as I do."

Although for Kiki and his relative, the priest, the old-time religion may have gone underground, there are younger men, especially in the coastal areas, who cannot cherish memories of initiation rites and of the *eravo* ceremonies simply because they have never seen them. And those who are growing up during this time of unsettling change may find it difficult to share Kiki's nostalgia for the old village life of Orokolo when everyone knew his place and life was comparatively serene.

Nevertheless, Kiki is fond of quoting the laws of the Orokolo community, believing that, amid all the innovation, their message is still relevant to the fundamental nature of human relationships. Add or subtract a few words and they bear a rather close resemblance to our own Ten Commandments. In this case there are nine:

> *You must not kill another man's pig.*
> *You must not take another man's wife.*
> *You must not tell lies.*
> *You must not steal from another man's garden.*
> *You must make your own garden.*
> *You must marry and have your own family.*
> *You must respect others.*
> *You must know your place in the community.*
> *You must love your elders.*

Rules of conduct like these are not always easy to follow, especially when the community has lost its stability: when the government has ordered pigs destroyed (instead of fencing them in) because they pose a sanitation problem, or when it induces the people to plant new crops in their gardens (rice and coffee in Orokolo) for which, as Kiki complains, there are no markets. The introduction of a cash economy and new patterns of authority have altered the social context of traditional loyalties. One's place in the community is no longer clearly defined, and the authority of the elders has withered away under colonial administration. To top it off, as Kiki points out, "Life in Orokolo has become uninspiring."

It is often said that primitive life in New Guinea—or anywhere, for that matter, was never very serene, that it was burdened with superstitious fears, natural dangers and lurking enemies. However true this may be, clear boundaries once determined where the perils lay—seen or unseen, imagined or real. Now the boundaries are only vaguely outlined. If New Guineans are to be led into some kind of national self-awareness, Kiki and his friends will have to establish new lines of demarcation, setting off the rights and wrongs, friends and enemies, and the aspirations and fears that can unify the entire territory. The mind of the village, the clan or the tribe must, in some sense, play a role in the national destiny. This requires the kind of political talent that Kiki has demonstrated.

Since his student days, Kiki has been searching out issues which both galvanize New Guineans into group action and set their identity and long-run interests apart from those of the Australian administrators. I asked him the natural question: how did a young man from a simple Stone Age community become the dynamic and controversial leader he obviously is today?

It was, he explained, an indirect route. He had run away from missionary school after the war. The missionaries had forgiven him but they suggested that he find a job, perhaps in Kerema, a coastal town and the local administrative district headquarters. Kiki's first job was as a "doctor boy," roughly equivalent to an orderly, in the Kerema hospital. The idea appealed to Kiki. He had imagined himself becoming qualified to return home and treat his people, healthy in most respects, but suffering severely from tropical ulcers. However, when it came down to handling bedpans Kiki was horrified, having been taught that a young boy who comes in contact with an older man's feces will fall prey to evil spirits, will no longer be able to receive power from the bush and will stop growing.

Prohibitions against contact with feces constituted only a sample of the communal prejudices Kiki had to overcome in order to make his way into the modern world. They were enough to cause him to leave his first job on the day that he was hired. He promptly applied to the district officer in Kerema for another job and was put to work as a "tea boy." This time the chief prohibition, a taboo enunciated by the white patrol officer who hired Kiki, was that he must never spill any of the liquid into the thing called a saucer. The penalty for spilling tea into the saucer, Kiki soon learned, was to have a cup of the boiling hot liquid hurled at his bare chest. Eventually Kiki mastered the art of serving tea and was moved up to the post of interpreter to a patrol officer on the Vailala River.

He would pass along the patrol officer's advice to the villagers: build roads, keep your houses apart as a precaution against fires, form a cooperative for selling copra, keep your village clean, lend us some men for work at the station—that kind of thing. During an expedition into Kukukuku territory, Kiki recalls interpreting a plea for obeying the coastal laws against fighting and killing, and having to tell these seminomads to stop moving around. The young interpreter was too tactful then to instruct the patrol officer on the reasons for Kukukuku migration; they were not simply restless, they were following the game.

Kiki had not given up his dreams of learning about medicine, and after a year of serving the patrol officer he went back to Kerema and asked for the doctor boy job. He was hired by Albert Speer, a hospital administrator who took an interest in Kiki's career: he made the young orderly aware of the larger political dimensions of Papua-New Guinea and its possible future under native rule, which Kiki had ever considered. Speer wanted Kiki, then about sixteen, to continue his secondary schooling in Australia, but the minister of territories vetoed the idea; young New Guineans were not then being encouraged to undertake higher education. (Kiki would have been the first to be thus educated in Australia.) Instead he went to school in Sogeri, near Port Moresby, and there he learned to speak English properly and became qualified as a teacher. When in his senior year he saw a notice inviting applications for medical training on the island of Fiji, he once again remembered his dream of curing the sick. With the support of his friend Speer, he was accepted. But at Suva, on Fiji, things did not go quite according to plan.

This was the first time that Kiki had to compete with young men from many parts of the South Pacific who had known English from infancy. "I found myself a baby among them," Kiki told me. Moreover, he became involved in matters that were not strictly medical on Fiji. For example, he sympathized with the lot of the poor Indian community there. It bothered him to discover that all the corpses he dissected belonged to lower-class Indians. There was never a Chinese corpse, Kiki remembers. He got to know the poor people, he discussed their problems with them, and he helped them to plow their fields and cut their hay. Kiki also discovered the Suva Trade Union. The idea of organizing for action was new to him. But he attended meetings and learned militant techniques that would be applicable in New Guinea communities where only a few years later he would abandon the frustrating path of individual complaints against discrimination in jobs and housing and form action-oriented groups instead. He was, in short, learning his true vocation.

Meanwhile, he failed his examinations but refused, he says, "to go home empty-handed." He was accepted as a student of pathology, and by 1956 was back in Port Moresby working as a laboratory technician, then as a welfare officer, then—after further schooling in the administrative college—as a patrol officer. He was by then an "administration man," but not for long.

It is worth mentioning that Kiki's advanced schooling introduced him to a problem common in Western societies: the necessity for postponing marriage and family life during a period of extended adolescence. This is something for which his upbringing in a traditional society could not have prepared him. But here again Kiki proved adaptable. He recognized that he was in danger of becoming a confirmed bachelor and as such would be subjected to "troubles with women," and thus be less likely to gain support for his projects or for his own advancement. He solved the problem while still on Fiji by writing to his cousin in Port Moresby and asking him to look for a prospective bride. His cousin sent back the address of Elizabeth, who was then in training to be a nurse; she was from Moripi and knew Kiki's Elema language. In a changing New Guinea, these qualities seemed adequate assurances of compatibility: mutual professional interests and no language barrier. After more than a dozen attempts, Kiki got off a long letter to her explaining that he had learned in Fiji what it meant to be treated on equal terms with white men for the first time in his life and that when he returned to New Guinea he would fight to end discrimination and advance the cause of the native New Guinean with trade unions, welfare societies and whatever political means he could devise. Elizabeth, incidentally, was too shy to reply without prompting from her sister and a second letter from Kiki. What she wrote at last was a simple "Yes, I like you."

Kiki left the administration service in 1967 to become secretary of the recently formed *Pangu Pati*. (*Pangu* is an acronym for the Papua-New Guinea Union; *Pati* means "party.") He was not really meant to be an administration supporter. His battles—whether in welfare societies or trade unions or as an individual—were never administration battles, and sooner or later the break had to come. The party is now Kiki's political home. It is the instrument with which he hopes to see Papua-New Guinea unified under black rule. Its program is an indication of the swift rise in both the expectations and the self-confidence of many New Guineans.

"The *Pangu Pati*," Kiki explained, "would like to see Papuan and New Guinean ministers soon take real executive positions that will affect the life of the country—not in external matters, but in the internal affairs of the land."

I asked Kiki if he didn't think that the New Guinean ministers presently in office were doing an adequate job.

"They are doing the best job they can under the system," he answered—he had already made it clear that he doesn't mean to attack individuals. "But we feel these ministers are not really responsible; they are not implementing the policies in which they themselves believe. They are made to implement the policies that have been worked out in Canberra. We've got to learn to govern ourselves, and we can only learn by doing it. We know that our people are not yet ready for independence, but independence could come to New Guinea anytime, whether we like it or not. The pressure might come from within, which I think unlikely—but the U.N. will probably force Australia to give early independence to New Guinea, and when that time comes we want to know what we are doing."

I wondered if Kiki's views were shared by people in other parts of New Guinea, for instance in the highlands, where there are large populations that have learned about the outside world only in the last few decades.

"The government has been telling us," Kiki said, "that we will get independence when the majority of the people want it. We know that a majority live in the highlands and they have only just been discovered. We, the minority, the politically sophisticated people, live down on the coast. Whether it is better to wait for the majority to become ready, or whether we on the coast should begin making the decisions, I am not sure."

Do all the people of New Guinea really want to belong to the same nation? What about the difference in languages—the more than 700 different dialects—the tribal enmities, the fears that a more-or-less homogenized New Guinean identity would conflict with traditional loyalties and beliefs? I threw these questions at Kiki at about the time some of his party colleagues arrived. After he had asked them to wait in the other room, he paced back and forth and then went on as if these questions were never very far from his thoughts.

"Our policy is this: we would like to see everybody in New Guinea speak one common language. They can also retain their local languages, but we would like to see Pidgin become universally used—for communication purposes, not for learning. English must be taught as the official language; it will be used for learning, for keeping records. But English cannot unify the people now in the way Pidgin can. What we want in the *Pangu Pati* is to see everybody think and feel as one—instead of a country that is segmented by so many tribes and languages."

Kiki admitted that this hope for a unified New Guinea may be premature. I agreed. I had already heard too many divergent attitudes expressed on the coast, along the Sepik in the northeast, and in the central highlands. The *Pangu Pati* may achieve its first step toward independence in the early 1970s: it may get home rule, that is. But it may take many more years before it can confront the world as an independent nation supported by a large population which believes that it shares important concepts, values and, possibly, simple economic and political interests. When that day does arrive it may be largely because of Kiki's relentless efforts. Whether Kiki will be a central figure in such a national society is difficult to say. There is an old expression commonly applied to radical politics: one must break eggs in order to make omelettes. This is undoubtedly true—sometimes painfully so—in the emerging, newly self-realized society. But there are egg-breakers and omelette-makers, and Kiki, it is just possible, may be a man who has found his role to be that of egg-breaker.

15 New Guinea—
The Central Highlands:
"It will all go . . ."

WHILE I WAS VISITING the biennial Mt. Hagen
show in 1969 I renewed my friendship of ten
years with Wamp, a highland chief whose views
on New Guinean independence contrast sharply
with those of Kiki. There was no better setting
for our talk than Mt. Hagen, which alternates with Goroka as the
setting for the most extraordinary display of tribal dancing,
music making and elaborate costumes to be found anywhere in
the world. At these shows the more adventurous (and generally
well-to-do) tourists—who are willing to fly through valleys with
vertical walls and around sudden peaks, and who don't mind
spending a few nights on beds of coffee sacks—can still see the
other New Guinea, the newly opened lands still teeming with
primitive life. One package tour advertises that "in the highlands
you may even shake hands with cannibals in the presence, of
course, of an ever-watchful patrol officer."

Here mingling with rich plantation owners, both white and

black, you can see axes and spears being whirled about in a wild exhibition and know that not long ago they were used as they had been intended—as murderous weapons. This is an epic scene that would have caused a Hollywood director to despair of ever duplicating: plumed warriors doing their *sing-sing* ritual victory and war-preparation dance; the ghostly mud men of Goroka; tugs of war, archery contests; pacified Kukukukus who must be kept apart from the rival Chimbus; men painted with ochre and wearing feathers, fishnets, shells, grass skirts.

The Mt. Hagen show makes its point: the highlands people are still furiously proud of their traditions. They are tribal men who are in no hurry to surrender their identities for the blurry prospect of achieving some kind of nationhood. Moreover, they are learning about the white man's world, and they do not mind telling you that there is much more that they want to learn before they join in an independence movement.

Wamp's point of view is typical of the highland attitude. He was now about fifty-three and had changed little in ten years. Short and stockily built, he has the large, almost semitic nose found on many Mt. Hagen men. The septum has been pierced through, although he no longer sports a bone in it on ordinary days. Wamp is a member of the Moggei group, and he was one of the first highlanders to become friendly with Europeans. He had met Mick Leahy and Jim Taylor when they first discovered the Wahgi valley more than thirty-five years ago. Wamp had served as *Tultal* (second in command) of the Moggei, succeeding Chief Ninji as *Luluai*. Wamp could have been a greater success in politics and might have even stood for the House of Assembly, but his Pidgin is too limited and he is too proud to allow himself to be placed in a responsible public office without the means to express himself. He is rich by Mt. Hagen standards—he is a coffee grower and raises cattle. When Wamp speaks, Mt. Hagen listens.

As head of the Mt. Hagen local government council, Wamp is the spokesman for some 350,000 people in the western highlands. He was wearing an immaculate white shirt, his councillor's badge, a pair of well-pressed brown slacks, and brown shoes. Not many months before he had stood up to a visiting delegate from the United Nations who had come to advocate independence for New Guinea. To the great satisfaction of the Australian administration and the local expatriates who regard him affectionately, Wamp made it clear that his people did not desire independence until they had been adequately educated.

When I asked Wamp to explain what he thought were the advantages and disadvantages of life today as contrasted with the life of the Moggei in his youth, he had an immediate answer. For one thing, he was quite happy to be done with tribal fighting. In the old days, Wamp recalled, one group would raid another; pigs would be stolen, houses would be ransacked, women would be carried off—all of which called for a "payback" or revenge raid. And so the feuding would continue, feeding on itself much in the style of the Jivaro clashes.

"These things," Wamp told me, "are already forgotten. Now, if a person breaks the law there is no payback; he must go to prison in Port Moresby. The only thing I'm going to keep is the traditional *sing-sing*. My children and grandchildren may go away to school and return, but they are going to be taught in the traditional way of the *sing-sing*. I might even teach white children born in New Guinea these traditional ways."

Wamp said that he would also like to keep the tradition of the highland pig feast. He felt confident that he could teach his children and grandchildren these things, and that they would pass along the customs to their own children. (Since Wamp has had seven wives and twenty-four children—of whom ten survive —his insistence on continuing these traditions carries added meaning.)

I could not be as confident as Wamp that the *sing-sing*, shorn of its ritual meaning, would long continue with the same style that was evident at the Mt. Hagen show. What seemed important to Wamp, however, almost as important as home rule was to Kiki, was the image of his people in the eyes of the world. It could be shameful, he thought, if his grandchildren should complete their technical and academic schooling and lose contact with the old ways. Let them forget war, but keep the war dance, he seemed to be saying; forget the tribal intimidation tactics, but keep the masks and paint. And why?

"When Europeans come and teach our children what they have been doing and they ask our children what their own people have done in the past, I want our young ones to have something to say. I don't want our children to be embarrassed by their ignorance of what went before. That would be bad."

Wamp reiterated his belief that his people were not yet ready to govern themselves. They needed more education—there was so much to be learned from Europeans, and they weren't sending enough teachers into the highlands. Wamp, while obviously proud of the show his people had put on at Mt. Hagen, remarked: "You see the way my people live now; they have not progressed enough. It may be 30 or 40 years before we are finished learning. Then we'll know about the things that are necessary for good government—things we, including myself, don't know—like building airplanes and working in factories."

Wamp surely speaks for more than the Moggei tribe when he acknowledges the awe in which he holds modern technology. Many primitive people, colonized by those with advanced technologies, have reached the conclusion that they could not achieve independence without proving their competence at the same game in which they had been beaten.

Without technological skills, Wamp believes, there can be no genuine national unity, no independence. One day industrial organization will replace the tribal life; men will share work and production goals, and their dreams will be consumer dreams. Cash may become the common language of New Guinea before English or Pidgin, inextricably binding the coast-dweller and the highlander together. Roads and air routes will thread villages together that once knew one another as fearful adversaries. Then New Guineans will face the outside world as economic equals. Economic independence will come, then political autonomy, and this, Wamp was saying, must all be preceded by an enormous increase in knowledge.

Wamp is disinclined to appear on the world stage before New Guineans have been well schooled in the drama of twentieth-century life. This separates him from someone like Kiki who is ready to begin raising the curtain now. Both men obviously have a feeling for their audiences, but Wamp, the conservative highlander, has known little of the coast-dweller's abrasive contacts with the white man, and partly in consequence he sees himself as upholding a tribal dignity that has never suffered a serious assault. He could never be comfortable in joining a Kiki-type protest; his dream is not to shake the administrative powers but to become their prize pupil.

As for the past, Wamp would prefer that its more violent aspects remain as obscure as possible. He likes to talk about pig feasts and *sing-sings*, but when the subject turns to intertribal raids he becomes reticent. His pride is nothing like that of the Jivaro chieftain who wants the world to know how many heads he has taken. Wamp has done his share of fighting over stolen women and livestock; as many as three tribes, he recalls, were enemies of the Moggei at one time. However, he stops short of discussing specific incidents; there are the authorities for whom he has an enduring respect; there is also the possibility of raking up old tribal antagonism—and buried hatchets—and there is even more sensitive consideration now: that of the Moggei, not to mention New Guinea's image in the eyes of the outsider.

While I was at the Mt. Hagen show I met Jim Dunbar, manager of Boroko Motors (W. R. Carpenter Organization) in the town of Mt. Hagen. Very few people are as qualified to give so useful, albeit so one-sided a view of a primitive community undergoing rapid economic change as the good-natured man who sells them automobiles and trucks.

"We sell the bulk of our stock—Fords and Datsuns—to natives who purchase on credit," said Dunbar, a slender Australian with a wry manner who sells "in round figures about 130 vehicles a year to these people."

"They get," he added, "the same credit terms as the expatriate. The vehicle, you know, is a status symbol with them. They use it for carting their coffee and their produce to the various local markets. They carry passengers, too." Dunbar went on to explain how these vehicles are purchased and what their eventual fate often is. "The vehicle is actually bought by the tribe (or 'line') or by a village. The procedure is that they ordinarily will bring a couple of hundred dollars in first, probably in shillings, and then you take the vehicle out and let them see it. After much pow-wow they begin to *bung*—*bung* means to collect money—from everybody in the village, and after they've got enough together for the initial payment we all go over to the headquarters of the organization in Mt. Hagen and count the money out. We give them a monthly arrangement, making it as clear as we can that the total interest charges will depend upon how quickly they complete the payments. Well, of course, the month goes by, and sometimes we have to go looking for them to get the installment. And then we see the vehicle! It's sometimes in quite a disreputable state, even after only a month—sometimes even less. We've delivered vehicles, you know, and the next day they're back. They've burned out the clutch or they've banged something. The native calls a collision 'fighting' another vehicle—'they fightem anotherfellow car' in Pidgin. Sometimes the whole top or side of the car is completely wrecked and has to be replaced. Then it's a matter for the insurance company which pays the claim—less a deductible amount that the driver has to pay himself, and that could be as much as $150.00, depending upon his age and length of driving experience."

I asked Dunbar what might happen if the car has been smashed up, and it's of no use to the driver or his people even though they must go on paying the installments for another two years.

"Whether the vehicle is still usable or if it's a total loss they have to go on paying the installments. It would be the same for you or me, wouldn't it?"

"But how," I wanted to know, "do you get them to understand that they haven't been cheated, or that there isn't something wrong with the system?"

"Well," Jim explained, "you have the administration to help you on these things. The patrol officers help to put them straight.

They'll insist, of course, that they should get some of their money back—'half-money' they call it—if something goes wrong with the vehicle. But we tell them, 'Look, you buggered it up yourself.' "

"And you can count on them to keep paying?"

"Well, intrinsically you can," Dunbar answered. "You've got to remember that what we have here in the highlands is an education—or rather, a re-education—program. We've been selling them vehicles on credit now for a few years, and they've come to understand that our credit system is different from their own traditional way in which they could take a whole lifetime before 'payback.' For instance, if a man buys a wife he pays a certain amount down in cash—in pigs, feathers or shells, but he doesn't have to finish paying for years, and to get used to paying monthly and promptly is, as I said, a whole re-education for them."

New Guineans like to restyle some of the machinery they buy, particularly vehicles, according to their own esthetic tastes and ceremonial traditions. Dunbar told me, "When you've completed all the negotiations, the purchase, and everything is signed and sealed, the very first thing they do is to decorate the vehicle with flowers and branches of trees. Well, they get any flowers that are handy to the village, and then you can hardly see the truck or utility for the foliage. And the great whoops of joy, the shouts, the hugging that go on among their own people when the vehicle arrives. They're so excited that they've got their vehicle, and of course they thank you profusely, although you've really *sold* them something, you know. Really, there's nothing quite like it anywhere in the world."

Another expatriate view of the changing New Guinean scene came from John Fox, an early explorer, prospector and farmer. We met during the Mt. Hagen festivities. Fox, who has lived in New Guinea for about forty years, was scornful of granting early independence to the territory. Fox's views, like those of Dunbar, are one-sided, but they are informed by years of first-hand experience. When a man like Fox says, "*We* know best," and that is generally his feeling about Australian rule in New Guinea, he is able to point to the very visible economic progress in the central highlands on the one hand and the worsening situation in West Irian, formerly Dutch New Guinea, on the other. He is not a naive man; civilization is not an unmixed blessing. It is, as he puts it, "unfortunately inevitable." Moreover, New Guinea is home for him, and like many other expatriates now rooted there, he has a vested interest in its future stability. "I mean," he says, "if we look after them, and the world leaves us alone, they'll be well looked after."

Fox would like to see New Guinea remain in Australian hands as a protectorate. "If we leave this country it could be disastrous. Somebody else will walk in: the Chinese, the Indonesians, or even the Japanese. The Japanese," Fox adds, "could do the best job of the lot, but I wouldn't like to see them here. They'd get the railway lines in, the whole place would be electrified, and then they'd never leave."

I asked Fox for his impression of the changes in New Guinea during the forty-odd years he has lived there, and his answer is worth reporting verbatim. It conveys the flavor and the personal style of his kind of pioneering breed, the men who drove in the opening wedge, who were followed by administrators, missionaries and salesmen, and who believe that their risk-taking entitles them to feel that the land is partly theirs.

"When we came here the beach boys," Fox began, referring to the northeastern coast-dwellers, "the beach boys were already sophisticated. They had the German administration there. But when you came up here to Mt. Hagen you saw the native in the raw, and he appeared to be a very friendly native. You couldn't trust him though. If you left your gear about, well—they'd just take the lot, and they'd probably do you over to get the stuff. But that was what you'd call business—from their point of view. They didn't hate us—we were just a novelty, a curiosity. We found natives all over the island, especially in the Wahgi Valley, that you didn't know existed. And they didn't even know about boiling water. It was all new to them. They used to stand around and watch us boil a billy. And they didn't really know how to prepare a pig. At the same time they were very friendly. Still they wouldn't be above putting you in the bamboo. I mean eating you: they'd slice a bit off you here and there and put it on the bamboo to cook. Oh, that's still going on. They're still eating one another only a few days' trek from here. As long as they stay in those isolated pockets up there, they'll be very independent."

It occurred to me that men like Fox were, in their own way, more nostalgic about New Guinea's primitive past than the indigenous people themselves, despite the fact that they had opened the door to change. Fox is more at home with the older generation of New Guinean than with the group he calls "the younger brigade." The old-timer chiefs, many of them now dead, were content to do "business" with the Australian—in one way or another—and Fox could join them in the kind of casual symbiosis, the predictable give-and-take in which a certain amount of petty theft and head-bashing was taken for granted and even the cannibalism was an acceptably spicy part of the scene. The trade-offs in labor and gold and freedom, with all the hazards, made it worthwhile. For men with pioneering tastes like Fox, the comforts of civilization are dubious at best. They are among the first to mourn the primitive's twilight. It is civilization, after all, that they came to New Guinea to escape.

"The younger brigade here," Fox went on, "seem to think that the U.N. is the Be All and End All. The U.N. is Everything, they say. Australia, they believe, is tied to the U.N. and whatever it says is law. And that's the big mistake, because the U.N. is talking all the time and they don't know what they're talking about! The U.N. has given these people false hopes. They say everything will be fine if they get home rule."

The very idea of home rule sends chills through Fox. He can see only a repetition of "what happened in Africa." (Clearly, the events in Africa early in the sixties have had a profoundly unsettling effect on people in colonial situations the world over.) Home rule, without a long and gradual preparation, opens the way to any number of unpredictable evils for the white settler.

Fox doesn't actually trouble himself about the loss of primitive culture as such. It is more, I think, the absence of civilization with its rules and restrictions and its pace and pressures that finds him such an enthusiastic defender of the New Guinean past. He hates to be crowded, and the world beyond, symbolized by the U.N., is beginning to crowd in on New Guinea. "The superstitions will go," he says. "The younger brigade will see to that. They will want to get modernized and show the U.N. that they're ready for home rule.

"And a lot of their fashions and superstitions will go. The pig feasts will go. I can't see them holding on to that. And I think all these *sing-sings* will go. It's a waste of time, you know. It's all very nice, but when they've got something else to think about, they'll see that they've only been wasting their time. They'll realize that they can do something better than that."

Fox will go too, of course, and when he and others like him disappear from the New Guinea scene the "younger brigade," who will by then be running things, will not be troubled by men of his stamp again. His rare kind is dying out—everywhere.

No picture of changing New Guinea would be complete without mention of the *kiap* or patrol officer, the representative of Australian authority. If he is to succeed in his task of watching over the peace and health of the native population, he must make at least a reasonable attempt to see life through their eyes. Because he works within a legal system imposed from the outside his sympathies with indigenous values must of necessity be somewhat limited.

On my most recent visit to New Guinea I looked up Keith McCarthy in Port Moresby, knowing that he, as much as anyone, was capable of getting beyond the restrictions of the white man's outlook while still being able to profit from the experience and mobility of an administration man. McCarthy, whom I had gotten to know on my previous visits to New Guinea, is neither an ordinary *kiap*, nor an ordinary man. He is now busily retired: he writes, paints and keeps himself trim. He is one of the legendary people whose lives were wrapped up with the rapid opening up of the New Guinea interior, having begun his career as a patrol officer in 1927 before the great majority of the New Guinean population was known to exist. He served in the central highlands, along the Sepik River, and in Rabaul. After the war (during which he was decorated for scouting and combat duty, and in the evacuation of Australian troops from Rabaul), he became a district commissioner, then a member of the New Guinea Legislative Council and, later, of its successor, the House of Assembly.

I told McCarthy that I was planning to write about the twilight of primitive life, and he said that he was afraid that it was a fact. "I say afraid," he added, "because too often we tend to come in with our Western culture and think that everything we bring the people is good. That of course is not so, although there are many things that we can bring them that are good—such as peace and health.

"I've never believed in the idea that primitive man was the Happy Savage," McCarthy went on. "Too often they lived in a world of fear from mortal enemies, from strangling superstition and sorcery—which you can still find in New Guinea today. But here they have worked out a culture of land division and a system of sharing things which I find something like the Sermon on the Mount: if you have something, share it with your brother. You don't share it with anyone else, of course. They worked out a way of survival."

"Maybe that system of survival is something that we could learn from," I suggested to Keith McCarthy. There was no argument. We both agreed that it didn't seem likely that Western civilization would attain the longevity of the primitive societies in Australia and New Guinea.

We spoke of the land tenure system in New Guinea society. The indigenes found it difficult to understand that land is something to be sold or exchanged, something to make money with. "The great idea here in New Guinea these days is Economic Progress. That's become the shibboleth. We Australians are telling them that the idea is to make money on things. We say: you will grow crops and sell them. But here's the rub. Most of the crops here are coconuts, cocoa or coffee; they're permanent—you don't plant one thing one year and something else the next. That means that the crops last longer than the man who plants them. In their traditional land tenure system when a man died his land did not go to the oldest son. If you belonged to a matrilineal society, for example, your land would go to your child's maternal uncle; the land remained in the clan, but not within the family as we know it. For us this is a hopeless mix-up, something very difficult for Western man to understand. So we say to them: change your whole system. Sell your land to the government, and the government will let you have it back on a long-term lease, and then you will have a wonderful thing called 'personal title' to it, and then—think of it—you will be able to leave those standing crops, those coconut trees, your coffee to your oldest son. And what's more, we tell them, once you have title to a piece of land, you can Borrow Money from the Bank. Well, it fits our idea of life very nicely. Not theirs. You've got people objecting to it."

McCarthy paused and lowered his voice slightly, adding, "Now I'm sounding like a New Guinean."

I agreed.

"Well, I think what we're asking of them is the bait on the hook. And the hook is going to lead them right to a rat race. There will be a lot of people wanting to join in the competition for land title. I know it sounds as if I should be accused of backward thinking, longing for the old days, and all that, but nevertheless I'm merely telling you what a majority of the people in this country are thinking at the present time."

Before we parted, McCarthy told me how a few months before he had seen some native art in Hanuabada that indicated for him how, as he put it, "things have cheapened here." McCarthy, a painter himself, had always loved the beautiful dobo posts, magnificently carved and painted in traditional colors: reds and umbers from clay, white from lime, black from lampblack. McCarthy had seen an old man working on two of these posts, and he had been pleased to see a group of younger men watching the craftsman. Some were lending a hand with the carving, and Mc- Carthy felt happy to know that in a small way, there in Hanu- abada where so much had changed, this bit of tradition might go on. The posts are about twelve feet high and are placed two feet in the ground. He asked the group when the painting would begin, and they told him, "Oh, we'll do that next week." When McCarthy returned the painting had already begun. What he saw upset him so that he recalled the incident vividly many weeks later. They had gotten synthetic enamel paint from a local hardware store, and they were sloshing on every available color from purple to pale pink—"all the colors of the rainbow," Mc- Carthy complained. "The whole thing had been ruined, really."

McCarthy does not like it said of himself that he is a backward- thinking type. Who does? But like other men who were drawn to New Guinea in the early—and still recent—days, perhaps for more reasons than they know, the loss of tradition, even a tradi- tion other than their own, can be unsettling.

16 New Guinea—The Sepik: Highway of Mechanical Dreams

I WAS ABLE TO RETURN to the Sepik River during my last trip to New Guinea and there, after a stopover at Wewak, I was taken in hand by Patrol Officer Frank Van Ousten. We had met at the airstrip in Ambunti and soon we were in his flat-bottomed metal boat, heading downriver to Pagui where he is based—a two-hour trip when the current is going our way.

Van Ousten is tall, a blue-eyed, blond Dutchman with a fairly decided accent. He's about thirty-eight, and the kind of dedicated, cooperative person you are likely to meet at the outposts. I met his wife and young daughter, and the next morning he and I made a trip in his river "truck," actually owned by the local village council. They'd gotten it, he told me, for $2,000, including the price of the motor. We traveled about eighty miles downriver to Chambri, a small island in the Chambri lakes. It was the dry season, so the water was low. I had seen this area at high water when it is covered with water lilies, and it is one of the most spectacular sights in the Sepik area. Because of the low water-level, the trip took us three and a half hours; during high water the distance can be negotiated in less than a half-hour. Van Ousten usually patrols an area of 120 miles up and down the river and 95 miles wide. We landed at Abom village, renowned for its fine pottery.

Since I had been there last the local councils had grown up; there were none here in the late fifties. Taxes were rising, water wells were being drilled, and the people were talking about to-morrow. I met with Father Pablo, a Chicagoan who has lived in the Sepik area for twenty years. We spoke about the school he had established, about the new airstrip, how it was becoming somewhat easier to get around. There are still no roads along the river, but cars and trucks are becoming a common sight. Toyota trucks seem to be the most popular there; the villagers will pool their resources, just as Jim Dunbar had told me, and head for Wewak to make the purchase. Delivery is made at Pagui, about ninety miles away, and there the car is based. To get to this distant parking lot the natives will paddle for one or two days in their canoes. Then they will tie up to a shaky pier and call for their driver—another native who has been sent to attend a driver-training course by his fellow villagers. They use the truck for carrying produce, for social affairs, to visit relatives and simply to show off. The truck, like the transistor radio, the automobile and the shotgun, has replaced the social prestige that once sur-rounded the superior warrior. It signifies that one has progressed and is in tune with the times. Americans and Australians some-times scoff at this status consciousness because, I think, they find it embarrassing to find their own foibles parodied in people who are so patently different.

The pottery was still being produced at Abom, and it was as fine as I had remembered it, but there were so many new impres-sions that I could not come away with my attention focused on any single experience. There was much talk of crop production, for one thing. Rice was being harvested at a rapid rate by comparison with other years. Coffee was making its appearance, and cattle raising was being encouraged. Van Ousten insisted that I look at a finely carved drum.

It was all taking longer than I had expected, and I was beginning to grow apprehensive about our trip back. It was already 4:30 in the afternoon, and I had no desire for an adventurous upriver ride of three and a half hours. (It was not until we got into the boat that I remembered that it took seven times as long to go upriver as down.) For a while the going was smooth, and I found myself hoping that the sun would forget to go down for a few hours. Then we saw some ominous clouds in the distance, and within a half-hour we were soaked to the skin by a torrential tropical rainstorm. In order to lessen air resistance, no cabin had been built on the boat. Consequently there was no shelter from the storm and, what is more, the boat took on about fifty gallons of water—necessitating our bailing in order to keep up our speed.

Slowed by the rain, we soon found ourselves traveling along in the dark, just as I had feared. There are many hazards in river travel at night; I was especially worried about our motor being knocked out as a result of a collision with trees or branches that had been blown down by the storm. Any number of things are usually floating along the river, and if the motor were fouled by floating debris we would have been at the mercy of the current and would have to float along until we reached a village. In the meantime, we would have been devoured by the Sepik mosquitoes, which are the most numerous and most voracious in the world. Recalling previous unsettling experiences along the Sepik, I wondered how anyone so experienced as this patrol officer could have set out without a spare motor. Luckily, we made our weary way back to Pagui late that night.

The next day we were off downriver again, heading for Kankanamun, when we encountered a former patrol officer heading in the opposite direction. We signaled to him and lashed our boats together in the middle of the river. His name was B. Kerry Leen, now deputy district commissioner of the East Sepik District. Although he had been a Sepik traveler for many years, he had once gotten himself into the very trouble that could have overtaken us the previous night. His outboard motor had broken down and he was forced to drift downriver helplessly. At night along the shore the mosquitoes went to work on him and he was in a deplorable condition by the time he reached a village. Leen suffered from anemia for months thereafter and had to be given a number of blood transfusions. This, I had no difficulty in reminding myself, could have been our fate too.

At that point we were 180 miles up the Sepik. Leaning across from one boat to the other, we talked about the flexibility of New Guineans who, in Leen's judgment, were better able to adjust to change than many Europeans he had seen. "Why I say this is that they are being taken out of their age-old ways of living and are being taught new skills, new methods, new ideas—and they are accepting them. And it's happening all within one generation. They are reaching a point that took European nations centuries to achieve. And then we get Europeans here who try to adjust to the New Guinean environment, and they just can't make it."

Leen admitted that there were matters in which the New Guineans found it difficult to put aside their traditional ways, for instance land tenure attitudes, which I had discussed with Mc-Carthy. "To us land is a saleable commodity," he said. "It's an asset. To these people it's entirely different. When I was a patrol officer, many times I had to purchase land for the Administration. Some of the reluctant sellers said, 'No, my father spilled his blood to win this land from that crowd over the hill there many years ago. Blood was spilled to keep this land. My mother bore me in the garden. I was born in that bush there.' Or they may say, 'My father is buried in the garden there.' So we come in and talk to them in legal jargon about rights, and purchases, and leases; it is completely baffling to these people. But in the end they do understand after many a long explanation that if the government wants to put a school here or a hospital there, they must have title to the land. They do understand that; they really are willing to learn."

Leen told me that there may be some important additions in the near future to the current Sepik River trade, which now centers around coffee, rice, cattle, timber, crocodile skins and artifacts. A number of companies, he said, are searching for oil and minerals here. Leen believes that it would be a good thing for the district if the companies should be successful in their search. I asked him if it might not bring about a too-rapid change. He believed that the Sepik people could handle the changes. "And think," he added, "of the employment that would be created. Aid posts and schools would spring up in the area, and it would bring the people a totally new economy."

I asked Leen what he thought of the home-rule movement in New Guinea, and he, like everyone else I had spoken with, had a strong opinion. The New Guineans didn't know when they were well off. If they were independent they couldn't expect to receive the $80 or $90 million in aid grants from Australia. Many New Guineans take as a matter of course the help they are now getting: free university education, free legal aid, free medical and dental treatment, free agricultural advice. Australians must pay for many of these services, and the time is not far off when New Guineans will have to pay fees for their schooling. Leen said that the money is there now. Along the Sepik families are earning comfortable incomes selling timber, crocodile skins and artifacts.

When Van Ousten and I reached Kankanamun we made our way to the men's ceremonial house there. This house-tamberan is the finest example in any of the villages along the Sepik and is probably the most famous. As we walked through the house-tamberan observing the richly carved garamuts, I saw a venerable old man sitting among the men in this sacred meeting place. I learned from Frank that he was Tanyaga, the head of the village, and one of the great Sepik leaders surviving from the old days. With us was a native police constable who spoke Pidgin, and he acted as interpreter. I learned that Tanyaga was about seventy-five years old and had been born there before the German occupation. He was already a young man by the time the Germans arrived. He had seen World War II come to the Sepik, and he had witnessed the broad changes under the present administration. He had talked with anthropologists, traders, soldiers and art collectors, and Frank told me that he had developed an astuteness that was highly prized by his own people as well as by visitors. He remains a powerful influence on the village even though he speaks no English and can neither read nor write.

There are forty-two elected councilors representing various villages in this area. These councilors are considered by the government to be the legitimate leaders of their villages. Yet at their meetings these leaders will often hold up an important vote until they have had a chance to discuss with elders like Tanyaga. He is regarded as a true leader, and all his people, young and old, male and female, revere him as one who was important in the past and is still to be respected.

When Tanyaga spoke to me, slipping between his own language and Pidgin, the other men of the house-tamberan listened in silence. Their faces seemed to mirror the same frustrations I had seen among such primitive peoples as the Bororos, the Chavantes and the exiled or subjugated Watusi. They had been sitting around doing nothing in particular, and now they were gathered around Tanyaga listening to him speak of his memories of the past—a time he called the golden age when life was full of meaning for his people. He said that his people were once complete men, proud of their accomplishments. Now the Australian administration is running things, and that is all right for the younger people, but it was no longer his time.

From Frank and Tanyaga I learned about the house-tamberan, the sacred place where the fighters and the leaders of the village met to plan their wars, their economy, their food production. The house-tamberan here, as elsewhere, was forbidden to all females and to the young on pain of death. In fact, if a woman came within hearing range of the flutes used in the house-tamberan ceremonies, she would pay for her indiscretion with her life.

Tanyaga, unlike Wamp, was far from reticent on the subject of wars and raids. He explained that around Kankanamun wars were fought for land and water, the basis for survival, not over the theft of replaceable women or livestock. Many of the surrounding villages, he told me, were envious because Kankanamun was richly endowed with land and had a beautiful lake well provided with fish. Several decades ago four nearby villages had combined forces in order to win for themselves access to the lake and land. Their plan was to attack the house-tamberan where the war councils were held. Because it was also a sacred place, to destroy it would, so the other villages decided, break the spirit of the defenders. The rest, they thought, would be easy.

When the Kankanamun people got wind of their enemies' intentions they built earth embankments which are still visible and barricaded themselves, successfully holding off the attack and eventually repelling the invaders. Both sides lost many men, Tanyaga said. I asked him how the dead had been disposed of. The enemies were thrown into the lake which they had so ardently coveted, while the warriors of Kankanamun were buried in the village or in the bush near where they had died. No prisoners were taken—attackers would wipe out whole villages, women and children included.

Convinced that I was genuinely interested in the history of his people, Tanyaga ordered one of the men to bring down from the upper loft in the house-tamberan a sacred pole, called a *Bengal*, which he displayed proudly. It had been laboriously carved from the heartwood of the sac sac tree. Hundreds of small sticks had been inserted into holes bored into the sacred pole. The *Bengal* was covered with cobwebs, indicating that it was rarely displayed in recent years, and Frank told me that I should feel honored at having been shown it. Each stick, about two inches long, represented one of the village men who had been killed in battle—the entire pole was about fifteen feet high. As we were looking at the pole and all the deaths it represented, Tanyaga seemed to read my mind. Were these really the good old days, I wondered? Yes, he told me, those days were better times, even with all the fighting, and despite the new schools, hospitals, air-fields and trucks.

Later, in Pagui, Frank told me about some of the pressures that are causing problems along the Sepik so that administrative officials were not able to keep up with the swift pace of change. Local government councils, begun in 1952, had reached a stage of development in which the native people were beginning to control their own affairs. The administrators were having to contend with the very lively demands of the indigenes expressed in their councils, through political parties and in the House of Assembly in Port Moresby.

The New Guineans, especially the growing numbers of the young, are clamoring to share the technology of the white man. They see or know about automobiles, airplanes, refrigerators and radios. They know that white men have landed on the moon. If all this is possible for white people, they are asking, why not for them? They will no longer fight over a lake—at least not in most cases—but they will stridently demand the commodities that have been dangled before their eyes.

The older people find in their magical sense a hoped-for path to obtaining the advantages of civilized life. Some have told Frank that their dead ancestors are building an enormous ship at a place that cannot be revealed. The ship is so large that it occupies a bay two miles long. In the middle of the bay was an island which the ancestors had to remove in order to make room for the ship. This vessel will bring them—once the white man leaves—all the gadgets and goodies, the mechanical dreams and devices that are now going to the white man. Some believe that in the harbors of Sydney, Darwin, Brisbane and elsewhere there are greedy white men who are changing the addresses on the shipments that their ancestors had intended for them. The so-called Cargo Cult takes many forms, and it is still very much alive in New Guinea. In one village in Frank's territory he was told that the Sepik will one day turn into a long concrete highway, and all freight will be delivered by motor truck instead of by boat. This notion is supported by the evidence that the ships belong to the white man, but the trucks in the area are invariably driven by natives.

Dreams like these belong to the older generation. The young have learned that they must work in the white man's way if they are to receive the white man's goods. They are getting the education for the jobs, but there are not enough jobs to satisfy the growing work force—a problem that disturbs leaders in emerging countries around the world.

Yet people in New Guinea seem to think that anything is possible, that it can be done one way or another through work, through magic or through revolt. The encouraging note is that they are sure a change will come. They have somehow managed to retain a faith that there is a real connection between what one wants in this world and what it is possible to get. The sad faces I saw in the Kankanamun house-tamberan along the Sepik reflect the vanishing glory of primitive life. It will indeed all go, as John Fox observed. But the point that New Guinea made for me is that everything need not go: not the people and their cultural history. Not so long as they carry over into the future the belief that they can continue to make their own decisions, make their own mistakes, take their own punishment, handle their own successes. This is what they have been saying.

Epilogue

FOR A LONG TIME we have looked at the primitive world as some kind of natural oversight, a past—even an embarrassing past—that refused to die, a part of nature that we had not quite straightened out—yet. But we supposed that it would be only a matter of time.

I have written this book to say that the time has come.

Whole populations have disappeared for a variety of causes, each having to do in one way or another with the thrust of civilization into their lives. Except in the very short run, I believe, there is little that can be done to reverse this process. The loss to man of his primitive roots is one thing that cannot be made good by pouring in more money, more volunteers, more scientific discoveries. And from the viewpoint of primitive man, civilization appears to be a disease for which there is no cure.

I believe this is a disaster every bit as compelling as the justly well-publicized environmental crisis. It is even less likely to be reversed.

We have been duly concerned about the disappearance of wild life, the alligators and okapi, the snowy egret and the bald eagle. I am concerned about them too, having spent much of my life observing and filming the animals of distant plains and forests. But now I am concerned about what seems the more urgent situation, the loss of human beings.

Let me put the matter squarely. What we have done, as a civilization, is not only to assist in the destruction of life systems that are incalculably old; we have participated in the banishment from earth of peoples whose right to exist and whose style of existence are as sacred as ours. We have also obliterated systems of survival that for all their variety and strangeness to us have been successful for others.

From these ways of life we might have been able to learn methods and values that could have taught us to serve each other, ourselves and our earth more wisely than we have hitherto. Perhaps we still can.

We have learned that victories over nature usually come at a high price. The primitive, too, is a conqueror of nature, although more often he seems to be its partner. He does it with all the seen and unseen resources of his wits, physical prowess and imagination. He has not, on the whole, had to pay dearly for his conquest.

There is no single "primitive way." The variety of his experience is as scattered and unclassifiable as human nature itself. I have always thought that the really important differences between civilized and primitive men are more in degree than in kind. They have had to do more—productively, ritually and imaginatively—with less material and often less space. And this is something we too had better begin to learn.

What it will mean to live in a world without the presence of our primitive heritage, I cannot say. It will not be safer or more embellished, however; of that I am sure. Nor will it be less lonely.

Index

Aborigines (Australia)
age-set, authority among, 181–182
arts of, 175
assimilation policy for, 161–192
attitudes toward property and land, 156, 157, 159, 181, 183–184
and Australian law, 181–183
beliefs about paternity among, 158–159
clans and "tribes" of, 154–155
Corroborees of, 156, 182
description and history of, 153–165
diversity of, 153–155
in government settlements, 157, 163–164, 177–180, 184, 188–189
initiation rites of, 173
lands of invaded, 155–157
languages of, 154, 172–173
marriage among, 157–158, 173–174
militancy among, 190–191
mixed bloods among, 160–161
origins of, 153
in "protection era," 161
sexual attitudes and exploitation of, 157–160, 187–188
sports in assimilation of, 150, 164, 168, 175, 176
survival of as issue, 149–153, 164, 174
"walkabout" of, 157, 162
and white paternalism, 161–162
Acculturation
of Aborigines, 161–192
of Eskimos, 79–88, 94, 99–102
and intermarriage, 99
of Jivaros, 34–47
of Masai, 144–146
in Mato Grosso, 70–73
in New Guinea, 197, 224–227, 231–233, 242–243
pace of as critical, 41, 55, 68, 70, 84, 134
role of language in, 41–42, 100–101, 171–173
See also Assimilation policies

Adamain (Jivaro shaman), 37–38, 40
Africa, nationalism vs. tribalism in, 106–115
Akpaliapik (Eskimo leader), 80–81, 82, 84
Alaska
first white men in, 89–90
native land claims in, 88, 103–105
population rise in, 83
social disorganization in, 90–92
Statehood Act (1958) of, 103
See also North Slope
Aleuts (Alaska), 90, 103
Alice Springs (Australia), 183, 185–188
Amazon River and basin
colonization of, 4–6
economic development in, 12–13
primitive depopulation in, 16
American Indians
achievements of, 7–8, 10
decimation of, 3–17
enslavement of, 4–6
moral values of, 8–9
white response to, 41, 164, 197
Americas (Western Hemisphere), first settlers of, 1–12
Animals
domestic, among Jivaros, 37–38
Eskimo game, 92, 93–94
in Ituri Forest, 116, 118, 119, 131
in Masai territory, 135, 136–137, 146–147
Aranda tribe (Australia), 188
Arawak Indians (Caribbean), 3
Aris, C. L., 153
Artifacts, folkloric objects
and cultural identity, 45, 150, 169, 211
as marketable, 45, 185, 211
and social change, 232–233
Assimilation policies
in Alaska, 99–100
in Australia, 161–192
in Canadian Arctic, 77–80
of Salesian missionaries, 41–47, 70–73

Index

Atahualpa, 10–11
Athapascan Indians (Alaska), 103, 104
Atkinson, Helen L., 103
Auca Indians (Ecuador), 13
Australia, Aborigines of, 149–192. *See also* Aborigines
Aweti Indians (Brazil), 58*n*
Aztec Indians (Mexico), 10

Baffin, William, 79
Bahutu tribe (Central Africa), revolt of, 109–112
Bambuti tribe (Congo). *See* Pygmies of the Ituri Forest
Bantu. *See* Walese Bantu tribe
Barrow (Alaska), Eskimos in, 94–100. *See also* North Slope
Batwa Pygmies (Central Africa), 109, 111, 127
Beachey, F. W., 89
Berndt, Catherine, 153–154, 159
Berndt, Ronald M., 153–154, 159, 164
Birth control, primitive use of, 66
Black militants, 44, 190, 191
Blackburn, Richard, 190
Boas, Franz, 9–10
Bolla, Father (Salesian missionary), 42–43
Bororo Indians (Brazil), 9, 53, 68, 134, 240
  decimation of, 16–17, 65
  funeral ceremonies of, 48–49, 65, 66
  loss of vitality among, 65–66
Brazil, 115
  charges of genocide in, 14–16
  economic development in, 12–13, 17, 67, 68–69, 70
  enslavement of Indians in, 4–5
  peonage in, 5–6, 69
  primitive depopulation in, 16–17, 57, 67
  rubber boom in, 5–6
  See also Mato Grosso
Brewer, Max, 98–100
Bryce, James, 6
Burundi, 111, 112. *See also* Rwanda-Burundi
Bushmen of the Kalahari Desert, 127
Byler, William, 86, 100–102

Calapalos Indians (Brazil), 51, 58*n*
Camayura Indians (Brazil), 114–115, 130
  change in character of, 63
  diseases among, 63–64
  docility and innocence of, 48, 58–60
  isolation of ended, 11–12
Caraja Indians (Brazil), 17
Casement, Roger, 5–6
Chance, Norman, 86–87
Chavante Indians (Brazil), 115, 134, 138, 240
  aggressiveness of, 11–12, 48, 58–60, 72
  bitterness of, 65–66
  isolated vs. integrated, 69, 70–73
  isolation of ended, 11–12, 16, 68
  missionary work among, 70–73
  pacification of, 51–53, 54, 66, 69
Cherokee Indians (United States), 7
Chimbu tribe (New Guinea), 222
Cintas-Largas Indians (Brazil), 15
Cities, towns. *See* Urban areas
Civilizado
  as modern conquistador, 12–16
  as pacifier, 53
  sexual attitudes of, 61
  in urban areas, 71
Civilization, relative levels of, 9–10. *See also* Western man
Cleland, Donald, 199, 212
Cleland, Rachel, 199
Colonialism
  in Africa, 108, 109, 134
  in Australia, 155–158, 161
  British, 134, 145–146, 147
  in South America, 4–5, 9, 10–11, 26
Columbus, Christopher, 2, 3, 10
Congo, anti-Western massacre in, 108, 124
Cowell, Adrian, 67
Craig Harbor (Ellesmere Island), 77, 79
Cultural identity
  and "desirability" of primitive traits, 44, 46, 115, 169, 170–171, 174–176
  effect of education upon, 37, 42–43, 79–80, 83, 99–102, 145, 169, 171–175, 200–201
  effect of language loss upon, 100–101, 171–173, 201

HÉANCE